What Pragmatism Was

AMERICAN PHILOSOPHY
John J. Stuhr, editor

EDITORIAL BOARD
Susan Bordo
Vincent Colapietro
John Lachs
Noëlle McAfee
José Medina
Cheyney Ryan
Richard Shusterman

What Pragmatism Was

F. Thomas Burke

Indiana University Press
Bloomington and Indianapolis

This book is a publication of

Indiana University Press
Office of Scholarly Publishing
Herman B Wells Library 350
1320 East 10th Street
Bloomington, Indiana 47405-3907 USA

iupress.indiana.edu

Telephone orders 800-842-6796
Fax orders 812-855-7931

© 2013 by F. Thomas Burke
All rights reserved

No part of this book may be reproduced or utilized in any form or by any means, electronic or mechanical, including photocopying and recording, or by any information storage and retrieval system, without permission in writing from the publisher. The Association of American University Presses' Resolution on Permissions constitutes the only exception to this prohibition.

∞ *The paper used in this publication meets the minimum requirements of the American National Standard for Information Sciences—Permanence of Paper for Printed Library Materials, ANSI Z39.48-1992.*

MANUFACTURED IN THE UNITED STATES OF AMERICA

Library of Congress Cataloging-in-Publication Data

Cataloging information is available from the Library of Congress

1 2 3 4 5 18 17 16 15 14 13

To the Memory of Michael Eldridge

Contents

	Preface	ix
	Acknowledgments	xiv
	Introduction: The Pragmatic Maxim	1
1	Peirce's Early Presentation of the Maxim	9
2	James's Presentation of the Maxim	13
3	Peirce's Later Versions of the Maxim	22
4	A Composite Sketch of the Maxim	36
5	Empiricism versus Pragmatism	65
6	Measurement and the Observer Effect	73
7	Perception and Action	80
8	Addams and the Settlement Movement	116
9	Truth, Justice, and the American Pragmatist Way	131
10	Twelve Misconceptions of Pragmatism	143
	Conclusion: Belief and Meaning	161
	Appendices	164
	Bibliography	184
	Index	203

Preface

Throughout his 2008 campaign and into the early months of his presidency, Barack Obama was both praised and condemned on various grounds for his professed "pragmatism."

> So my whole goal over the next four years is to make sure that whatever arguments are persuasive [are] backed up by evidence and facts and proof that they can work, that we are pulling people together around that kind of pragmatic agenda. (Obama 2009)

Just the fact that a U.S. president would claim to be a pragmatist calls attention to the importance of the question of what pragmatism is. Any U.S. president, Obama or otherwise, perhaps should indeed be a pragmatist, in some sense of that term. Such a claim is worthless, though, if we do not know what it means to make it. It is worse than worthless when, for whatever purpose, the meanings of the terms 'pragmatist', 'pragmatism', and 'pragmatic' are so distorted or misused as to promote rather than dispel confusion. The latter point assumes, of course, that we might know how to use those terms properly. So how do we do that? What is pragmatism?

There are numerous possibilities if we can believe what we read in the political news media.

For instance, a common view seems to be that to profess pragmatism simply means that one would avoid dogmatic ideology for its own sake in favor of commonsense post-partisan (pluralistic) practicality (Berkowitz 2009; Bronsther 2009; CBS News 2012; Cohen 2010; Critchley 2008; Dionne 2009a;b; Goldberg 2010; Gordon 2009; Hamburger and Wallsten 2009; Hayes 2008; Lerner 2009; Lim 2009; Lizza 2007; Lowry 2009; Packer 2008; Payne 2008; Rivas 2009; Salam 2008; Schultz 2009; Sunstein 2008; Worsnip 2012; Zelizer 2012). In one form or another, this is apparently at least part of what Obama means by it (as in wanting to be "pulling people together around [a] pragmatic agenda").

It is also common to think that pragmatism means that policy decisions are to be made on the basis of *what works*—on the basis of what is effective in getting things done (Aboulafia 2009d; Hayes 2008; Ignatius 2007; Koopman 2009; Kroft 2008; Lowry 2009; Schultz 2009; Worsnip 2012; Wickham 2008). This also comes through in some of Obama's statements, including the preceding quote (Obama 2009).

To some the latter characterization suggests an emphasis on means, not ends—that is, a focus on instituting effective means to achieve given ends (Reich 2009). To others it entails a problem-oriented focus on ends, consequences, results, as the measure of what works (Hayes 2008; Kantor 2009).

An emphasis on "results" may suggest a kind of data-driven evidence-based empiricism (Dionne 2009a; Engel 2002; Payne 2008; Revesz and Livermore 2009; Sunstein 2002; 2008), while others would deny such a suggestion if empiricism simply means an exclusive emphasis on the techniques of game theory, decision theory, risk assessment, or cost-benefit analysis (Acronym Required 2010; CPR 2008; Mooney 2009; Shapiro and Schroeder 2008). Either way, empiricism does not preclude a concern only for what works to successfully promote preconceived favored agendas or partisan causes (Berkowitz 2009; Gerson 2009).

Or is pragmatism simply a kind of anti-intellectual practicality (Bronsther 2009)? It might be worse than that. To some, any emphasis on "what works" may signify only a concern for expediency at the expense of principle (Hayes 2008), often as if principle and expediency exclude one another—a matter made all the worse if it is only self-serving vote-winning political expediency at issue. This often seems to be what real-world politics is ultimately about—the pragmatist being one who readily accepts this fact and strategizes accordingly (saying or doing whatever one must, rational or not) for political advantage (Aboulafia 2009b;c; Dionne 2009b; Lim 2009; Lizza 2007; Packer 2009; Smith 2008; Weisberg 2009). Obstructionist tactics designed by one faction solely to prevent or undermine an opponent faction's successes are labeled as "pragmatic" if not "pragmatist" in this latter sense.

This may suggest to some an ethical and philosophical emptiness and, thus, a lack of moral leadership (Aboulafia 2008; Bronsther 2009; Critchley 2008; Gerson 2009; Goldberg 2010; Packer 2009; Reich 2009; Worsnip 2012). Pragmatism in this sense "takes our hope away and tells us that all we can do is muddle through" (Fish 2010).

On the other hand, pragmatism to some means open-mindedness, epistemological modesty, an appreciation of human fallibility, and prudent flexibility in solving problems—versus dogmatic adherence come what may to rigid moral ideals or political agendas (Aboulafia 2009a;d; Hayes 2008; Kloppenberg 2011; Schultz 2009; Sunstein 2008).

This in turn suggests to some a kind of waffling opportunism, giving no weight to overarching ideals at all (Gerson 2009; Hamburger and Wallsten 2009; Landler and Cooper 2011; Sunstein 2008).

And on it goes.

A pragmatist may indeed be any of these things; but it is not clear that any of these things, alone or together, really tell us what pragmatism is. Minimally, if this quick survey is any indication, the meaning of the word 'pragmatism' is in need of clarification.

It is hoped that a philosophical look at the historical origins of pragmatism as a distinctively American philosophical standpoint will help to correct this problem. That is in any case what this book is about—the nature of pragmatism as reflected in its historical origins.

One cannot be sure what Obama means by the term 'pragmatism'; but one thing that it should mean, we will come to see, is that one's concepts—and thus one's ideologies and their constituent principles—are not as clear as they could be until one has operationalized them (and if that cannot be done, then those concepts and principles are to that extent unclear). Pragmatism is after all a philosophical stance or attitude that includes a certain view about the contents of our concepts, asserting that it is not enough to know how concepts are formally related to one another but that we also need to know how they work on the ground when applied in concrete situations (Engel 2002; Kantor 2009; Lizza 2007; Obama 2008b; Schultz 2009). In particular, costs and benefits associated with a given regulation cannot be evaluated in any reliable and veridical sense without our being able to specify what one will have done to gauge such values (the problem perhaps not being so much that values are quantitative in nature but that no ways of objectively and routinely measuring such quantities are available). It is this latter operationalist feature of pragmatism that one does not see enough of in the press. It also indicates how and why it is rather hard actually *to be* a pragmatist and not just to brandish the term about to gain rhetorical points, or worse, to try to legitimize self-serving policies.

> Of course, the answer to the slavery question was already embedded within our Constitution—a Constitution that had at its very core the ideal of equal citizenship under the law; a Constitution that promised its people liberty, and justice, and a union that could be and should be perfected over time.
>
> And yet words on a parchment would not be enough to deliver slaves from bondage, or provide men and women of every color and creed their full rights and obligations as citizens of the United States. What would be needed were Americans in successive generations who were willing to do their part—through protests and struggle, on the streets and in the courts, through a civil war and civil disobedience and always at great risk—to narrow that gap between the promise of our ideals and the reality of their time. (Obama 2008a)

For Obama, whether as a "clear-headed" realist or merely as a self-interested political strategist, these statements may be the expedient things to say in a speech on "race" in the midst of a campaign for the U.S. presidency. In fact, though, and in spite of any such political expediency, these statements point to an important defining feature of pragmatism as it plays out in political arenas—the view, namely, that real meaning is ultimately manifested in concrete worldly actions and their tangible results.

In colloquial terms, this says that it may be easy to talk the talk, but the talk is empty of real content if you cannot walk the walk. The point here is not just that one should walk one's talk—not just that one should *do* something and not just talk about it. The point rather is that one does not really know what one is talking about except *in terms of* such doing. Pragmatism is a logical and thus normative view about the nature of the semantic and pragmatic contents of one's words, not a moral admonition about practicing what one preaches.

To understand what this means, we need to put the newspapers and magazines down for a bit and try to get accustomed to working through some rather dense philosophical texts. Throughout the following chapters, at certain junctures, there will be some long quotations from primary texts—in particular, from the writings of William James and Charles Sanders Peirce but also from the likes of Jane Addams, J. J. Gibson, Immanuel Kant, and others. By supplying and discussing numerous snippets from their actual writings, we will be better able to avoid vague and elliptical allusions to what the authors *allegedly* said. It is hoped that readers will be inspired to find and read the original texts in their entirety. It is assumed that many readers will not yet have actually read these texts, in which case this may be a first opportunity to see how pragmatism was originally conceived. Even if one has seen these classical passages before, perhaps it would be good to see them again. Somewhere in all of the politicking, this material is getting lost.

A Note about Page Citations

Many passages from the works of Peirce and James will be quoted here. The works of both of these philosophers have been reissued in one or more critical editions that will be cited here. In particular, James's work has been collected and reissued by the Harvard University Press. References to James's work will cite the original year of publication but will list page numbers from the Harvard University Press edition. For example, a passage from page 67 of James's 1897 *Will to Believe* will be cited as "James 1897, HUP:67." One exception to this rule will be anything cited in either James's 1907 *Pragmatism* or his 1909 *The Meaning of Truth*. These books were issued separately by Harvard in 1975 and then again in combined form in 1978. Page citations from either of these works will refer to the 1978 combined edition, indicated by "PMT" in place of "HUP."

The publication of Peirce's work has a somewhat more colorful history, but the citation format is fairly straightforward. For a long time the standard sources for citing Peirce's work were the *Collected Papers* (CP), published (also by Harvard) in eight volumes beginning in 1931. In 1981, the Peirce Edition Project at Indiana University began to publish the *Writings of Charles S. Peirce: A Chronological Edition* (WP). This definitive edition of Peirce's writings is projected to include something on the order of thirty volumes though fewer than a third of that number have been published as of the present date. Meanwhile the Peirce Edition Project has put out two valuable selections of Peirce's writings that span his career, *The Essential Peirce* in two volumes (EP1 and EP2). Almost all of the passages from Peirce's writings that are quoted or cited here can be found in the latter two volumes; and when that is not the case, they can be found in the chronological *Writings*. References to Peirce's work will thus cite the original year of publication (or the date of the manuscript, if unpublished) but will list page or chapter numbers from the *Essential Peirce* volumes, indicated by "EP1" and "EP2," respectively. For example, a passage from page 230 of Peirce's 1903 "Pragmatism as the Logic of Abduction" will be cited as "Peirce 1903f, EP2:230." Citations to the *Writings* will be indicated by "WPN" in place of "EP1" or "EP2" for respective volume N in the WP series.

Acknowledgments

My views have changed over the course of writing this book, largely under the influence of discussions with a number of people at the Atlantic Coast Pragmatism Workshop, held yearly so far in various locations in Virginia, Maryland, and the Carolinas (and soon to expand further up and down the coast). As a result of these discussions, I have had to comb through the text from start to finish a number of times to make changes; and I probably have not corrected everything that needs to be corrected.

In particular, Mike Eldridge's insisting that my view of pragmatism "*is too narrow*" was finally heeded, though I'm not sure that the current broader version will have been to his liking. He looked over an early version of the manuscript but sadly and unfortunately passed away before letting me know anything in detail about what he thought about it.

Others attending the ACPW at least once who have positively influenced my thinking about pragmatism one way or another include Brian Butler, Marilyn Fischer, Russell Goodman, Jacob Goodson, Mike Jostedt, David LoConto, Rosa Mayorga, Bill Rogers, Mark Sanders, Charlene Haddock-Seigfried, Jayne Tristan, Seth Vannatta, and probably others whom I have failed to list.

Special thanks also to Stephen Everett for many useful conversations while he was completing a dissertation on Dewey's externalist philosophy of mind. His questions and suggestions after reading earlier versions of the present manuscript have led to important revisions and improvements. More significantly, his own work on Dewey's externalism has helped me to clarify and hone my own thinking about how best to characterize pragmatism.

Another major influence on what is written here was the December 3, 2006 *Philosophy Talk* discussion of pragmatism where John Perry and Kenneth Taylor discussed pragmatism with John McDermott (Taylor and Perry 2006). If anyone knows what pragmatism is, McDermott does. Yet somehow I came away from that interview feeling frustrated. McDermott was spot on, yet the interview as a whole was confusing about what pragmatism is or why anyone would think that way. In spite of their ability to make things simple and understandable, it seemed that Taylor and Perry kept missing the point, pressing some challenging not-so-simple issues that cannot be cleared up in a few minutes on air whether you are a pragmatist or not. Just what pragmatism is in the first place has to be more obvious. Or so I thought. This book is essentially the result of trying to point out what I originally thought was "so obvious."

This work has been supported in part by an Associate Professor Development Award in 2010 from the College of Arts and Sciences at the University of South Carolina.

Chapter 8 is an expanded version of a paper "Empiricism, Pragmatism, and the Settlement Movement" that originally appeared in *The Pluralist* 5(3), Fall 2010, reprinted here by permission of the University of Illinois Press.

Chapter 9 stems from a paper "Truth, Justice, and the American Pragmatist Way" presented at the 2012 Atlantic Coast Pragmatism Workshop in Williamsburg, Virginia, and again at the 2012 Inland Northwest Philosophy Conference at the University of Idaho. A different version of that paper will appear in *Pragmatism, Law, and Language*, ed. Graham Hubbs and Douglas Lind (London: Routledge, 2013).

Last but not least, I am indebted to Dee Mortensen and especially Marvin Keenan at Indiana University Press for invaluable support, tolerance, and patience in seeing the publication of this book through to its completion.

What Pragmatism Was

INTRODUCTION
The Pragmatic Maxim

Trying to change the way the word 'pragmatism' is commonly used particularly in reference to political attitudes is probably an exercise in futility. Journalists, politicians, and philosophers alike seem equally mistaken about the meaning of the word. Nevertheless, this book is an attempt to clarify what the word means by looking at some key texts in the earliest history of pragmatism as a quintessentially American philosophical movement.

By key texts in the "earliest" history of pragmatism one means certain seminal works of Charles Sanders Peirce and William James. The following will not be a survey of the history of pragmatism such as one finds in Thayer 1981, Flower and Murphey 1977, or Schneider 1946. Nor will it be the kind of topical overview that one finds in Bernstein 2010 or Talisse and Aikin 2008, both of which are highly recommended. Rather, the aim here is to characterize *and reconcile* what Peirce and James originally meant by "pragmatism" independent of subsequent developments throughout the 20th century and around the world.

The view of pragmatism promoted here is, first, that it involves a certain conception of *belief*, namely, that our beliefs about the world determine how we in fact act in the world insofar as they reflect "rules of action" embodied in established habits. How and why that is the case of course requires some explication and argumentation, and that is not an easy task given that it depends on whose version of pragmatism you are talking about. As such, this conception of belief is not itself a full-fledged theory of belief but only puts some constraints on such theories. In any case, second, a certain conception of *meaning* is alleged to follow from this conception of belief, namely, a conception of meaning formulated by the so-called pragmatic maxim. What this maxim says, it turns out, is also not easy to pin down and in fact can be given at least two distinct readings. Clarifying this ambiguity of the pragmatic maxim is the central focus of this book.

In recent decades pragmatism has come to be identified with a kind of *inferentialism*—largely under the influence of philosophers like Richard Rorty and Robert Brandom—though it may be misleading to put it so simply. We will see below that inferentialism is essentially a contemporary take on pragmatism as it was originally promoted by William James. Namely, what a given belief *means* depends essentially on what may be inferred from it in conjunction with other established beliefs. Thus the content of a belief is essentially determined by its logical consequences. At the same time, this is a take on James's version of pragmatism that reflects later analytic sensibilities that are not uniquely pragmatist—as exemplified, for instance, in the work of Wilfrid Sellars and Willard van Orman Quine. The aim of this book is not to disparage or otherwise downplay inferentialism but to balance it with a different but equally important aspect of the pragmatic maxim that was originally emphasized by Charles Peirce. Namely, the maxim also promotes a kind of *operationalism*. Operationalist aspects of pragmatism have been eclipsed if not forgotten altogether for a number of reasons, but we will have a better, more complete understanding of what pragmatism is if we can clarify both its inferentialist and operationalist commitments. Clarifying the operationalist character of pragmatism is of special importance given that it is less well understood (even when acknowledged) as an aspect of pragmatism.

James is credited with putting pragmatism on the philosophical map. He has strongly influenced how we conceive of pragmatism today, though his initial aim may have been simply to publicize and promote the views of a down-on-his-luck friend, namely, Peirce. James explicitly cited and summarized Peirce's derivation and discussion of what is now referred to as the *pragmatic maxim*, thus baptizing a philosophical movement that originated as much with Peirce as with James.

Peirce's original statement of this "maxim of pragmatism" was not labeled as such but was described rather as "a rule for attaining [a high] grade of clearness of apprehension":

> Consider what effects, which might conceivably have practical bearings, we conceive the object of our conception to have. Then, our conception of these effects is the whole of our conception of the object. (Peirce 1878a, EP1:132)

James (1907c, PMT:29) restated this rule almost verbatim as part of a summary of Peirce's presentation of it, labeling it "the principle of Peirce, the principle of pragmatism." Later, Peirce described "the maxim of pragmatism" as "a mere maxim of logic" (1903a; 1903f) and otherwise later referred to it as a *maxim* (1905b; 1907a; 1913). And so it has come to be known as the pragmatic maxim.

It is generally agreed that James inaccurately interpreted Peirce's early thought on the subject to such a degree that, for better or worse, the pragmatist tradition was essentially founded on a misunderstanding that has persisted to the present day (see Perry 1948, 281; Ayer 1968, 3, 8, 40; Talisse and Aikin 2008, 11). The following discussion examines this claim by comparing some familiar pieces of text—one being the first half of James's "What Pragmatism Means" (1907c) and another being the second section of Peirce's "How to Make Our Ideas Clear" (1878a). These texts clearly indicate where exactly the disagreement lies. In particular, a pragmatist conception of belief functioned for Peirce as no more than a conception of belief, whereas for James it was transformed into "a theory of truth." In light of this difference, we can show, secondly, that there are two different though legitimate ways to interpret the pragmatic maxim, one emphasizing inferentialist themes (as James did) and one emphasizing operationalist themes (as Peirce did).

It is not unreasonable to think that each of these themes is part of what the pragmatic maxim says; but because the two have not been properly distinguished, neither has been properly understood, and the pragmatic maxim has effectively been rendered incomprehensible. For the most part, in Rorty's formidable wake, contemporary references to pragmatism tend to be oriented to inferentialist pragmatism—whether in academic journals, textbooks, or mass media. This is a mistake insofar as it is one-sided and incomplete. This mistake—this one-sided misconception—will be something of a tragedy, if it persists, insofar as it would mean the loss of an ingenious bit of philosophical thought worthy of further exploration.

As we seek to clarify these two different readings of the pragmatic maxim, it is important to understand that pragmatism is not and never was a single doctrine. On this point, a noteworthy characterization of pragmatism was spelled out by Richard Bernstein in his 1988 presidential address to the Eastern Division Meeting of the American Philosophical Association. In that address he denied that the pragmatist tradition was a doctrine or even a method. He characterized it rather as "an ongoing engaged conversation consisting of distinctive—sometimes competing—voices" (Bernstein 1989). As such, he highlighted five *themes* running through this tradition qua conversation: (1) anti-foundationalism, (2) a thoroughgoing fallibilism, (3) an emphasis on the social character of self and the need to nurture a critical community of inquirers, (4) recognition of the ubiquity of contingency and chance and thus of the precariousness of life, and (5) pluralism with regard to traditions, perspectives, and orientations in philosophy, science, and culture at large. Bernstein is right to identify such common themes in the views of Peirce, James, John Dewey, George H. Mead, and others as a way of saying what pragmatism is. On the other hand, one might wonder if such themes are enough by themselves to say what is distinctive about pragmatism as such. That is, are any one or more of these themes sufficient and/or necessary features of pragmatism? How does one justify an answer to that question? What other themes need be added to Bernstein's list?

We do not want to pursue these questions here, that is, not as a way of saying what pragmatism is or what it originally *was* in the work of Peirce and James. In regard to saying what pragmatism originally was, the body of work of Peirce and James by itself takes precedence over the larger "conversation" that it spawned. As such, pragmatism might be characterized relatively simply as already indicated, namely, as a conception of belief and a corollary conception of meaning. More accurately, though, and here the messiness immediately shows itself, the respective conception of belief was from the start a matter of contention, and the corollary conception of meaning was at best equivocal. Nevertheless, the range of considerations at play in this motley mix was constrained. The fact that it involved a fairly distinctive take on the two key notions of *belief* and *meaning* suggests that we might be able after all to give a single composite portrait of what pragmatism was for Peirce and James.

It should be noted that little attention will be given here to John Dewey or George H. Mead, both being prominent second-generation classical American pragmatists. A few connections with Dewey's work will be mentioned in passing given that that work to a great extent exemplifies the kind of synthesis of Peirce's and James's views of pragmatism that is being promoted here. Support for such a claim deserves a monograph all to itself. For the present, the major focus will be on Peirce and James, and moreover on a limited set of writings crucial to the emergence of pragmatism as a going concern.

An alternative to Bernstein's claim that pragmatism is neither a doctrine nor a method but rather a conversation sporting certain distinctive themes is the claim that it is neither a doctrine nor a method but rather a philosophical stance or attitude or style. Recently, van Fraassen's (2002) characterization of empiricism as a *stance* "rather than a thesis" reflects a similar idea, where a stance is an "attitude, commitment, approach, [or] cluster of such ... [that] may involve or presuppose some beliefs, but cannot be simply equated with having beliefs or making assertions about what there is" (47–48). Van Fraassen (48n14) in turn points to similar recent discussions of philosophical attitudes, for example, by Fine (1984) and Crasnow (2000). This distinction between philosophical attitudes and philosophical doctrines would quickly and easily allow us to dispose of critical strategies aimed at undermining pragmatism as a particular body of doctrines. Characterizing pragmatism as an attitude or stance allows a variety of views on just about any philosophical topic. Pragmatism when regarded as a philosophical stance or style cannot then be directly confirmed or refuted but will merely fail or succeed in ways that philosophical styles fail or succeed.

Thus it is tempting to characterize pragmatism as a philosophical attitude or stance or temperament, as James (1907b) put it, that encompasses a number of perhaps incompatible doctrines. It would seem to be well in line with Peirce's and James's own statements that what characterizes this attitude or stance, while not a particular doctrine, is adherence to the pragmatic maxim. Peirce described this maxim as a "mere maxim of logic instead of a sublime principle of speculative philosophy" (1903a, EP2:134–135), where "logic can gain not the slightest support from metaphysics" (1903c, EP2:179). On Peirce's view, "pragmatism is, in itself, no doctrine of metaphysics, no attempt to determine any truth of things. It is merely a method of ascertaining the meanings of hard words and of abstract concepts" (1907b, EP2:400). Similarly, according to James, the pragmatic maxim gives us "a method only ... an attitude of orientation" rather than any particular doctrine (1907h, PMT:31–32). On James's view, pragmatism "represents a perfectly familiar attitude in philosophy, the empiricist attitude ... in a more radical and in a less objectionable form than it has ever yet assumed. ... At the same time [pragmatism] does not stand for any special results. It is a method only" (1907h, PMT:31). Pragmatism by these accounts is not a particular philosophical doctrine but a philosophical *stance* placing constraints on how any given doctrine is to be spelled out and otherwise promoted. If the pragmatic maxim is in some way supposed to indicate what pragmatism is as a philosophical attitude, then it would be in effect (as we will see below) an attitude about how to clearly define one's terms.

As much as one might try to push this characterization of pragmatism as *merely* an attitude reflected in the pragmatic maxim, there is an equal and opposite effort out there to pursue Bernstein's strategy of identifying common substantive themes if not theses that characterize pragmatism. It might be countered—to maintain the privileged status of the pragmatic maxim—that any such themes and theses would count as essential features of pragmatism only to the extent that they are consequences of adopting the pragmatic maxim as a fundamental methodological principle. It would certainly be nice to know which themes and theses satisfy that requirement. But the fact is that the consequence relation to a large extent goes the other direction: the pragmatic maxim, by Peirce's own lights, would appear rather to be a *corollary* of any collection of theses that promotes a certain conception of belief.

Specifically, we will see in the next chapter that Peirce's formulation of the maxim was *derived* from a certain conception of (a particularly tight relationship among) belief, habit, and action that might just as well be elevated to the status of being the basis for a pragmatist doctrine. This is essentially what James did, though he added his own twist to that doctrine by rendering it as a theory of truth. This is a questionable move that in any case evidences the contentiousness at the heart of the earliest pragmatist "conversation." Working in terms of a certain conception of belief adapted from Alexander Bain (1855; 1859) and James Fitzjames Stephens (1863) by way of his friend Nicholas St. John Green (see Peirce 1906b; 1907b, EP2:399; Menand 2001, 225, 354), Peirce originally presented the maxim as a principle pertaining to how our thinking may best be concretely grounded in the real world—a principle couched in terms of activities and their tangible results—in explicit contrast with Cartesian (or Kantian) epistemology. James recast this conception of belief as a conception of truth, and pragmatism ever since has been the mess that it is.

Despite their mutual emphasis on the pragmatic maxim as somehow being the key to understanding what pragmatism is, James and Peirce thus were originally and forever at odds about what pragmatism is. Peirce expressed this disagreement sometimes indirectly (1903a, EP2:134) and sometimes not so indirectly (Peirce 1905a, EP2:334–335; 1913, EP2:457). One of the strongest statements of his dissatisfaction with James's version of pragmatism came in the year following the publication of James's *Pragmatism* (1907h), in a passage that specifically targeted James's earlier *Will to Believe* (1897) as the source of the problem (see in particular James's fourth chapter, "Reflex Action and Theism," originally published in 1881):

> In 1871, in a Metaphysical Club in Cambridge, Mass., I used to preach this principle as a sort of logical gospel, representing the unformulated method followed by Berkeley, and in conversation about it I called it "Pragmatism." In November 1877 and January 1878 I set forth the doctrine in the *Popular Science Monthly*; and the two parts of my essay were printed in French in the *Revue Philosophique*, volumes 6 and 7. Of course, the doctrine attracted no particular attention, for, as I had remarked in my opening sentence, very few people care for logic. But in 1897 Professor James remodelled the matter, and transmogrified it into a doctrine of philosophy, some parts of which I highly approved, while other and more prominent parts I regarded, and still regard, as opposed to sound logic. About the time Professor Papini discovered, to the delight of the Pragmatist school, that this doctrine was incapable of definition, which would certainly seem to distinguish it from every other doctrine in whatever branch of science, I was coming to the conclusion that my poor little maxim should be called by another name; and accordingly, in April 1905, I renamed it *Pragmaticism*. I had never before dignified it by any name in print, except that, at Professor Baldwin's request, I wrote a definition of it for his *Dictionary of Psychology and Philosophy*. I did not insert the word in the *Century Dictionary*, though I had charge of the philosophical definitions of that work; for I have a perhaps exaggerated dislike of *réclame*. (Peirce 1908, EP2:448)

Some of these remarks may be somewhat disingenuous; but here and elsewhere, time and again, Peirce makes it clear that the pragmatic maxim is key to understanding what pragmatism is. James clearly would agree. Yet what were those "prominent parts" of James's writings on pragmatism that Peirce regarded "as opposed to sound logic"? Perhaps we will never know, though I will try to show here at least indirectly (1) that Peirce would never have endorsed James's theory of truth as anything other than a theory of rational believability, and (2) that James leaned toward a flexible *inferentialist coherentism* that, on its surface, did not comport well with Peirce's promotion of a kind of *operationalist quasi-foundationalism*—namely, an operationalist fallibilism that dismissed Cartesian or Kantian forms of absolutism but otherwise promoted some kind of systematicity of knowledge. If such "ism" jargon sounds unintelligible, then never mind. The important point for now is that Peirce and James had fundamental disagreements that were ultimately reflected in their understanding and use of the pragmatic maxim. James and Peirce had different takes on the conception of belief at the heart of pragmatism, and consequently they interpreted the corollary pragmatic maxim differently. We need to better understand these early disagreements between James and Peirce. They reflect distinctions that lie at the very core of pragmatism as a philosophical stance.

In the next few chapters, we will examine Peirce's version of the pragmatic maxim and summarize James's interpretation and application of it, highlighting commonalities as well as key differences. We will then consider an integrated twofold (double-aspect) version of the maxim that accommodates the differences between Peirce's and James's respective interpretations.

In the second half of the book we will work through several related topics that help to clarify what this twofold reading of the pragmatic maxim amounts to. First, we will contrast the pragmatist stance with a couple of twentieth-century analytic attitudes concerning the nature of empirical verification. Namely, we will contrast it with Quine's so-called holism and his first-order extensionalism—the key difference in the latter case being one between Quine's primary emphasis on first-order "things" versus pragmatism's primary emphasis on action and (sensible) effects. Quine's views in large part were defined by a *holistic* conception of verification that was developed in response to logical-positivist atomistic conceptions of verification. The latter position was well represented by Carnap. We will therefore review and amend Putnam's comparison of pragmatism and Carnap's sensationist empiricism—the key difference in this case being that Carnap neglects the *interactive* (or enactive) nature of observation and measurement. The moral here is that "enactivist" aspects of pragmatism (reflecting Peirce's operationalist conception of pragmatism) provide an alternative kind of response to atomistic forms of empiricism besides Quine's holism (the latter being more closely aligned with James's inferentialist view of pragmatism).

To promote a better appreciation of the contrast between pragmatism and empiricism, we will, for the record, survey a range of examples of the "observer effect" as evidence for a conception of observation and measurement as interactive rather than as the workings of a passive, detached spectator. Citing various forms of enactivism in cognitive science and looking in particular at some of the details of Gibsonian ecological psychology, we will argue further that ordinary sensory perception is similarly interactive. If Gibson was right about the nature of perception, then it is clear that the operationalism at the heart of pragmatism reflects fundamental features of human nature and is relevant to more than just the professional practice of science (or politics).

Next, to complement Putnam's contrast between pragmatism and Carnap's kind of empiricism, we will examine a particular case of a proposed analysis of the methods and organization of the so-called *settlement movement* during the Progressive Era in the United States. At first this may seem like something of a detour, but it is important to see that this analysis (Simkhovitch 1906) is clearly an empiricist analysis, not a pragmatist one. This example will help to draw a sharp contrast between pragmatism and empiricism if prior discussion at that point does not already accomplish that feat. More to the point, it helps us to more clearly distinguish two different conceptions of *action* that are at the heart of the disagreement between Peirce and James.

The characterization of pragmatism that is promoted here will be further supported with more examples showing how to employ the pragmatist method. In particular, we will quickly review some of the examples already considered and then show how to define the words 'knowledge', 'democracy', and 'justice' in similar ways. The latter two examples are instructive in that, like Peirce's definition of the words 'reality' and 'truth', their meanings when operationalized turn on the fact that they represent *ideals* of one sort or another.

At that point we will address various competing conceptions of pragmatism that are often found in mass media publications—especially recent publications addressing "pragmatism" as relevant to U.S. presidential politics. The aim is to establish why none of these common conceptions of "practical" political pragmatism quite do justice to pragmatism as originally formulated by Peirce and James. This is not merely an incidental difference of word usage reflecting a disconnect between academia and the real world. Journalists and politicians have gotten it wrong regarding what they think they mean by the word 'pragmatism' particularly as it relates to politics in the United States. It is a chronic, deeply rooted mistake; but it ought to be corrected.

ONE

Peirce's Early Presentation of the Maxim

To understand what pragmatism is, we first have to understand what the pragmatic maxim says. Peirce's earliest statement of the pragmatic maxim is in some sense the definitive statement of that maxim, but its ambiguous formulation has generated considerable misunderstanding over the years. With some care, though, we can make some sense out of it.

When James initially publicized pragmatism (1885; 1897; 1898), he indeed cited and discussed Peirce's original 1878a presentation of this maxim. Succinct statements of the maxim can be and have been given in just a few lines. Here is Peirce's first published statement:

> It appears, then, that the rule for attaining the third grade of clearness of apprehension is as follows: Consider what effects, which might conceivably have practical bearings, we conceive the object of our conception to have. Then, our conception of these effects is the whole of our conception of the object. (Peirce 1878a, EP1:132)

It is clearly not a simple matter to determine what these few lines actually say. They are the conclusion of an argument that is aimed (as the title of Peirce's paper indicates) at establishing standards of "clearness" of thought (of apprehension, of ideas, of conceptions—Peirce employs all of these terms in this paper) over and above Cartesian rationalist standards of *clarity* and *distinctness*—the latter supposedly being exemplified by Euclid's axiomatic development of geometry. Peirce characterizes the latter two notions, respectively, as *familiarity* and *precise definability in abstract terms*. These are then alleged to be inadequate standards by themselves, the point being that a large proportion of our ideas are not amenable to clarification using purely formal axiomatic methods (1878a, EP1:125–127).

In spite of the limitations of purely rationalist standards of "clarity," the question of how to make our ideas clear *is* nevertheless a logical matter, Peirce claims, where logic is broadly conceived as a study of the "guiding principles of reasoning"—including a survey of inductive and abductive as well as deductive forms of inference (Peirce 1877; 1878b). According to Peirce, logical theory requires an examination of the various forms of inference as they function together in inquiry. Hence Peirce's discussion leading up to the statement of the maxim focuses largely on the nature of inquiry, drawing initially on the results of the earlier 1877 paper in which it is concluded that (among other things) the method of *scientific* inquiry is the best method of "fixing" or securing belief. This conclusion is alleged to "lead, at once, to a method of reaching a clearness of thought of a far higher grade than [mere] 'distinctness'" (1878a, EP1:127).

We need not get into too many details of Peirce's arguments in the crucial 1878a paper except to note that they begin with some general considerations of the nature of thought (inquiry, reasoning) in service to securing workable beliefs in the face of particular doubts, questions, or moments of indecisiveness. Peirce had already argued (1877) that thought (inquiry) is only a response to a felt need to address some doubt or indecision or question—to remove the doubt, resolve the indecision, answer the question—such that "the production of belief is the sole function of thought. ... The soul and meaning of thought ... can never be made to direct itself toward anything but the production of belief" (Peirce 1878a, EP1:127–129). The "motive of thought" is just the appeasement of doubt. Belief is to doubt what an answer is to a question. In making such claims, Peirce is quick to point out that the notions of doubt and belief are to be conceived broadly, pertaining to any kind of issue whether profound or mundane. This would include anything from what to have for dinner to whether or not to use taxpayers' money to bail out a failed banking system or automobile industry.

Peirce claims further that belief has just three properties: first, we are aware of it; second, it assuages doubt; and third, "it involves the establishment in our nature of a rule of action, or, say for short, a *habit*" (Peirce 1878a, EP1:129). In fact, rules of action fully determine beliefs. That is, the "final upshot" of any completed inquiry is the securing of some manner of action, the exercise of some volition, how that plays out being set by the rules of action established by that inquiry.

Thus two beliefs are different only if the respective habits which they involve are different. If two beliefs would appease the same doubt by way of the same rules of action, then no other attitude or regard for them can make them different beliefs, "any more than playing a tune in different keys is playing different tunes." Peirce summarizes the result of this first phase of his argument as follows:

> [T]he whole function of thought is to produce habits of action [*sic*]; and that whatever there is connected with a thought, but irrelevant to its purpose, is an accretion to it, but no part of it. ... To develop [a thought's] meaning, we have therefore, simply to determine what habits it produces, for what a thing means is simply what habits it involves. (Peirce 1878a, EP1:131)

There are several substantive claims here which Peirce takes a few pages to develop (1878a, EP1:127–131). These may be summarized as follows:

A. The *sole* function of thought in a given instance is to produce some respective belief in response to a given doubt.
B. The formation of a belief is the establishment of a habit.
C. A habit is just a rule of action.

D. The *content* of a belief is fully determined by the rules of action established in the formation of the belief.

On this basis, we have the following:

E. The *whole* function of thought is to produce habits or rules of action.
F. To determine the meaning of *the object of a thought*, one need only determine what habits it involves. Thus:
G. To determine the meaning of *a thought*, one need only determine what habits it produces.

The next phase of the argument therefore homes in on the nature of *habit*. As an established "rule of action," a habit is a capacity to act in some particular way that is triggered by suitable circumstances and that, when triggered, yields characteristic "sensible results." Both the circumstances and the results are in some way *sensible*:

> Now, the identity of a habit depends on how it might lead us to act, not merely under such circumstances as are likely to arise, but under such as might possibly occur, no matter how improbable they may be[—no matter if contrary to all previous experience]. What the habit is depends on *when* and *how* it causes us to act. As for the *when*, every stimulus to action is derived from perception; as for the *how*, every purpose of action is to produce some sensible result. Thus we come down to what is tangible and [conceivably] practical, as the root of every real distinction of thought, no matter how subtle it may be; and there is no distinction of meaning so fine as to consist in anything but a possible difference of practice. (1878a, EP1:131)

This gives us two more key claims:

H. As determining a way of acting, a habit is wholly identified by the sensible circumstances in which it is triggered and the sensible results that follow from acting in that way.

On this view, a habit, as a rule of action, might be specified in terms of a relation between initial and subsequent sensible circumstances. It is not clear how the domain and range of such a mapping are to be determined, though they need only be conceivable, not actual or even actualizable in real terms (e.g., drilling out several 700-mile-long core samples on the surface of the dwarf planet Pluto and analyzing each of them for iron content there on the spot). Peirce's notion of *habit* would otherwise appear to be neutral as to the material realization of any given habit, assuming that such details would go beyond what is "sensible." A given habit is distinguished rather by the fact that certain appropriate tangible results of respective actions would be produced in particular tangible circumstances. Thus:

I. The meaning of (the object of) a thought can be cast wholly in terms of a relation between a range of possible tangible initial conditions and a range of possible tangible results, i.e., wholly in tangible, practical terms.

It follows that if two allegedly different "meanings" are nevertheless cast in exactly the same tangible, practical terms, then they are in fact indistinguishable, at least so far as any "real distinction of thought" is concerned.

Peirce illustrates this conception of meaning briefly with the example of transubstantiation of the elements of the sacrament, a minimal point being that, if one holds that the substance of bread and wine literally changes into flesh and blood while all sensible qualities of the substance remain as before, then one is dealing with ideas that lack clearness beyond merely formal "distinctness."

At this juncture, Peirce quickly runs backwards through the various notions he has just discussed as a way of tying up the argument:

> Thus our action has exclusive reference to what affects the senses, our habit has the same bearing as our action, our belief the same as our habit, our conception the same as our belief; and we can consequently mean nothing by [a given conception] but what has certain effects, direct or indirect, upon our senses; and to talk of something as having all of the sensible characters of wine, yet being in reality blood, is senseless jargon. ... I only desire to point out how impossible it is that we should have an idea in our minds which relates to anything but conceivable sensible effects of things. Our idea of anything *is* our idea of its sensible effects; and if we fancy that we have any other we deceive ourselves, and mistake a mere sensation accompanying the thought for a part of the thought itself. It is absurd to say that thought has any meaning unrelated to its only function. It is foolish [to argue] about the elements of the sacrament, if [there is agreement] in regard to all their sensible effects, here [and] hereafter. (Peirce 1878a, EP1:131–132)

With these results on the table, Peirce then states the pragmatic maxim as a "rule for attaining the third grade of clearness of apprehension" (see page 9 above for the exact quote). This maxim and Peirce's supporting argument in its favor did not receive much attention after its publication in 1878a—not until James managed successfully to publicize it some twenty years later.

Later we will peruse some of Peirce's other versions of the pragmatic maxim along with some of his later examples of how to use it. First, though, we will consider James's treatment of this earliest version of the maxim.

TWO

James's Presentation of the Maxim

James cited Peirce's 1878a article several times in the two decades following its publication (James 1881; 1885; 1898), though it was the 1898 lecture at the University of California at Berkeley that seems to have ignited broad interest in pragmatism as such. Here we want to look at his retrospective look at pragmatism some ten years later in 1907h. It is this later writing that is typically regarded as the core statement of James's views on what pragmatism is. At that point he had certainly had time to sort out some thoughts on the subject, and the result taken as a whole is something that in many respects went beyond what Peirce was willing to endorse.

James began his "What Pragmatism Means" (1907c) with a straightforward example of "the pragmatic method" at work. This is his well-known discussion of someone trying to "go round" a squirrel on a nearby tree. The issue he deals with is hardly profound, though it may be used effectively to illustrate the "pragmatic method." Here is the issue in James's own words:

> Some years ago, being with a camping party in the mountains, I returned from a solitary ramble to find everyone engaged in a ferocious metaphysical dispute. The *corpus* of the dispute was a squirrel—a live squirrel supposed to be clinging to one side of a tree-trunk; while over against the tree's opposite side a human being was imagined to stand. This human witness tries to get sight of the squirrel by moving rapidly around the tree, but no matter how fast he goes, the squirrel moves as fast in the opposite direction, and always keep the tree between himself and the man, so that never a glimpse of him is caught. The resultant metaphysical problem now is this: *Does the man go round the squirrel or not?* (James 1907c, PMT:27)

Whether this "metaphysical problem" is a particularly subtle one is beside the point—or rather, what James is perhaps claiming on that score is that the point he is about to make applies as much to the subtlest metaphysical disputes as it does to this relatively mundane semantic dispute about the phrase 'go round'.

It is not hard to understand the dispute. As James puts it, the man goes around the tree, and the squirrel is on the tree; yet the man never manages to get anywhere that is not in front of the squirrel. James's solution, when asked to cast the deciding vote, was that whoever is right depends on what one "practically means" by the phrase 'going round'. This may seem to be the obvious (trivial) reply to *any* merely semantic dispute. But notice that James appeals not just to what one "means" but to what one *"practically* means" by the phrase 'going round'. One could "practically" mean two different things, yielding two different answers to the question. If one means being to the north, then west, then south, then east, then north again of the squirrel, the answer is yes. If one means being in front, then being to one side, then being behind, then being to the other side, then being in front again of the squirrel (from the squirrel's point of view), the answer is no. There is no dispute once the two meanings of the phrase are properly (practically) clarified. Of key importance here is the fact that each of the two meanings can be operationally (and thus practically) specified—in terms of the use of a magnetic compass or else in terms of geometrical angular measurements taking a plane parallel to the squirrel's abdomen as the basis for a fixed coordinate system. An answer to the question is geared to what essentially could be *measured* once we have specified which kinds of measurement procedures to use. The two different meanings are ultimately distinguished on operational grounds.

More generally, this is supposed to illustrate a method that is applicable across the board to any kind of debate that might be interminable due to semantic confusions:

> The pragmatic method in such cases is to try to interpret each notion by tracing its respective practical consequences. What difference would it practically make to anyone if this notion rather than that notion were true? If no practical difference whatever can be traced, then the alternatives mean practically the same thing and all dispute is idle. (James 1907c, PMT:28)

It is at this point that James cites Peirce as the author of this pragmatic method, summarizing the latter's 1878a presentation of the pragmatic maxim as follows:

> Mr. Peirce, after pointing out that our beliefs are really rules for action, said that, to develop a thought's meaning,, we need only determine what conduct it is fitted to produce: that conduct is for us its sole significance. And the tangible fact at the root of all our thought-distinctions, however subtle, is that there is no one of them so fine as to consist in anything but a possible difference of practice. To attain perfect clearness in our thoughts of an object, then, we need only consider what conceivable effects of a practical kind the object may involve—what sensations we are to expect from it, and what reactions we must prepare. Our conception of these effects, whether immediate or remote, is then for us the whole of our conception of the object, so far as that conception has positive significance at all. (James 1907c, PMT:28–29)

There is no explicit mention here of Peirce's relational conception of *habits* as rules of conduct. Peirce also did not claim to provide a method for attaining *perfect* clearness but rather just a (far) superior grade of clearness. Likewise, conceptions presumably may have some degree of positive significance without this superior grade of clarity. Other than that, James arguably has summarized Peirce's point fairly well. Note, in particular, the initial emphasis on conduct and practice, and on sensations as "effects of a practical kind," namely, as effects of conduct.

Writing in 1907, James recalls his 1898 lecture at UC Berkeley (twenty years after Peirce's original paper) where he discussed the principle of pragmatism. He does not mention that in 1885 he published a paper on "the function of cognition" (only about five years after Peirce's paper and almost fifteen years prior to the UC Berkeley lecture) in which the pragmatic maxim plays a crucial conclusive role. Namely, it helps to provide a kind of common ground that justifies our sense "that we all know and think about and talk about the same world" and thus explains why we do not "[fly] asunder into a chaos of mutually repellant solipsisms" (1885, PMT:195–196). James's argument in the final pages of that article may or may not work; but what is important for us presently is the marked emphasis that is given there to percepts, sensations, sensible things, etc., as being

> the mother-earth, the anchorage, the stable rock, the first and last limits, the *terminus a quo* and the *terminus ad quem* of the mind. To find such sensational *termini* should be our aim with all our higher thought. ... We can never be sure we understand each other till we are able to bring the matter to this test. ... "Scientific" theories ... always terminate in definite percepts. You can deduce a possible sensation from your theory and, taking me into your laboratory, prove that your theory is true of my world by giving me the sensation then and there. (1885, PMT:197)

We may safely ignore the deductive fallacy of affirming the consequent in the last sentence, or replace 'prove that your theory is true of my world' with something like 'show that your theory is confirmed in my world'. The point here rather is the emphasis on sensible results as the overriding if not ultimate test of scientific theories. James quotes a bit of Peirce's discussion and presentation of the pragmatic maxim in 1878a as support for this point. It would appear for the most part that Peirce and James are on the same page here so far as pragmatism is concerned.

To return to the 1907 article, after citing Peirce explicitly, James continues this emphasis on the sensible effects of experimental and observational activities. He quotes the views of the chemist Wilhelm Ostwald who made the point in 1905 that many theoretical controversies in science might never have begun

> if the combatants had asked themselves what particular experimental fact could have been made different by one or the other view being correct. For it [might then appear] that no difference of fact could possibly ensue; and the quarrel [be] as unreal as if, theorizing in primitive times about the raising of dough by yeast, one party should have invoked a "brownie," while another insisted on an "elf" as the true cause of the phenomenon. (James 1907c, PMT:30)

On the surface, it would seem that there is nothing new here to which contemporary philosophy of science is not now well attuned.

The thing to note is that, up to this point, James and Peirce seem to be in agreement concerning the notion of practical consequences. Namely, "consequences" are tangible if not sensible in nature, and they are "practical" in the sense that they are the effects of actions (operations, practices, modes of conduct) in "your laboratory" or in the world more broadly. Peirce would say, as we have noted, that the meaning of (the object of) a thought is determined by what habits it (involves) produces, where a habit, as an established way of acting, is identified by the sensible circumstances in which it is triggered and the sensible effects that follow from acting in that way. This is essentially an operationalist conception of practical consequences.

At this juncture, though, it becomes increasingly obvious that James is proceeding toward a different conception of practical meaning and thus effectively loosens if not loses his hold on an operationalist action/effect conception of practical consequences. Granted, he emphasizes again the empiricist (versus rationalist) attitude that pragmatism represents (1907c, PMT:31) while reiterating the notion that pragmatism presents not a doctrine but a method—a method, if Peirce has any say in the matter, of *defining* one's terms and clarifying one's concepts so as to specify, in particular, what it amounts to for an object to fall under a given concept. James, on the other hand, now characterizes this method more vaguely as designating a certain attitude—"the attitude of looking away from first things, principles, 'categories', supposed necessities; and looking toward last things, fruits, consequences, facts" (1907c, PMT:32). Rather suddenly, it would seem, the emphasis is placed on consequences in a quite broad sense with little or no regard for sensible *practicality*—with no regard, that is, for consequences as sensible effects of concrete activities. For better or worse, this diverges from Peirce's more specific notion of "sensible effects."

Surprisingly, at this point James moves beyond a presentation of the pragmatic maxim toward promoting the idea that pragmatism also designates "a certain *theory of truth*"—that it includes, after all, a doctrine and not just a method (1907c, PMT:32–33). This is a significant step on James's part. Peirce invariably linked pragmatism with the pragmatic maxim as its central if not sole defining feature. James, on the other hand, characterizes pragmatism as "first, a method," as designated by the pragmatic maxim, "and second, a genetic theory of what is meant by truth" (1907c, PMT:37).

We will examine this move on James's part below, but quickly, it would appear that he is mistaken in characterizing what he is talking about here as a theory of truth. What he is talking about rather is a theory of *warranted believability* (Ayer 1968, 189), and that theory essentially draws on a kind of inferentialism. As such, he is reformulating if not reinventing the theory of belief on the basis of which Peirce derived the pragmatic maxim. This yields two innovations on James's part. First, it promotes the idea that pragmatism is more than just a methodological maxim. That is, it also includes a background doctrine—a certain conception if not a theory of belief. Second, in light of James's take on that conception of belief, it characterizes the scope of the pragmatic maxim so as to include inferentialist as well as operationalist factors. That is, to clarify our ideas (to clearly define our terms, etc.), we need to consider not only the operationalization of those ideas but also the fact that their meanings equally hinge on the consequences of their being integrated into our current stock of beliefs. The conjunction of a given belief with other beliefs will have consequences, and those consequences help to constitute the meaning of the given belief. As such, its meaning is determined in part by its believability which in turn substantially depends on its systemic coherence with one's overall stock of beliefs.

Again, in making the move to present a pragmatist theory of truth, James is actually circling back around to issues that Peirce dealt with in "The Fixation of Belief" (1877), including preliminary results that were instrumental to the argument in the second section of "How to Make Our Ideas Clear" (1878a) that eventually led to the statement of the pragmatic maxim. One may think that James is pressing ahead into new territory when in fact he is highlighting a doctrine (a theory of reasonably justified believability mislabeled as a theory of truth) that was essential after all to Peirce's brand of pragmatism. In particular, James holds up scientific method as the premier method of justifying our beliefs (1907c, PMT:33-34) just as Peirce identified scientific method as the single best method for "fixing" our beliefs (as opposed to mere tenacity, appeals to authority, or *a priori* reasoning).

But wait. Looking more closely at what James makes of this emphasis on scientific method, it appears that he is promulgating methods of respecting convention and conceptual coherence—closer to Peirce's second and third methods for fixing beliefs that were pretty much discredited by Peirce in favor of full-fledged scientific method. Namely, after noting the variability and fallibility of candidate beliefs on almost any given subject of any import, James states that

> "truth" in our ideas and beliefs means ... *that ideas (which themselves are but parts of our experience) become true just in so far as they help us to get into satisfactory relation with other parts of our experience*, to summarize them and get about among them by conceptual short-cuts instead of following the interminable succession of particular phenomena. Any idea upon which we can ride, so to speak; any idea that will carry us prosperously from any one part of our experience to any other part, linking things satisfactorily, work securely, simplifying, saving labor; is true for just so much, true in so far forth, true *instrumentally*. (James 1907c, PMT:34)

James's use of the word 'experience' here, by his own account, encompasses the whole fabric of one's beliefs. The notion of a new idea helping one to "get into satisfactory relation" with the rest of one's experience thus suggests merely a coherentist notion of truth. The metaphors of "riding" an idea, of being "carried" by it, of its "linking" things, etc., moreover suggest, e.g., one's being beholden to the kinds of commitments and entitlements that play such a key role in Brandom's so-called inferential role semantics (Brandom 1994). The coherence here includes a coherence of the valid (inferrible) consequences of any new claim (whether you are aware of them or not) conjoined with those of pre-existing ideas and beliefs.

One can see how unsympathetic critics like Moore (1907) and Russell (1909) would have a field day with these kinds of statements particularly when taken out of context. Besides merely a coherence theory of truth, it would appear that

James is also allowing an opportunistic do-whatever-works-in-the-moment theory of truth. A fair and honest reading of the text easily shows, though, that James is already aware that that would not be acceptable. The "working" of the ideas cannot be just in the moment.

Specifically, though he does not cite Peirce in this instance, James (1907c, PMT:34) cites Schiller's and Dewey's use of Peirce's doubt/belief picture of inquiry, emphasizing the idea that settling into a *new* opinion or fixing a *new* belief is generally accomplished in response to some strain (contradiction, doubt) that gives salience to the candidate opinion as a potential solution to the respective problem posed by the initial conflict. James's point is that any such new opinion must be evaluated and can be sustained only in light of one's current stock of beliefs as a whole (or else the discrepancies would eventually revive the problem and opinion would not remain settled).

> The result [of the conflict] is an inward trouble to which his mind till then had been a stranger, and from which he seeks to escape by modifying his previous mass of opinions. He saves as much of it as he can, for in this matter of belief we are all extreme conservatives. So he [eventually finds some new idea] which he can graft upon the ancient stock with a minimum of disturbance of the latter, some idea that mediates between the stock and the new experience and runs them into one another most felicitously and expediently.
>
> This new idea is then adopted as the true one. ... It marries old opinion to new fact so as ever to show a minimum of jolt, a maximum of continuity. We hold a theory true just in proportion to its success in solving this "problem of maxima and minima." ...
>
> [Note] the part played by the older truths. ... Their influence is absolutely controlling. Loyalty to them is the first principle—in most cases it is the only principle; for by far the most usual way of handling phenomena so novel that they would make for a serious rearrangement of our preconceptions is to ignore them altogether, or to abuse those who bear witness to them. (James 1907c, PMT:35)

This hardly warrants criticisms of pragmatism as being epistemologically shortsighted or opportunistic. Even for James it is not enough to show merely in the moment "a minimum of jolt, a maximum of continuity." The acceptability of a new opinion must be such as to solve this two-variable optimization problem in a robust way. Fallibility is the norm, of course, but the standard of acceptability of new opinion is a *very*-long-range standard.

This is all well and good as a response to Russell and Moore on the issue of truth as being what works "momentarily"; but now consider two things.

(1) As already mentioned above, why think that James's theory of truth is actually a theory of *truth*? This is more likely what bothered Russell, Moore, and a multitude of others who could not stomach the plasticity of truth allowed by James's theory, even if it respects "ancient" beliefs. Substitute the phrases 'justified belief' or 'warranted believability' pretty much wherever James speaks

of truth and this aspect of pragmatism would be judged differently. The notion that pragmatism may presuppose a certain theory of belief (e.g., as utilized in a doubt/belief conception of inquiry) is both obvious and uncontentious. The same can be said for the notion that pragmatism is concerned with discerning the best ways of justifying beliefs. James essentially baptized pragmatism and then shot it in the foot by speaking of truth where he should have spoken (and where Peirce *did* speak) of belief.

(2) At this point James's discussion has shifted full bore toward systemic, inferentialist considerations with only implicit attention to the grounding of one's system of beliefs in concrete actions and their sensible effects. The overriding concern seems rather to be with the preservation of "the older stock of truths with a minimum of modification, stretching them just enough to make them admit the novelty, but conceiving that in ways as familiar as the case leaves possible" (James 1907c, PMT:35).

> A new opinion counts as 'true' just in proportion as it gratifies the individual's desire to assimilate the novel in his experience to his beliefs in stock. It must both lean on old truth and grasp new fact; and its success ... in doing this, is a matter for the individual's appreciation. When old truth grows, then, by new truth's addition, it is for subjective reasons. We are in the process and obey the reasons. That new idea is truest which performs most felicitously its function of satisfying our double urgency. It makes itself true, gets itself classed as true, by the way it works; grafting itself then upon the ancient body of truth, which thus grows much as a tree grows by the activity of a new layer of cambium. ... Purely objective truth, truth in whose establishment the function of giving human satisfaction in marrying previous parts of experience with newer parts played no rôle whatever, is nowhere to be found. The reasons we call things true is the reason why they *are* true, for 'to be true' *means* only to perform this marriage-function. (James 1907c, PMT:36–37)

It is difficult to accept the notion that, for example, sensible and propositionally formulated evidence used to test some hypothesis may be accepted as true or rejected as false solely "for subjective reasons," as if the latter were sufficient to validate the determination of the proposition's truth-value. Nevertheless, the idea of an opinion's "working" sounds here like a matter of its working to preserve coherence of the new and the old and nothing more. If pragmatism recommends a method for clarifying what one *means* by a given term, and if James is in fact applying that method to the notion of truth here, then it would appear that an opinion falls under the concept 'true' just to the extent that it works to permit some kind of "marriage" between itself and older opinions that fall under that concept.

Applying this revised pragmatic method to the notion of truth itself is just what James does in a later chapter, "Pragmatism's Conception of Truth" (1907f), and the results again echo coherentist rather than operationalist themes:

> Pragmatism ... asks its usual question. "Grant an idea or belief to be true," it says, "what concrete difference will its being true make in anyone's actual life? How will

the truth be realized? What experiences will be different from those which would obtain if the belief were false? What, in short, is the truth's cash-value in experiential terms?

The moment pragmatism asks this question, it sees the answer: *True ideas are those that we can assimilate, validate, corroborate and verify. False ideas are those that we cannot.* That is the practical difference it makes to us to have true ideas; that, therefore, is the meaning of truth, for it is all that truth is known-as.

This thesis is what I have to defend. The truth of an idea is not a stagnant property inherent in it. Truth *happens* to an idea. It *becomes* true, is *made* true by events. Its verity *is* in fact an event, a process: the process namely of its verifying itself, its veri-*fication*. Its validity is the process of its valid-*ation*.

But what do the words verification and validation themselves pragmatically mean? They again signify certain practical consequences of the verified and validated idea. It is hard to find any one phrase that characterizes these consequences better than the ordinary agreement formula—just such consequences being what we have in mind whenever we say that our ideas 'agree' with reality. They lead us, namely, through the acts and other ideas which they instigate, into or up to, or toward, other parts of experience with which we feel all the while—such feeling being among our potentialities—that the original ideas remain in agreement. The connexions and transitions come to us from point to point as being progressive, harmonious, satisfactory. This function of agreeable leading is what we mean by an idea's verification. (James 1907f, PMT:97)

The crux of the issue here is James's characterization of "verification and validation." The emphasis James places here on the process or event of an idea becoming or being made true requires nothing that might not be realized in one's armchair. This is, for all we know, the dynamics of abstract cognition, not the dynamics of laboratory operations. James does not intend any such thing; yet what he actually says about truth here does not require anything other than a rationalist psychology of belief. "James broadened the application of Peirce's maxim by including among the 'practical consequences' of a proposition the *psychological* effects of *believing* it" (Talisse and Aikin 2008, 15). Some of his statements too easily sound as if the application of the pragmatic maxim has been *shifted* rather than broadened.

One might argue that the next couple of pages in the latter lecture bring James back around to concrete operationalist themes when he distinguishes primary, original verifications from remote, indirect verifications:

Our experience meanwhile is all shot through with regularities. One bit of it can warn us to get ready for another bit, can "intend" or be significant of that remoter object. The object's advent is the significance's verification. Truth, in these cases, meaning nothing but eventual verification, is manifestly incompatible with waywardness on our part. Woe to him whose beliefs play fast and loose with the order which realities follow in his experience: they will lead him nowhere or else make false connexions.

By "realities" or "objects" here, we mean either things of common sense, sensibly present, or else common-sense relations, such as dates, places, distances, kinds, activities. Following our mental image of a house along the cow-path, we actually come to see the house; we get the image's full verification. *Such simply and fully verified leadings are certainly the originals and prototypes of the truth-process.* Experience offers indeed other forms of truth-process, but they are all conceivable as being primary verifications arrested, multiplied or substituted one for another. (James 1907f, PMT:97)

This is all well and good—not incorrect so far as it goes—but it only goes as far as, say, Carnap's appeal ultimately to the "knowledge-by-acquaintance" contained in so-called protocol sentences. The truth process finally stops with opinions each of whose truth individually stands on its own, with no account of what that amounts to. This simply begs the question. It pushes the question of truth down—puts it off—to some allegedly primitive level and then just stops, as if that were conclusive. There is nothing here of the activities of experimentation and observation that yield sensible results (Peirce 1878a, EP1:131–132)—nothing that points to an operationalist reading of the pragmatic maxim. The only "workings" this suggests are the systemic workings of a rationalist psychology of belief grounded in certain instances of immediate and irrefutable belief.

James's notion of *verification* is indeed the main culprit here. It rests not on the workings of "laboratory" procedures or generalized extrapolations thereof but on the workings of a rationalist psychology, e.g., the workings of discourse and inference. An operationalist reading of the pragmatic maxim says rather that so-called protocol sentences would have to be reports of specific objects falling under given concepts, their truth resting on the objective possibility of acquiring expected sensible effects of certain observation (e.g., measurement) activities. The "working" of such laboratory-like activities to yield expected sensible results is somehow lost in whatever James means by the "progressive, harmonious, satisfactory" workings of new and old ideas.

THREE
Peirce's Later Versions of the Maxim

James's application of the pragmatic method to the notion of "truth" is in stark contrast with Peirce's application of the maxim to the notions of "reality" and "truth" (1878a, section 4). Immediately after presenting the pragmatic maxim, Peirce (1878a, EP1:132–139) worked through several examples to show how that maxim may be employed to clarify various "conceptions." He looked at various concepts from physics—namely, *hard*, *weight*, *force*—before tackling two notions related (as he put it) to "logic"—specifically, our concepts of *reality* and *truth*. Peirce's discussions of the physics examples are not entirely easy to follow, and he later rejected what he thought were nominalistic aspects of his treatment of the first one (1905b; 1905d; 1911). Nevertheless, there is a common pattern throughout the discussions of these examples, namely: one must identify various distinctive "conceivable effects" that would serve as evidence of an instance of the given conception, where these effects are to be characterized as possible results of respective conceivable actions.

For example, the surface of something that is *hard* would *not* show *scratch marks* (result) if *scratched* (action) by a good many other substances. That and similar conditional claims constitute what it means to say that something is hard. The degree of meaningfulness of such claims, then, is correlated with one's ability to comprehend the respective actions and the expected results, for example, if one were capable of performing those actions.

The concept of *weight* is just as easily operationalized in fairly common terms. Namely, something with *weight* is something that would *drop* (a sensible effect) as a result of *letting it go* (an action of removing a force opposing the force of gravity). Of course, this employs other concepts that also beg for clarification.

Peirce's way of handling the concept of *force* appeals to Newtonian mechanics and related bits of mathematics (like vector geometry). Newtonian mechanics, based on three elementary laws of motion, is made up of a system of relations among a number of vector and scalar quantities (position, distance, duration, velocity, acceleration, mass, momentum, force, energy, etc.), some that are directly measurable and any of which may be manipulated directly or indirectly. Variations in any one of these variables will induce corresponding variations in others as prescribed by that system of relations. For instance, a Newtonian conception of *a force acting on a body with constant mass* can be characterized solely in terms of the acceleration of that body. If such acceleration is not directly sensible in itself (e.g., if one's own body is not the body in question), it may be cast in terms of the sensible results of measurements of distances and durations.

We should be able to generalize this method for defining concepts in terms of conceivable effects and respective actions that would bring them about, to a point that it should work across the board, from economics or sociology or cultural anthropology to physics or chemistry or any other area of concern, scientific or otherwise.

To better appreciate this claim, it is useful to peruse some of Peirce's later remarks on what pragmatism is, including other examples as well as various reformulations of the maxim itself. Peirce reformulates the maxim in later works, with various changes in content and emphasis that may not be obviously consistent from one formulation to the next. But the experimental, perceptual, sensible, operational gist of this account of meaning—that "there are no conceptions which are not given to us in perceptual judgments" (1903d, 223) and that "what we think is to be interpreted in terms of what we are prepared to do" (1903a, 142)—persists in all of these formulations. It is instructive to survey some of these formulations, presented below roughly in the chronological order in which they appeared in Peirce's publications and unpublished notebooks.

One perhaps must appreciate Peirce's wry if not bitter sense of humor to comprehend the following formulation:

> Pragmatism is the principle that every theoretical judgment expressible in a sentence in the indicative mood is a confused form of thought whose only meaning, if it has any, lies in its tendency to enforce a corresponding practical maxim expressible as a conditional sentence having its apodosis in the imperative mood. (Peirce 1903a, EP2:134–135)

These remarks are part of some opening remarks in the first of a series of lectures given by Peirce at Harvard over the course of three months in 1903. He says here that the meaning of any meaningful declarative theoretical judgment (*theoretical judgments only?*) is expressible in the form of a conditional sentence whose consequent is some kind of command or mandate. The latter could be regarded more generally as a set of instructions: to achieve this or that, *do such and so*; or, if this or that other is to occur, then *do thus thusly*; and so forth. On the face of it, this seems too simple as an account of the meanings of theoretical judgments. This formulation of the maxim is at best a slogan that requires a good deal of elaboration.

From the same series of lectures, a formulation that is more easily understood goes as follows:

> The last lecture was devoted to an introductory glance at Pragmatism, considered as the maxim that the entire meaning and significance of any conception lies in its

> *conceivably* practical bearings,—not certainly altogether in consequences that would influence our conduct so far as we can foresee our future circumstances but which in *conceivable* circumstances would go to determine how we should deliberately act, and how we should act in a practical way and not how we should act as affirming or denying the conception to be cleared up. (Peirce 1903b, EP2:145)

This formulation of the maxim contains more careful qualifications that resist reduction to simplistic slogans. This formulation is again somewhat cryptic insofar as it was supposed to be a brief summary of points made in a previous lecture. But note the emphasis on what is *conceivable* rather than what is actual or even foreseeable by "us" at a given time in given circumstances of entertaining a given conception. The meaning and significance of a conception lies in practical bearings not limited to what might actually be born out but encompassing any conceivable action in any respective conceivable circumstances pertinent to that conception. The point here is to highlight the notion of "practical bearings" as the fundamental notion in a theory of meaning while at the same time denying *exclusive* emphasis on practical bearings *actually* born out in our experience. The pragmatic maxim is thus cast so as to accommodate counterfactual "practical bearings."

We find the following remarks at the end of the same series of lectures in which the two preceding formulations of the maxim appear. These remarks help to explicate the maxim insofar as it appeals to the practical bearings of "sensible effects":

> I do not think it is possible to fully comprehend the problem of the merits of pragmatism without recognizing these three truths: *first*, that there are no conceptions which are not given to us in perceptual judgments, so that we may say that all of our ideas are perceptual ideas. This sounds like sensationalism. But in order to maintain this position, it is necessary to recognize, *second*, that perceptual judgments contain elements of generality, so that Thirdness is directly perceived; and finally, I think it of great importance to recognize, *third*, that the abductive faculty, whereby we divine the secrets of nature, is, as we may say, a shading off, a gradation of that which in its highest perfection we call perception.
>
> But while, to my apprehension, it is only in the light of those three doctrines that the true characteristics of pragmatism are fully displayed, yet even without them we shall be brought, although less clearly and forcibly, to nearly the same opinion. (Peirce 1903d, EP2:223–224)

These three claims are what Peirce elsewhere refers to as his three "cotary" propositions, namely, propositions that finally get to the point: "*Cōs, cōtīs* is a whetstone. They appear to me to put the edge on the maxim of pragmatism" (1903f, EP2:226). The first two claims are reminiscent of what James refers to as "radical empiricism" (1909a, PMT:172–173), a connection we need not pursue presently. But we do need to acknowledge how broadly Peirce conceives of perception. This speaks against interpreting his views on meaning along modern sensationist or contemporary verificationist lines:

To return to [earlier discussions of] the dog. My perceptual judgments of dogs have contained sundry general elements and these I have generalized by abductions chiefly, with small doses of induction, and have thus acquired some general ideas of dogs' ways, of the laws of caninity, some of them invariable so far as I have observed, such as his frequent napping, others merely usual, such as his circling when he is preparing to nap. These are laws of perceptual judgments, and so beyond all doubt are the great majority of our general notions. It is not evident that this is not the case with all general notions. If, therefore, anybody maintains that there are any general notions which are not given in the perceptual judgments, it is fair to demand that he should prove it by close reasoning and not expect us to accept unsupported assertions to that effect nor to assent to it without some better than vague remarks to convince us that it is so. . . .

It is now generally admitted, and it is the result of my own logical analysis, that the true maxim of abduction is that which Auguste Comte endeavored to formulate when he said that any hypothesis might be admissible if and only if it was verifiable. Whatever Comte himself meant by verifiable, which is not very clear, it certainly ought not to be understood to mean verifiable by direct observation, since that would cut off all history as an inadmissible hypothesis. But what must and should be meant is that the hypothesis must be capable of verification by induction. Now induction, or experimental inquiry, consists in comparing perceptual predictions deduced from a theory with the facts of perception predicted, and in taking the measure of agreement observed as the provisional and approximate, or probametric, measure of the general agreement of the theory with fact.

It thus appears that a conception can only be admitted into a hypothesis insofar as its possible consequences would be of a perceptual nature; which agrees with my original maxim of pragmatism as far as it goes. (Peirce 1903d, EP2:223–225)

Such remarks point to the fact that, for Peirce, the "logic of perception" is the logic of abductive inference, and that "the true doctrine concerning Pragmatism whatever it may be is nothing else than the true Logic of Abduction" (Peirce 1903d, EP2:224). This twist in the early development of pragmatism is perhaps unique to Peirce. We need not delve into the enigma of abductive inference, as interesting as that would be. One thing this connection between pragmatism and abduction entails, though, is that a theory of justifiable belief, if grounded finally in perception, is grounded in judgments that are inherently ampliative and fallible. Moreover, Peirce describes a kind of abductive regress at bottom that makes for a solid though endlessly analyzable *foundation* for belief:

On its side, the perceptive judgment is the result of a process, although of a process not sufficiently conscious to be controlled, or to state it more truly, not controllable and therefore not fully conscious. If we were to subject this subconscious process to logical analysis we should find that it terminated in what that analysis would represent as an abductive inference resting on the result of a similar process which a similar logical analysis would represent to be terminated by a similar abductive inference, and so on *ad infinitum*. This analysis would be precisely analogous to that which the sophism of Achilles and the tortoise applies to the chase of the tortoise by

Achilles, and it would fail to represent the real process for the same reason. Namely, just as Achilles does not have to make the series of distinct endeavors which he is represented as making, so this process of forming the perceptual judgment, because it is subconscious and so not amenable to logical criticism, does not have to make separate acts of inference but performs its act in one continuous process. (Peirce 1903f, EP2:227)

These remarks of course reveal intriguing though not entirely clear differences between Peirce's open-ended fallibilist conception of perception and Quine's less weighty references to irritations of nerve endings and/or to excitations at the periphery of one's web of belief (1960; 1973)—or Carnap's notion of sense data simply as given (1928).

Peirce's emphasis on "sensible effects" in various statements of the pragmatic maxim clearly should not be equated with these later forms of analytic empiricism. In particular, the latter are unable to accommodate the abductive nature of perception. That is perhaps a tall order for any theory of belief or meaning, but Peirce at least acknowledges the ampliative nature of perception. Twentieth-century analytic empiricism does not do that, or it does so differently by way of such notions as the theory-ladenness of observation (Hanson 1958, 19). James also falls short in this regard to the extent that he too easily accommodates Carnap's kind of empiricism in an effort to promote inferentialist pragmatism.

In some way that remains unclear, Peirce's conception of the abductive nature of perception is tied up with the emphasis on sensible effects as effects of actions in the world rather than as mere surface irritations or nerve-hits received out of the blue. At the end of the series of lectures in which the preceding discussion of pragmatism appeared, we find the following:

> [A]gainst unclear and nonsensical hypotheses, whatever aegis there may be in pragmatism will be more essentially significant for [the pragmatist] than for any other logician for the reason that it is in action that logical energy returns to the uncontrolled and uncritical parts of the mind. His maxim will be this:
>> The elements of every concept enter into logical thought at the gate of perception [broadly conceived as indicated above] and make their exit at the gate of purposive action; and whatever cannot show its passports at both those two gates is to be arrested as unauthorized by reason.
>
> (Peirce 1903f, EP2:241)

This comes dangerously close to endorsing a form of empiricism that we will contrast with pragmatism below (chapters 5–8). Perhaps Peirce is as much mistaken here as James was in eventually succumbing to a relatively common run-of-the-mill form of logical empiricism; but the theme to emphasize here is Peirce's recognition that it is actions in the world, as well as their sensible effects, that ground our beliefs. Pragmatism emphasizes the role of action (e.g., experimentation) as a logical foundation, not simply as an extra-logical application of detached rational thought.

Two years after the 1903 Harvard lectures on pragmatism, Peirce published a couple of articles in *The Monist* where, once again, he reconsiders how best to characterize pragmatism and, consequently, how best to formulate the pragmatic maxim:

> Endeavoring, as a man of that [experimentalist] type would, to formulate what he so approved, [I] framed the theory that a *conception*, that is, the rational purport of a word or other expression, lies exclusively in its conceivable bearing upon the conduct of life; so that, since obviously nothing that might not result from an experiment can have any direct bearing upon conduct, if one can define accurately all the conceivable experimental phenomena which the affirmation or denial of a concept could imply, one will have therein a complete definition of the concept, and *there is absolutely nothing more in it*. For this doctrine [I] invented the name pragmatism. (Peirce 1905a, EP2:332)

Note the emphasis here on experimentation, not just armchair manipulations of beliefs. Notice also that Peirce does not say here that complete definitions of concepts can always be given (though surely that is achievable in simple and/or artificial cases). Echoing statements quoted earlier, the point is that we may master various conceptions as easily as Achilles overtakes the tortoise though complete definitions of those conceptions may not be articulable. The more important point is the claim about what goes into constituting such a definition, lying "exclusively in [a conception's] conceivable bearing upon the conduct of life" which ultimately is expressed in terms of "conceivable experimental phenomena."

At the beginning of the second of the 1905 *Monist* articles, Peirce explicitly restates the maxim qua maxim, immediately after quoting the 1878a version:

> I will restate [this maxim] in other words, since ofttimes one can thus eliminate some unsuspected source of perplexity to the reader. This time it shall be in the indicative mood, as follows: The entire intellectual purport of any symbol consists in the total of all general modes of rational conduct which, conditionally upon all the possible different circumstances and desires, would ensue upon acceptance of the symbol. (Peirce 1905b, EP2:346)

Again Peirce identifies "conduct" (in this case, conduct that is rational) as keyed conditionally to various possible circumstances in the world. The earlier emphasis on "sensible effects" is all but missing here, though Peirce makes this connection explicitly toward the end of the article in his discussion of the *real* hardness of diamonds:

> [W]e must dismiss the idea that the occult state of things (be it a relation among atoms or something else), which constitutes the reality of a diamond's hardness can possibly consist in anything but in the truth of a general conditional proposition. For to what else does the entire teaching of chemistry relate except to the "behavior" of different possible kinds of material substance? And in what does that behavior consist except that if a substance of a certain kind should be exposed to an agency of a certain kind, a certain kind of sensible result *would* ensue, according to our

experiences hitherto. As for the pragmaticist, it is precisely his position that nothing else than this can be so much as *meant* by saying that an object possesses a character. (Peirce 1905b, EP2:357)

It is in the first of the two 1905 *Monist* articles, by the way, that Peirce labeled his own view as "pragmaticism" (1905a, EP2:334–335) in light of disagreements with other views of pragmatism held by proponents and critics alike (see page 6 above). In what was supposed to be a third paper for *The Monist* in 1905, we find the following characterization of Peirce's "pragmaticism." In this passage, Peirce is attempting to explain what he takes the then current view of pragmatism to be as developed by James, Schiller, and others, and how his original conception of pragmatism differs. The quotation is somewhat long, but it deserves careful reading:

> After a good deal of reflection and careful rereading, I have come to think that the common pragmatistic opinion aforesaid is that *every* thought (unless perhaps certain single ideas each quite *sui generis*) has a meaning beyond the immediate content of the thought itself, so that it is as absurd to speak of a thought in itself as it would be to say of a man that he was a husband in himself or a son in himself, and this not merely because thought always refers to a real or fictitious *object*, but also because it supposes itself to be interpretable. If this analysis of the pragmatistic opinion be correct, the logical breadth of the term *pragmatist* is thereby enormously enlarged ... [*so* broadly as to embrace Royce, Leibniz, Ockham, Aquinas, Aristotle]. ... If we wished to exclude the general body of such logicians from the ranks of this school, we should have to describe the latter, no longer as consisting of those who hold to the doctrine that every thought has a meaning beyond its immediate content, but as confined to those who specially insist upon certain consequences of this doctrine, when the unity of their opinion would lose its definiteness.
>
> The contents of most logic books is a syncretistic hodgepodge, and it is difficult to detect any differences but those of detail between one book and another. It is certain, however, that there have been, and still are, many logicians who in regard to our primary and simple thoughts would protest against the theory that they have any exterior meaning. "The meaning!" these logicians would exclaim, "That *is* precisely the concept!" The refutation of this opinion will make us pragmatists, according to my analysis. In order to establish *pragmaticism*, it will be necessary further to show that if the ultimate interpretation of a thought relates to anything but a determination of conditional conduct, it cannot be of an intellectual quality and so is not in the strictest sense a *concept*. (Peirce 1906a, EP2:361–362)

The earlier parts of this passage show Peirce's awareness of the fact that "pragmatism" has taken on the shape of a Jamesian inferentialism—a view that when fully developed, with no other constraints or qualifications, would not align well with what Peirce had originally intended. Giving up on salvaging the term 'pragmatism', he instead states that his pragmaticism is indeed a form of pragmatism, but then it is something more specific. Besides the inferentialism, pragmaticism also calls for the "interpretation of a thought" ultimately in terms of "a determination of conditional conduct." Peirce is essentially saying here that, as of 1905 or earlier and despite its origins, pragmatism has lost its operationalist orientation.

A couple of years later, in 1907, Peirce attempted yet again to characterize pragmatism, this time in a manuscript that failed to be accepted for publication. The following quotation, like the last one, is rather long, but it portrays a more conciliatory, less confrontational attitude on Peirce's part—employing a strategy whereby he simply attributes his operationalist emphasis on experimental activity to "all pragmatists":

> Suffice it to say once more that pragmatism is, in itself, no doctrine of metaphysics, no attempt to determine any truth of things. It is merely a method of ascertaining the meanings of hard words and of abstract concepts. All pragmatists of whatsoever stripe will cordially assent to that statement. ... All pragmatists will further agree that their method of ascertaining the meanings of words and concepts is no other than that experimental method by which all the successful sciences (in which number nobody in his senses would include metaphysics) have reached the degrees of certainty that are severally proper to them today;—this experimental method being itself nothing but a particular application of the older logical rule, "By their fruits ye shall know them." ... The most prominent of all our school and the most respected, William James, defines pragmatism as the doctrine that the whole "meaning" of a concept expresses itself either in the shape of conduct to be recommended or of experience to be expected. ... I understand pragmatism to be a method of ascertaining the meanings, not of all ideas, but only of what I call "intellectual concepts," that is to say, of those upon the structure of which arguments concerning objective fact may hinge. ... Intellectual concepts, however,—the only sign-burdens that are properly denominated "concepts,"—essentially carry some implication concerning the general behavior either of some conscious being or of some inanimate object, and so convey more, not merely than any feeling, but more, too, than any existential fact, namely, the "*would-acts*" of habitual behavior; and no agglomeration of actual happenings can ever completely fill up the meaning of a "would be." But that the *total* meaning of the predication of an intellectual concept consists in affirming that, under all conceivable circumstances of a given kind, the subject of the predication would (or would not) behave in a certain way,—that is, that it either would, or would not, be true that under given experiential circumstances (or under a given proportion of them, taken *as they would occur* in experience) certain facts would exist,—*that* proposition I take to be the kernel of pragmatism. More simply stated, the whole meaning of an intellectual predicate is that certain kinds of events would happen, once in so often, in the course of experience, under certain kinds of existential circumstances. (Peirce 1907b, EP2:400–402)

We thus see in this later formulation of "the kernel of pragmatism" a slightly revised expression of operationalism in terms of possible "events" that might result from "the '*would-acts*' of habitual behavior ... in the course of experience, under certain kinds of existential circumstances." This is something other than James's ultimate appeal (in some instances) to primitive beliefs. It ties our meanings more tightly to the potential effects of our actions in the world.

Peirce's various formulations of the pragmatic maxim display its complexity (it remains unclear what it actually says!) though he never lost sight of its original operationalist character. These various formulations also indicate that the first formulation in 1878a, though somewhat cryptic, remains as good a formulation as any that he composed in subsequent years, especially if brevity is the aim.

Given these various formulations of the pragmatic maxim, we may more clearly grasp what it says by considering some of Peirce's examples and illustrations of how to apply it. We have already noted that the latter half of the 1878a article in which the maxim was first published was devoted to just such examples, including applications of the maxim to the words 'reality' and 'truth' after first applying it to some terms from physics. We will look at the 'reality' and 'truth' examples shortly, particularly to contrast Peirce's pragmatist definition of the word 'truth' with James's theory of truth. Before we do that, first consider an especially informative illustration of how to use the pragmatic maxim in the sciences, this time involving a notion from chemistry. Unlike the physics examples in the 1878a article, it is short and to the point:

> If you look into a textbook of chemistry for a definition of *lithium*, you may be told that it is that element whose atomic weight is 7 very nearly. But if the author has a more logical mind he will tell you that if you search among minerals that are vitreous, translucent, gray or white, very hard, brittle, and insoluble, for one which imparts a crimson tinge to an unluminous flame, this mineral being triturated with lime or witherite rats-bane, and then fused, can be partly dissolved in muriatic acid; and if this solution be evaporated, and the residue be extracted with sulphuric acid, and duly purified, it can be converted by ordinary methods into a chloride, which being obtained in the solid state, fused, and electrolyzed with half a dozen powerful cells, will yield a globule of a pinkish silvery metal that will float on gasolene; and the material of *that* is a specimen of lithium. The peculiarity of this definition—or rather this precept that is more serviceable than a definition—is that it tells you what the word lithium denotes by prescribing what you are to *do* in order to gain a perceptual acquaintance with the object of the word. (Peirce 1903g, EP2:286)

This is an operational definition, loud and clear. It is not insignificant that this illustration appears in the third section of "A Syllabus of Certain Topics of Logic," an unpublished supplement to Peirce's Lowell lectures (November 1903). These notes range far and wide to extend his semiotic theory (see the editor's notes, EP2:267) to cover any non-trivial concept, whether it be in chemistry, political science, or otherwise. It is a telling fact that he introduces this *lithium* example at a juncture where he is presenting an account of the meanings of general terms:

> The ordinary doctrine [regarding categorical propositions] makes the copula the only verb, and all of the other terms to be either proper names or general class-names. The present author leaves the *is* as an inseparable part of the class-name; ... [A]lmost every family of man thinks of general words as parts of verbs. (Peirce 1903g, EP2:285)

Immediately thereafter Peirce presents the *lithium* example not in terms of what such a substance *is* but in terms of how it reacts to what one *does* with it. Regarding general class-names in particular, after presenting the lithium example, he makes the following general remark:

> Every subject of a proposition, unless it is either an Index (like the environment of the interlocutors, or something attracting attention in that environment, as the pointing finger of the speaker) or a Subindex (like a proper name, personal pronoun, or demonstrative) must be a *Precept*, or Symbol, not only describing to the Interpreter what is to be done, by him or others or both, in order to obtain an Index of an individual (whether a unit or a single set of units) of which the proposition is represented as meant to be true, but also assigning a designation to that individual, or, if it is a set, to each single unit of the set. (Peirce 1903g, EP2:286)

We should especially appreciate the emphasis here on descriptions of "what is to be done" (etc.) as the content of any "subject of a proposition." Most notably this discussion does *not* so much concern "conversational pragmatics." Peirce is making a more fundamental point about basic word definitions—the discussion as a whole pointing to the fact that what does all the work here is essentially the pragmatic maxim: i.e., that a serviceable definition will "[prescribe] what you are to *do* in order to gain a perceptual acquaintance with the object of the word."

The *lithium* example is worth close scrutiny though it is complicated. Substantial effort would be required to generalize the example to fairly large parts of chemistry. Einstein's operational foundations for special relativity (1916) display how complicated (and far-reaching) things can get just with measurement activities involving clocks, measuring rods, and the like. Applications in economics and related social sciences will be even more of a challenge for obvious reasons.

Peirce's discussion of reality and truth in this regard (in his 1878a article) is, on the other hand, surprisingly straightforward and rather simple (once you see how it is done). If we are to clarify our concept of reality (to clearly define the *term* 'reality'), we should do so in terms of its sensible effects and practical bearings. We should be able to "operationalize" the concept of reality just as with any other concept. Peirce does that, smartly but in an understated way, in terms of inquiry as a kind of operation that leads to the fixation of beliefs. In this case, the relevant actions are "inquiries" and the sensible effects are "consequent beliefs."

How does he do this? The concept of reality is quite broad, and its effects should be stated in respectively broad terms. On Peirce's account, reality may consist of that whose characters are independent of our thought of them, but, he says, "[t]he only effect which real things have is to cause belief, for all sensations which they excite emerge into consciousness in the form of beliefs" (1878a, EP1:137). That claim is debatable, but the point here is that beliefs are now playing the role of "sensible effects" at least so far as a definition of the word 'reality' is concerned. Reality generates appearances and ultimately beliefs, and these are "sensible"—perhaps "tangible" would be a better term here—in the broad (radical, non-sensationist) sense captured in Peirce's three "cotary" propositions (see page 24 above).

We should thus be able to articulate what we mean by the word 'reality' in terms of such effects. This is a remarkable point on Peirce's part, namely, to note that such considerations *illustrate* the pragmatist method, or more specifically, the method of operationalizing one's terms. The *lithium* example might tempt one to think that the pragmatic maxim is applicable only in terms of *laboratory* activities. The laboratory is a good source of examples because it is a controlled environment designed for clearly specifiable procedures and protocols that lend themselves easily to operational definitions; but there is nothing in Peirce's various formulations of the pragmatic maxim saying that laboratory activities exhaust the range of operational definitions.

So, in the case of defining the term 'reality', the actions are "inquiries" and the sensible effects are "consequent beliefs." A complication immediately arises from the fact that beliefs may have various sources, real and unreal. Thus further clarification of the concept of reality will rely on distinguishing true belief (belief in the real) and false belief (belief in what is not real). Defining the term 'reality' thus hinges on definitions of the terms 'truth' and 'falsity'. As applied to opinions, truth and falsity are defined in terms of methods by which opinions are formed and maintained. Here Peirce draws on an earlier discussion of different methods of settling belief (1877). While the methods of tenacity, authority, or *a priori* reasoning are by their own internal standards unreliable, "the ideas of truth and falsehood, in their full development, appertain exclusively to the scientific [or experiential] method" (EP1:137). Peirce's method of science is the only one of the four with an intrinsic concern for distinguishing truth and falsity. Thus, we can clarify the notion of *truth* in terms of the operations and effects of inquiry; but it will be specifically in terms of the methods of *scientific* inquiry.

On this basis, still aiming to clarify the term 'reality', Peirce offers his infamous definition of the term 'truth' utilizing the pragmatic maxim. Truth is defined in terms of processes of scientific investigation (the requisite actions) in response to questions or doubts, and the resulting solutions (namely beliefs as sensible effects) that these processes yield. What we *mean* by the terms 'truth' or 'true opinion' is just what would result if such investigations were to be carried out to a point that no further resolution were possible—namely, if they were to be carried out perfectly (Talisse 2007).

In Peirce's words, "[t]he opinion that is fated to be ultimately agreed to by all who investigate, is what we mean by the truth." This statement has led to much confusion; but here, using a bit of hermeneutic license, it is taken to mean that the word 'truth' signifies (expresses, denotes) some kind of *ideal*. That is, if an ideal is "a conception of something in its perfection" and thus "a standard of excellence" (Oxford American Dictionary 2011), then the "something" in the case of 'truth' would have to be the carrying out of scientific inquiry. (In the case of any word that can be defined operationally and whose meaning admits of a standard of excellence, the "something" would just be the carrying out of the respective operations in accord with how they allegedly determine the meaning of that word.)

How else might we define 'truth' in terms of the activities of inquiry? There may be multiple ways to do that, but the point here is to show how to use the pragmatic maxim to define such words. The agreement-in-the-limit-of-perfect-scientific-inquiry definition says (only) what we *mean* by the term 'truth', not that we can actually carry out such processes of investigation perfectly or attain such final agreement. Such agreement in the indefinite long run is *conceivable* in terms of the practices of inquiry, and that is enough to *clarify* the concept of *truth*. (See chapter 9 below for further discussion in light of applying this manner of definition more broadly.)

With this pragmatist clarification of the concept of 'truth', we can complete the definition of the term 'reality'. Namely: "the object represented in this [unavoidable] opinion is the real" (1878a, EP1:138–139). We thus conceive of reality as being what we would come to represent in a perfect resolution of opinions (particularly through use of scientific methods), rather than as something *behind* a veil of appearances. We could just as well be rid of the veil metaphor altogether. This puts science and practical processes of intelligently guided experience in the limelight as our best hope for grasping reality and dispelling false opinions.

The important point here, again, is that Peirce has used the pragmatic maxim to clearly articulate the concepts of *reality* and *truth*. He has not yet provided epistemic criteria for deciding truth values (he does that elsewhere) nor has he defined the term 'truth' in terms of the particular results of particular processes of actual investigation. He has defined the word 'truth' rather in terms of a conceivable idealization of such processes and results, as if they could be pursued without constraints or limits on time and resources. The Achilles-and-tortoise metaphor may be apt here, in some cases, in that, practically speaking, we may complete such infinite resolutions in fairly short order, in real time. On the other hand, Peirce does seem to gear this idealization to long-range developments in the ongoing work of a changing community of scientific inquirers (spanning generation after generation, etc.). Indeed the "workings" of any particular new opinion of any one individual will often be essentially negligible when measured against such idealizations. Such an ideal limit is nevertheless conceivable in practical terms though not always in here-and-now *practicable* terms. The idea of a true opinion is *clearly defined* in this way even if many true opinions, so defined, may themselves be ever beyond our present grasp.

Similarly for the term 'reality'. The idea of reality as Peirce presents it is clear enough—as that which is independent of what we may think it to be but which can be investigated indefinitely—even if we do not investigate matters *forever* in actual practice. Reality is what we would come to not by lifting the veil of processes and results of scientific or experiential method but by pursuing those practices without resource limitations—or rather, that is what we should say we *mean* by the word 'reality' when pressed to give a definition.

It is perhaps thought that, since we are not able in fact to investigate matters to a point of infinite resolution, the ideal-limit-of-inquiry definition requires that we achieve something that we cannot actually achieve. Indeed, in many cases, various realities will not be investigatible *at all* in any way that we can actualize. Nevertheless, *conceivability* of pertinent practical bearings and not their actualization is all that is *required* in such definitions—of 'reality' and 'truth' or of any other words defined in accordance with the pragmatic maxim.

Thus the belief that there are iron ore deposits somewhere in the interior of Pluto is by Peirce's lights true or not depending on what the interior of Pluto is really like. One does not have to go to Pluto and actually perform appropriate chemical analyses on various core samples to conceive of such analyses being performed. We very well know what it *means* to claim that there *are* iron ore deposits in the interior of Pluto, even if we do not yet have the wherewithal to figure out workable engineering details for actually getting at it. The belief that Caesar kept his sword dry when he crossed the Rubicon is true or not depending on what really happened at that historical juncture. One does not have to be able to provide evidence of such realities for the provisions of evidence to be conceivable. We know in just such terms what we mean by each of the various concepts used to formulate such beliefs. We have to say what we mean in terms of investigatory practices, but a belief is true because of what is real, not because we have implemented those practices. This is the case even if our current beliefs fall short of a complete grasp of the particular reality insofar as the investigatory activities and such that we are now capable of conceiving fall short of what would be possible in an unlimited progressive development of investigatory practices.

We can see then that Peirce's definitions of 'reality' and 'truth' are not unserviceable in the here and now just because of the perfectionist element of idealization that is built into them.

Consider the following analogy. We define so-called real numbers as ideal limits. We can approximate irrational numbers to any degree practicable, but we need not question their *reality* (in the broader metaphysical sense) just because of the practical finitude of any such approximation effort. The first few digits in the decimal expansion of π are what they are and will never be undone as more and more decimal places are calculated—they *really* are the actual early digits in that expansion. That much of reality (being what will be preserved in the limit) is thus directly and openly accessible here and now, not exclusively at the end of all possible future calculations of later digits in the expansion.

Peirce's definitions of 'reality' and 'truth' allow that realities and respective truths in general are accessible in much the same way. We routinely carry out early stages of such idealized inquiry as we solve day-to-day problems, achieving limited but practicable results that would only be preserved in resource-unlimited inquiry. For example, suppose you want a beer. You go to the refrigerator where you now have to decide which objects therein are bottles of beer and which are not. In all of about half of a second or less, you will probably complete as much of a scientific inquiry as is needed to make the decision. You may not have pursued your inquiry to the point of infinite resolution; but so far as you have taken it, to that extent you have *some* direct and open grasp of reality inside the refrigerator— a direct if only partial grasp of what would be discerned as the result of resource-unlimited inquiry. No further inquiry will undo what you have found to be the case (assuming you have not made a mistake and grabbed a ketchup bottle). Your belief is limited in its content relative to what a complete scientific inquiry would reveal, but it is fully true so far as that partial content is concerned. This much of reality, moreover, does not reside behind some veil of appearances. It is directly and openly accessible.

Peirce took the term 'pragmatism' from Kant's term *pragmatisch* (1905a). More substantively, he explicitly stated that he "was led to the maxim by reflection upon Kant's *Critic of Pure Reason*" (1902b). He did not endorse Kant's views across the board. In fact, he was emphatically critical of Kant on numerous grounds (see, e.g., 1907b, EP2:424). Nevertheless he found in Kant (and in the modern emergence and refinement of scientific method) the seeds of a viable theory of meaning. Kant appealed to a principle requiring empirical grounds for applications of concepts to objects of experience in objectively valid judgments. Strawson (1966, 16, 145, 241–243) refers to this requirement as the principle of significance. This Kantian principle anticipates Peirce's pragmatic maxim, though Peirce rejected Kant's picture of human mental faculties and, in particular, the picture of how a faculty of understanding imposes structure on a manifold of sensibility. Peirce asserted though that "sensible effects of things" may be appealed to as grounds for objectively valid judgments precisely because they *and* the activities which produce them constitute the contents of our thought. The bottom line is this: the pragmatic maxim presents an experimentalist, empiricist view of conceptual content that is necessarily operationalist in character.

FOUR

A Composite Sketch of the Maxim

With Peirce's and James's explanatory remarks and interpretive differences in front of us, it is not exactly easy to determine what the pragmatic maxim actually says or, consequently, what pragmatism is. Nevertheless this chapter will present what is meant to be a constructive, inclusive synthesis of the two kinds of pragmatism represented respectively by Peirce and James.

A composite portrait of pragmatism begins to emerge as we bring together various results from preceding chapters. Namely, pragmatism would appear to be a philosophical stance or attitude with essentially two defining characteristics. These are (1) a certain normative conception of *belief* and (2) a methodological principle (the so-called *pragmatic maxim*) regarding *meaning* that itself has two aspects, operational and inferential. Together these various features of pragmatism suggest that we distinguish not just a third but also a *fourth* grade of clarity beyond Descartes' two grades of "clear and distinct" ideas.

Belief

A pragmatist conception of belief was spelled out (roughly) by Peirce in "The Fixation of Belief" (1877). It was extended by James in *Pragmatism* (1907h) as a theory of *truth* that, as argued in earlier chapters, would have been better cast as a treatment of rational and/or justified and/or warranted belief. Peirce, of course, did not exactly acknowledge (though he should have) that the background conception of belief from which he derived his "principle of pragmatism" is itself an aspect of pragmatism. He tended rather to characterize pragmatism solely in terms of the pragmatic maxim—so that *pragmatism*, as a corollary of that conception of belief (1907b, EP2:399), was cast solely as "a method of ascertaining the meanings" of abstract concepts (1907b, EP2:401). In this regard, with hindsight that neither of them had, we could say that neither Peirce nor James quite got this first aspect of pragmatism right: James mislabeled it and Peirce did not give it its due. Yet some minor adjustments of each of their positions yields a composite conception of belief that comports with both of their respective views in every substantively important way.

It was noted earlier that Peirce was working with a certain conception of belief adapted from Alexander Bain (1855; 1859) and James Fitzjames Stephens

(1863) by way of his friend Nicholas St. John Green (see Peirce 1906b; 1907b, EP2:399; Menand 2001, 225, 354; Wiener 1946, 220, 223). Officially, Peirce originally presented the pragmatic maxim as a principle pertaining to how our thinking may best be concretely grounded by way of experimental methods (1907b, EP2:400–401)—a principle that could thus be easily interpreted in terms of activities and their sensible results. But also recall the statement by Peirce (quoted on page 6 above) that "[i]n 1871, in a Metaphysical Club in Cambridge, Mass., I used to preach this principle as a sort of logical gospel, representing the unformulated method followed by Berkeley, and in conversation about it I called it 'Pragmatism'" (1908, EP2:448). Whatever it was that Peirce was calling by the name 'pragmatism' in 1871 surely had as much or more to do with his discussions with Green, James, Chauncey Wright, and others concerning the nature of belief. This claim is supported by the fact that much of the content of "The Fixation of Belief" (1877) and "How to Make Our Ideas Clear" (1878a) appeared in some earlier drafts of chapters for a book on logic (1872, WP3:14–61). The material there is focused on the nature of belief (versus doubt, etc.) and reality (as the object of the one final opinion that all would come to who carry out their research far enough—an objective and decidedly Darwinian conception of the "fixation" of opinion, according to Wiener 1946) with at best only faint hints of the kinds of concerns targeted by the pragmatic maxim, for instance, in some inconclusive remarks about meaning (1872, WP3:38–39). It is arguably the case—in light of Fisch's careful but tentative study (EP2:546n7; Fisch 1964; 1981)—that these drafts, in whole or in part, were what Peirce was referring to in 1907b (EP2:400) when he mentioned that, as a "souvenir" of the Metaphysical Club discussions, he had drawn up "a little paper expressing some of the opinions that I had been urging all along under the name of pragmatism." Assuming this is an accurate portrayal of actual events, it would clearly show that Peirce's "pragmatism" was originally concerned with (a doctrine concerning) the nature of belief and a proper conception of reality and not so much with the yet-to-be-formulated pragmatic maxim as a methodological principle.

This thesis is further supported by Peirce's various statements that he appropriated the name 'pragmatism' from Kant's first *Critique*. Speaking about himself in the third person, Peirce describes some issues concerning his choice of the label as follows:

> Some of his friends wished him to call it *practicism* or *practicalism* (perhaps on the ground that πρακτικός is better Greek than πραγματικός). But for one who had learned philosophy out of Kant, as the writer, along with nineteen out of every twenty experimentalists who have turned to philosophy, had done, and who still thought in Kantian terms most readily, *praktisch* and *pragmatisch* were as far apart as the two poles, the former belonging in a region of thought where no mind of the experimentalist type can ever make sure of solid ground under his feet, the latter expressing relation to some definite human purpose. Now quite the most striking feature of

the new theory was its recognition of an inseparable connection between rational cognition and rational purpose; and that consideration it was which determined the preference for the name *pragmatism*. (Peirce 1905a, EP2:332–333)

Thus, while the words 'pragmatic' and 'pragmatism' do not appear in the 1878a article "How to Make Our Ideas Clear" where the pragmatic maxim first appeared in print, we are to believe that the term 'pragmatism' originated with Peirce years earlier based on his readings of Kant. These readings no doubt included Kant's views on the nature of belief.

Specifically, toward the end of Kant's *Critique of Pure Reason*, in chapter II (The Canon of Pure Reason) of part II (Transcendental Doctrine of Method), Kant distinguished two kinds of practical ("theoretically insufficient") belief: pragmatic belief and moral belief. Peirce rejected this distinction and adapted the term 'pragmatism' to stand for the view that, from the perspective of late-nineteenth-century statistics-savvy post-Kantian science, all belief is pragmatic in a Kantian sense—which is to say, there is just one kind of belief, and Kant's description of pragmatic belief comes closest to saying what that is:

> But it is only from a *practical point of view* that the theoretically insufficient holding of a thing to be true can be termed believing. This practical point of view ... in reference to *skill* [is] concerned with optional and contingent ends. ... Once an end is accepted, the conditions of its attainment are hypothetically necessary. This necessity is subjectively, but still only comparatively, sufficient, if I know of no other conditions under which the end can be attained. ... In [this] case my assumption and the holding of certain conditions to be true is a merely contingent belief. ... The physician must do something for a patient in danger, but does not know the nature of his illness. He observes the symptoms, and if he can find no more likely alternative, judges it to be a case of phthisis. Now even in his own estimation his belief is contingent only; another observer might perhaps come to a sounder conclusion. Such contingent belief, which yet forms the ground for the actual employment of means to certain actions, I entitle *pragmatic belief*. ... The usual touchstone [of pragmatic belief] is *betting*. ... [P]ragmatic belief always exists in some specific degree, which, according to differences in the interests at stake, may be large or may be small. (Kant 1781/1787, A823–825/B851–853)

We cannot legitimately claim—and we do not want to claim—that Peirce endorsed this particular characterization of pragmatic belief in detail. Peirce was, after all, merely appropriating the label, not endorsing the larger Kantian edifice of which this conception of belief was a part. Rather, looking only at Kant's survey of two possible kinds of belief, this is the one of the two that most closely corresponds to what Peirce wanted to endorse as a conception of belief in general. Pragmatic belief in Kant's view is always tentative and speculative though based on possibly extensive experience with the subject matter of the belief (e.g., as physicians are supposed to have). To say that all belief is like *betting* is hardly enough to tell us what pragmatism is for Peirce, though it helps to map out the philosophical space in which he intended to work and to cordon off certain conceptions (e.g., infallible certitude) that have at best a marginal place in that work. In any case, it indicates that the nature of belief was at the core of Peirce's early conception of "pragmatism."

Before turning to other matters, it is worthwhile to further clarify why a label like 'practicalism' was not acceptable to Peirce. Peirce rejected the label 'practicalism' as associated with Kant's use of the term *praktisch*—meaning "practical" as in the *Kritik der praktischen Vernunft* (1788) where Kant argues that pure practical reason alone (free of empirical considerations) is able to dictate a rationally and thus universally valid moral imperative, namely, *the* categorical imperative. Peirce opted instead for 'pragmatism', associated with Kant's use of the term *pragmatisch*, meaning "pragmatic" as in prudential, pertaining to prudent action (based on past experience) aimed at promoting some purpose at hand if not securing one's well-being in general (Kant 1785; 1788). This is problematic (given Kant's Machiavellian conception of prudence—see chapter 10 below), but it is enough for now. In the latter part of the first *Critique* cited above, each of the two different kinds of belief are characterized from "a practical point of view." Namely, belief may be characterized (only) from "a practical point of view" in reference either to *skill* or to *morality*, Kant claims, as if these denote mutually exclusive considerations. The passages quoted above concern only belief as regards skill. Peirce can accommodate those kinds of statements at least roughly. Kant's description of belief in regard to morality, on the other hand, is problematic because of what it assumes about the nature of moral belief as having a kind of certainty:

> This practical point of view ... in reference to *morality*, ... [is concerned] with ends that are absolutely necessary. ... Once an end is accepted, the conditions of its attainment are hypothetically necessary. ... [This necessity] is sufficient, absolutely and for everyone, if I know with certainty that no one can have knowledge of any other conditions which lead to the proposed end. In [this] case my assumption and the holding of certain conditions to be true is a ... necessary belief. ... [Regarding] *moral belief* ... it is absolutely necessary that something must happen, namely, that I must in all points conform to the moral law. The end is here irrefragably established, and according to such insight as I can have, there is only one possible condition under which this end can connect with all other ends, and thereby have practical validity, namely that there be a God and a future world. I also know with complete certainty that no one can be acquainted with any other conditions which lead to the same unity of ends under the moral law. Since, therefore, the moral precept is at the same time my maxim (reason prescribing it should be so), I inevitably believe in the existence of God and in a future life, and I am certain that nothing can shake this belief, since my moral principles would thereby be themselves overthrown, and I cannot disclaim them without becoming abhorrent in my own eyes. (Kant 1781/1787, A823–829/B851–857)

This gets us to the point of why Peirce would reject the label 'practicalism'. Moral belief is a *practical* matter, as is pragmatic belief. The terms 'practical' and 'pragmatic' are thus distinct notions for Kant. The more comprehensive label 'practicalism' would be inappropriate, Peirce would say, because such a label would also subsume Kant's notion of moral belief. But one cannot "know with certainty" what other kinds of knowledge others may have, in which case this Kantian conception of moral belief is vacuous if not incoherent. If we cannot be sure of the universality of the "moral law" to which Kant alludes here, then we cannot know with complete certainty what Kant claims we can know with complete certainty.

To shed further light on this distinction between 'praktisch' and 'pragmatisch' in Kant's discussion of the "practical employment of Reason," consider the following remarks that appear several pages prior to those quoted above. They are of interest here not for what they say about belief as such but what they say about Kant's uses of the terms 'praktisch' and 'pragmatisch':

> By 'the practical' I mean everything that is possible through freedom. When, however, the conditions of the exercise of our free will are empirical, reason can have no other than a regulative employment in regard to it, and can serve only to effect unity in its empirical laws. Thus, for instance, in the precepts of prudence, the whole business of reason consists in uniting all the ends which are prescribed to us by our desires in the one single end, *happiness*, and in coordinating the means for attaining it. In this field, therefore, reason can supply none but *pragmatic* laws of free action, for the attainment of those ends which are commended to us by the senses; it cannot yield us laws that are pure and determined completely *a priori*. Laws of this latter type, pure practical laws, whose end is given through reason completely *a priori*, and which are prescribed to us not in an empirically conditioned but in an absolute manner, would be products of pure reason. Such are the *moral* laws; and these alone, therefore, belong to the practical employment of reason, and allow of a canon. (Kant 1781/1787, A800/B828)

A few pages later, Kant again links the term 'pragmatic' (as opposed to 'moral') with the notion of prudence:

> Happiness is the satisfaction of all our desires, *extensively*, in respect of their manifoldness, *intensively*, in respect of their degree, and *protensively*, in respect of their duration. The practical law, derived from the motive of *happiness*, I term pragmatic (rule of prudence), and that law, if there is such a law, which has no other motive than *worthiness of being happy*, I term moral (law of morality). The former advises us what we have to do if we wish to achieve happiness; the latter dictates to us how we must behave in order to deserve happiness. The former is based on empirical principles; for only by means of experience can I know what desires there are which call for satisfaction; or what those natural causes are which are capable of satisfying them. The latter takes no account of desires, and the natural means of satisfying them, and considers only the freedom of a rational being in general, and the necessary conditions under which alone this freedom can harmonise with a distribution of happiness that is made in accordance with principles. This latter law can therefore be

based on mere ideas of pure reason, and known *a priori*.

I assume that there really are pure moral laws which determine completely *a priori* (without regard to empirical motives, that is, to happiness) what is and is not to be done, that is, which determine the employment of the freedom of a rational being in general; and that these laws command in an *absolute* manner (not merely hypothetically, on the supposition of other empirical ends), and are therefore in every respect necessary. I am justified in making this assumption, in that I can appeal not only to the proofs employed by the most enlightened moralists, but to the moral judgment of every man, in so far as he makes the effort to think such a law clearly. (Kant 1781/1787, A806–807/B834–835)

We see here, of course, why Peirce would want to adapt the term 'pragmatic' to his own ends without buying wholesale into Kant's overall view of these matters. For one thing, the whole issue of *thinking clearly* and what it actually gains you is something Peirce will eventually address in "How to Make Our Ideas Clear," and the result will not support Kant's Cartesianesque appeal to clarity in regard to the assumption that "there really are pure moral laws."

Secondly, Peirce's pragmatism does not carry with it an association with "happiness" as a generic end except in the loose sense that fulfilling purposes is in a way satisfying but where a particular end in view will usually not be satisfaction as such but rather fulfillment of a given purpose (balancing the checkbook, earning the advanced degree, passing legislation on financial reform, etc.). The establishment of a belief, moreover, is characterized by Peirce as an intended response to doubt—always having such a purpose of removing doubt. The removal of doubt carries with it a kind of satisfaction to the degree that doubt is unsettling, but to say that pragmatism is concerned with achieving happiness misses the point. What pragmatism is concerned with is the nature of belief formation, and what belief formation is supposed to achieve is removal of doubt.

Third, again, Peirce would not acknowledge the existence of "pure practical laws, whose end is given through reason completely *a priori*." He thus would simply not endorse the notion of "moral laws" in Kant's sense. The point here, of course, is not to jettison or otherwise marginalize moral beliefs and moral laws (in some sense of those phrases) but, rather, to distinguish *Kant's characterization of them* (because of the elements of certainty and absolute necessity) from what Peirce called pragmatic laws and pragmatic beliefs. Moral beliefs, from a practical point of view, would *also* be matters of skill, as it were, and thus are "concerned with optional and contingent ends"—involving, for example, "betting" as to *how* to develop *which* personal character traits that ultimately will yield achievement of *eudaimonia*; or "betting" as to the precise formulations of rules of ethical conduct; or "betting" as to what kinds of consequences of our conduct can be identified as objectively preferable and how to compare and balance such preferences. That is to say, the observation that all belief is what Kant calls pragmatic belief encompasses but does not favor any particular normative ethical theory, allowing instead that the "ends" at issue may be virtues, duties, or the immediate consequences of one's actions. Pragmatism would thus be in itself an ethically neutral attitude that nevertheless is supposed to be applicable to any ethical stance.

Interestingly, the term 'pragmatic' is used in different ways by Kant across the first *Critique* (1781/1787), the *Groundwork* (1785), and the *Anthropology* (1798). Gregor's introduction to her translation of the *Anthropology* indicates several ways that Kant used the term 'pragmatic', *none* of which corresponds to how Peirce ultimately used it or to his related conception of belief. Peirce rather gave the term a new twist as reflected in the account of his conception of belief that we have already outlined above in chapter 1.

The main point we have been attempting to establish here is that a particular conception of belief, derived in part from an assessment of Kant's "Doctrine of Method" in the first *Critique*, constituted an important aspect of what we should think of as Peirce's pragmatism. In later years Peirce always pointed to the pragmatic maxim as the essence of pragmatism; but in earlier years, as in his discussions with Green and others, the focus was more likely the nature of belief.

Meaning

As we have seen in earlier chapters, the pragmatic maxim has been stated and interpreted in multiple ways. James summarized Peirce's argument and interpreted and used his maxim in ways that Peirce apparently abhorred. Peirce himself motivated and reformulated the maxim a number of times in the decades following its first formulation. Nevertheless, adherence to some version of this maxim is a common feature of their respective views that arguably goes a long way toward making those views pragmatist, no matter how much they disagreed otherwise.

We should note that pragmatism (in keeping with the etymology of the word itself) emphasizes practices or actions as much as it does effects or consequences. This may not be obvious from Peirce's emphasis on conceivable effects with "conceivable practical bearings" in 1878a, but it is apparent in later restatements, for example, in references to a concept's "conceivable bearing upon the conduct of life," or to the specification of the "rational purport" of a word in terms of types of experimentation and experimental phenomena, or to analyzing the meanings of predicates in terms of "habits of conduct" (1903a; 1905a; 1905b; 1907b).

We have seen that, in his writings on pragmatism after 1877, Peirce emphasized that the clarification of concepts (ideas, meanings) should be cast in terms of results of activities associated with objects falling under the given concept. We are to say what the word 'wine' means in terms of expected qualities resulting from appropriate kinds of actions (looking, smelling, tasting, etc.). We are to say what the word 'hard' means by describing how hard things would react to various kinds of interactions with them (poking, prodding, pounding, scratching, etc.). We are to say what the word 'reality' means by describing what would result from certain kinds of interactions with whatever is "independent of what we may think it to be" (activities of resolving doubt, fixing beliefs, etc.). The emphasis here, again, is on interactions with the *objects* falling under the given concept—an emphasis, again, that too easily suggests a kind of nominalism (blind to the *reality* of possibilities—and thus to the hardness of a diamond that is never actually poked or scratched) that Peirce later was careful to reject as irrelevant to a proper understanding of the maxim (in favor rather of an extreme "scholastic realism") (1871; 1905b; 1905d; 1911).

On the other hand, James (1898; 1907c) entertained a differently oriented notion of the maxim that included cognizance of systemic consequences of holding particular beliefs in particular contexts. Beyond mere factual verification of a belief, emphasis was also put on the influences of believings upon other believings in terms of their combined consequences and, respectively, on how accepting a new belief affects subsequent behavior by virtue of affecting one's overall corpus of beliefs. These latter considerations allegedly factor into the meanings of the concepts that constitute the belief. The meaning of the phrase "rainy weather" in circumstances of rainy weather will include references to a preparedness to carry an umbrella, etc., and not just references to barometer and rain gauge readings. The meaning of the word 'true' in specific circumstances of holding a given belief will include reference to how that belief comports (which is to say, "works") in those circumstances with other current beliefs. The meanings of the words 'wine' and 'blood' will depend on the consequences of their use in particular circumstances, not solely on chemical analyses or directly sensible characteristics. Indeed, the meanings of words like 'God' may involve virtually no laboratory-like verification procedures but hinge entirely on larger systemic affects of respective beliefs.

Between the two original classical American pragmatists (Peirce and James), there are therefore at least two notions of "practical effects" or "practical bearings" at work in their conceptions of "the maxim" of pragmatism. We can summarize these as follows insofar as the maxim is the cornerstone of an account of meaning:

1. An *operationalist* reading of the pragmatic maxim emphasizes interactions with objects falling under a given concept—requiring an operational, exploratory, evidence-oriented account of word meaning (for example, explaining what the word 'hard' means by saying how hard things would react to various interactions with them, or defining a word like 'real' in terms of the results of inquiries).

This reading of the maxim constitutes an alternative to a merely representational theory of semantic truth conditions—not an alternative to truth-conditional semantics as such but an alternative to a standard extensionalist notion of truth conditions. This reading in effect recommends an *operational* account of "satisfaction"—a key notion underlying Tarski's theory of truth for a first-order language (1936a; 1936b; 1944).[1] The so-called *causal* account of reference (Kripke 1980) somewhat weakly addresses such concerns, most notably in the form of "grounding" links in "designating chains" (Devitt 1981). This requires more than an overly simple Bridgmanesque "operationalism" (Bridgman 1927; Putnam 1981a; Chang 2009) in that we have to deal with more than just sets of operations to define our terms; and it is not a logical-positivist "verificationism" (Ayer 1959; Carnap 1928; 1936), which focuses on the testability of *consequences* of hypotheses while offering no independent, principled account of satisfaction (other than a standard Tarskian account for first-order languages). An operationalist reading of the maxim rather promotes a quasi-foundationalism (to be contrasted with Sosa's 1980 distinction between foundationalist and coherentist epistemologies) in allowing that hierarchical systems of beliefs may well be grounded operationally even if neither "absolutely" nor "atomistically." On still other fronts, some aspects of *enactivism*, both in education theory (e.g., Bruner 1960) and in cognitive science (e.g., Hurley 1998; Maturana and Varela 1992; Noë 2004; Rowlands 2006; Varela et al. 1991), are not incompatible with this reading of the pragmatic maxim insofar as they place activity at the center of learning and cognitive development.

The second reading of the pragmatic maxim has a different focus and emphasizes a different notion of "consequence":

2. An *inferentialist* reading of the pragmatic maxim emphasizes repercussions of beliefs upon other beliefs and, respectively, upon one's subsequent manner of conduct—requiring a functional, inferential-role account of word meaning (for example, saying what the word 'God' means by saying how belief in such a thing affects one's way of life, or saying what a symbol like '∈' means by examining its manner of use as part of a vocabulary for a given axiomatic system).

To say that this second reading of the maxim involves a "psychology of belief" may not be inappropriate if the latter is understood broadly to include a range of epistemological and cognitive-scientific concerns, from linguistics and especially pragmatics to theories of cognition and perception.[2] Brandom's inferentialism (1994; 2000; 2008) is in line with this kind of pragmatism. Focusing largely on relations within and among "vocabularies," etc., Brandom (2008) characterizes what he is doing as an alternative kind of semantics—a variation on the theme of inferential- or conceptual-role semantics (Brigandt 2010; Sellars 1953; 1974). Quine's "holism" (1951) and "ontological relativism" (1968) and Putnam's "internalism" (1981a) link the truth of statements to their formulation and interpretation relative to larger conceptual or linguistic frameworks while giving only nominal

---

[1] What follows in this paragraph is mere name-dropping, though the intention is to connect this first reading of the pragmatic maxim with recent trends in philosophy that may be more familiar to some readers.

[2] Again, here is some more name-dropping to highlight connections with more recent philosophical trends.

attention to *experiential* inputs (the latter being of primary importance for an operationalist semantics). Classical "speech act theory" (Austin 1962; Searle 1969) as it emerged in the early and mid-twentieth century among "ordinary language philosophers" at Oxford, focusing on what we *do* with words, emphasized utterances rather than beliefs as such but otherwise promoted what we might call a pragmatic inferentialism. More recently, Boersema (2009, 234) explicates a functionalist account of reference and names that "places the underlying emphasis on what reference and names *do*, not simply what they *are* as part of a conceptual analysis." Regarding Sosa's 1980 distinction between foundationalist and coherentist epistemologies, this second reading of the maxim would appear to be more in line with coherentism, broadly conceived.

The difference between operationalist and inferentialist pragmatism reflects a major difference between Peirce and James so far as their respective conceptions of pragmatism go. The first of these conceptions highlights the basic gist of Peirce's notion of "conceivable practical bearings," pertaining to how *things* in the world behave, while the second highlights James's, pertaining to how *we* behave in the world—though one can certainly find both of these themes in Peirce's writings about pragmatism if not James's as well. (From an externalist perspective, it is not clear that this should be so much of a distinction as might be thought.)

For a case in point, it may be remarked that the assessment of James's view of pragmatism in chapter 2 above is born out in other chapters of *Pragmatism*, for instance, where he "pragmatically considers" some classical metaphysical problems (James 1907d;e). The latter lectures are a good source of illustrations of what James thinks the pragmatist method is. He examines several thorny philosophical issues in operationalist-friendly terms—substance versus attributes, matter versus spirit, personal identity, evolution versus intelligent design, free will versus determinism—though in each case (1) any appeal to "sensible effects" is merely empiricist and not operationalist in character, and (2) the discussion of each issue ultimately focuses on inferrible consequences of relevant beliefs, respectively, rather than on operational results.

James's treatment of "the mystery of the Eucharist" (James 1907d, PMT:46–47), for instance, contrasts in a telling way with Peirce's discussion in "How to Make Our Ideas Clear" (Peirce 1878a, EP1:132–133; also see page 12 above). For Peirce it was meant to serve as an illustration in the argument that led finally to his statement of the pragmatic maxim as "the rule for attaining the third grade of clearness." He did not intend "to pursue the theological question" but only to use it "as a logical example." His only point was that we have no idea what we are talking about (it is "senseless jargon") to distinguish wine and blood as different *substances* while at the same time asserting that all of their respective *attributes* may in some cases be identical to the attributes of wine. At that point in Peirce's argument, he wants to assert that we can have ideas of a thing *only* in terms of its sensible attributes, so that the notion of two different substances underlying or having identical attributes is logically incoherent.

James later used the same example to make a point rather about how it is possible to "pragmatically" clarify the idea of substance, at least in the case of the Eucharist, in spite of the fact that the attributes of the wafer do not change. He acknowledges that a substance/attribute distinction derives from a linguistic subject/predicate distinction *and* from the otherwise unjustified tendency to reify whatever it is for which we think we have names. Peirce essentially says as much but stops there with the point that we simply *cannot* do that if such reified concepts are to have third-grade clarity (and that we *should not* do that if we want all of our concepts to be at least that clear). But James continues. Assume that you already believe in the *real presence* of Christ on independent grounds. The substance-idea "breaks into life, then, with tremendous effect" once this independent belief is combined with the belief that a substance can separate from its attributes and take on entirely new attributes. Specifically, given that the wafer has changed though none of its attributes have changed, it must be only the substance that has changed. A further effect-qua-consequence of this inference, then, is the highly compelling belief that one who takes the sacrament "now feeds upon the very substance of divinity." One might be inclined to call this latter belief a "cognitive effect" rather than a "sensible effect," but it is nevertheless a tangible result (a belief, as it were) that influences how one subsequently behaves, and this ties the belief to our on-going practices so that it may be counted among the practical consequences of taking the substance-idea seriously.

One key difference in their conceptions of *attributes* may explain the difference between Peirce's and James's respective treatments of the *substance-idea*. It was only James who actually used the Scholastic "substance/attribute" terminology in this context. Peirce spoke only in terms of "sensible effects"—as possible "qualities" of things, but more importantly as results *produced* by manipulative actions intended specifically to produce sensible effects. James, on the other hand, regards attributes in a fairly pedestrian if not exactly Scholastic manner as "accidental" properties, etc., with nothing said about how they might be *produced* as sensible effects. Practical effects, as such, may be produced in other ways. Namely, James is willing to regard beliefs derived (inferred, produced inferentially) from other beliefs as practical effects. Peirce was thinking like an operationalist. James was not only thinking like an inferentialist but made it explicitly clear in this example, at least, that inferential considerations can override operational considerations.

Four Grades of Clearness

Rather than try to choose which of these notions is *the* correct one, it is advisable to conclude that the pragmatic maxim as commonly stated is ambiguous as to how one should regard the notion of "practical bearings," with at least two readings both of which are legitimate (thank you, Michael Eldridge). The two ways of regarding this notion may easily be (and have been) conflated and thus confused one for the other, but they are obviously different. That difference needs to be understood and acknowledged. We do not have to make an exclusive choice as to which version is the correct version. Originally (ironically) Peirce was not as clear as he could have been. The maxim was stated ambiguously. We might therefore simply acknowledge and promote a dual reading of the maxim.

Or perhaps not; but it is not at all obvious that either of these two readings of the maxim could legitimately take precedence over the other. One could reasonably argue that Peirce's original presentation is definitive, bracketing the fact that it is difficult to determine what he actually meant. That is, one could argue that an operational semantics takes precedence over an inferential pragmatics when it comes to capturing the core content of the pragmatic maxim insofar as the latter eventually comes around to depending on the methodological details of the former, e.g., if pragmatism is not to collapse into mere empiricism. Inferentialism may *require* operationalist grounding in this regard if it is to succeed at all, much less count as something distinct from a standard empiricist inferential-role semantics. Some aspects of inferentialist pragmatism, likewise, might be developed as a special case of operationalist pragmatism to whatever extent various dynamic aspects of discourse and inference could be cast as "operations" with "sensible effects" (as in conversational uses of words). This possibility is discussed briefly below (and in appendix B).

This raises the question of whether inferentialist pragmatism might be reducible to operationalist pragmatism. That might not work in the end (for reasons to be touched on later), in which case we should acknowledge that the notion of "practical bearings" that plays a key role in Peirce's earliest formulation of the pragmatic maxim has two interpretations—operational versus inferential—as previously spelled out. Or it might work out after all (for other reasons to be touched on later), in which case we should acknowledge that the kind of operationalism that is advocated in Peirce's earliest formulation of the pragmatic maxim is a somewhat uncommon brand of operationalism.

To finish this line of thought, consider some of the consequences of distinguishing *pragmatism* and *empiricism*. It might seem after all is said and done that there is no substantial distinction between pragmatism and empiricism. British, Austrian, or American empiricism, despite nuances of style and emphasis, are all just empiricism. This issue will be examined further in later chapters, though we have already shown previously in chapter 2 how James's version of pragmatism is hardly different at bottom from a Carnapian sensationist empiricism (Ayer 1968, 317). As such, a Jamesian psychology of belief can be developed independently of operationalist considerations—specifically, along strictly sensationist empiricist lines—and thus it may be susceptible to standard criticisms to which it might not otherwise be subject. In effect, James's way of developing a "theory of truth" took liberties with Peirce's "mere maxim of logic." Peirce was of course able to *apply* the pragmatic maxim to the *concept* of truth, but that is different from claiming that pragmatism is or includes a theory of truth. One could conceivably define the word 'truth' in multiple ways using the pragmatic maxim, suggesting possibly different theories of truth. For example, there were a few choice points in Peirce's discussion of the words 'reality' and 'truth' where one might make different choices, slight or not so slight; or one might begin entirely differently in terms of a different array of defining types of *actions* and their characteristic *effects*.

What James should have claimed perhaps was an extension of operationalist methodology to include inferentialist factors. That would not have been out of line with Peirce's conceptions of habit, belief, inquiry, etc., not to mention his distinctive theory of "signs." Such an extension would not be a theory of truth as such but a theory of an idea's *working* in ways not captured solely by operationalist considerations. A normative treatment of beliefs "working" in the course of ongoing experience requires consideration of scientific (and non-scientific) methodology if not perhaps a theory of intelligence as well. This eventually goes beyond mere semantics (and thus an operationalist reading of the pragmatic maxim), but it need not extend beyond logical or methodological considerations to include psychological or epistemological doctrine. How that would work in detail needs to be worked out, perhaps in the form of a normative theory of inquiry.

One may compare and contrast James's radical empiricism, Dewey's theory of experience, Mead's philosophy of "the act," and Peirce's "new list of categories" and his semiotic theory of cognition to appreciate the variety of psychological and epistemological doctrines that are compatible with the pragmatic maxim. It would be difficult if not futile to try to make sense of this range of views without nailing down the distinctive double-aspect pragmatist "stance" at the core of all of them. On one hand, one reading of the pragmatic maxim stipulates that we "operationalize" our terms (words, concepts) in order to achieve greater clarity of meaning. On the other hand, this clarification of one's terms is done usually in the interest of addressing pertinent issues (resolving pressing doubts, pursuing some inquiry, etc.) where acting in accordance with certain beliefs yields consequences that bear one way or another on resolving those issues—such that the warrantability (versus "truth"?) of those beliefs in the given context hinges on their workability in just that regard. At least for Peirce, this warrantability will be tied to the use of scientific methods (broadly conceived) to address the issue(s) at hand—methods that Dewey sometimes referred to more generally as methods of intelligence, marked by openness to any feasible hypothesis, emphasis on rational systematic coherence of one's beliefs on the whole, reliance on experimental/observational testing of any proposed hypothesis, and so forth. But, science and intelligence aside, the point here is that beliefs as brought to bear in given instances will have instrumental force in certain contexts that will in itself say as much about what those beliefs *mean* as does the operationalization of the vocabularies in terms of which those beliefs are couched. These two notions of meaning reflect the two ways of reading (the two aspects of) the pragmatic maxim.

Perhaps we should take a cue from Peirce's 1906a reconciliation of pragmatism and pragmaticism (essentially inferentialist pragmatism and operationalist pragmatism, respectively; see page 28 above). We might summarize this reconciliation in present terms by saying that pragmatism is inferentialist but that it also has to be more than that to be *distinctively* pragmatist, namely, it must also be operationalist. That is to say, pragmatism as such is *both* operationalist and inferentialist in what is meant by "sensible effects" and "practical bearings."

But we can perhaps do even better to reconcile these two aspects of pragmatism. First note that Peirce later may have backed off from his claim that pragmatism is only a method, identifying the two doctrines of Critical Common-Sensism (1905b, EP2:346–354) and Scholastic Realism (1905b, EP2:354–359) as "essential consequences" of the "principle of pragmaticism"—unless we were to regard these *also* as attitudes rather than as doctrines?

Of greater interest here is the fact that that article begins with a reformulation of the pragmatic maxim that sounds decidedly more inferentialist than operationalist:

> Pragmaticism was originally enounced in the form of a maxim, as follows: *Consider what effects that might conceivably have practical bearings you conceive the objects of your conception to have. Then, your conception of those effects is the whole of your conception of the object.*
>
> I will restate this in other words, since ofttimes one can thus eliminate some unsuspected source of perplexity to the reader. This time it shall be in the indicative mood, as follows: *The entire intellectual purport of any symbol consists in the total of all general modes of rational conduct which, conditionally upon all the possible different circumstances and desires, would ensue upon the acceptance of the symbol.*
> (Peirce 1905b, EP2:346; emphasis added)

Words may be symbols. Sentences may be symbols. On this account, the meaning of the word 'lithium' (when a symbol), for instance, will include any "general mode of rational conduct" that "would ensue upon [its] acceptance," e.g., in an utterance of sentences like "lithium is white" or "this is lithium." This reformulation of the maxim would have to allow if not emphasize effects of a given symbol's acceptance relative to a larger framework or system of symbols—a matter of how it might affect "rational conduct" by virtue of its being a part of such a framework. This interpretation of Peirce's statement above is not unreasonable, and it does seem to turn on how symbols work as parts of symbol systems. That "general modes of rational conduct" which contribute to such meanings might include precepts characteristic of operational definitions is not ruled out, but the latter surely would not exhaust "the entire intellectual purport" of a given symbol.

Earlier in the same article Peirce emphasizes the role of "deliberate conduct" as the key to understanding the pragmatic maxim, rather than "sensible results" as such:

> Now the theory of Pragmaticism was originally based, as anybody will see who examines the papers of November 1877 and January 1878, upon a study of that experience of the phenomena of self-control which is common to all grown men and women; and it seems evident that to some extent, at least, it must always be so based. *For it is to conceptions of deliberate conduct that Pragmaticism would trace the intellectual purport of symbols; and deliberate conduct is self-controlled conduct.* (Peirce 1905b, EP2:348; emphasis added)

This suggests inferentialist sentiments that could very easily accommodate, for instance, James's manner of handling the idea of *substance* (see page 45 above).

In this same article, Peirce presents some illustrations of how to employ this maxim and in so doing squarely offers up none other than operational definitions in at least two cases (specifically, in saying what the word 'diamond' means as part of reconsidering his discussion of the meaning of the word 'hard' in 1878a).

But he also takes on the harder word 'time' (1905b, EP2:357–359). There are no references to the use of clocks. Much of the focus rather is on time as a kind of "objective modality," the past being associated with actuality and the future with possibility and necessity. We will not go into the details here though we will sample some of the language he uses. The interesting point is that Peirce's discussion of the idea of *the future*, for instance, is inferentialist in a somewhat surprising way. If we regard his characterization of that idea as operational in nature, then one of the key operations he is appealing to here is none other than the activity of *inferring*:

> Pragmaticism consists in holding that the purport of any concept is its conceived bearing upon our conduct. ... How does the Future bear upon conduct? The answer is that future facts are the only facts that we can, in a measure, control; and whatever there may be in the Future that is not amenable to control are the things that we *shall* be able to infer, or *should* be able to infer under favorable circumstances. ... It is natural to use the future tense (and the conditional mood is but a mollified future) in drawing a conclusion or in stating a consequence. "If two unlimited straight lines in one plane and crossed by a third making the sum ... then these straight lines *will* meet on the side, etc." It cannot be denied that acritical inferences may refer to the Past in its capacity as past; but according to Pragmaticism, the conclusion of a Reasoning proper must refer to the Future. For its meaning refers to conduct, and since it is a reasoned conclusion must refer to deliberate conduct, which is controllable conduct. But the only controllable conduct is Future conduct. As for that part of the Past that lies beyond memory, the Pragmaticist doctrine is that the meaning of its being believed to be in connection with the Past consists in the acceptance as truth of the conception that we ought to conduct ourselves according to it (like the meaning of any other belief). Thus, a belief that Christopher Columbus discovered America really refers to the future. (Peirce 1905b, EP2:358–359)

By this account, an exclusively future fact is *necessary* if it is not actual but could be inferred from what is *actual*, namely, from past facts. A future event is otherwise at best *possible*. Presumably we could talk of the necessity of past/actual facts in the sense that they are inferrible from temporally previous actual facts, which leaves intact the association of *necessity* with the future mode. The important point here is that these modes of time as a kind of objective modality are defined and distinguished in terms of conceivable inferences.

Note that, on this view, a belief that Christ died on a cross for the benefit of all of us and that the divine is really present in consecrated bread and wine will also refer to the future in just the way that a belief that Columbus discovered America does. The meaning of the conclusion that one "now feeds upon the very substance of divinity" (etc.) refers to deliberate and thus controllable conduct, i.e., to future conduct. It would appear that Peirce is now sanctioning precisely the line of argumentation that James employed in providing a "pragmatical" definition of the term 'substance'.

The suggestion that Peirce could be regarding inference itself as a kind of operation (just as he treated inquiry as an operation in his definition of 'reality') strongly supports the notion that inferentialism might well be reducible to operationalism. This may seem too easy. More study is needed here. Suffice it to say that this 1905 article clearly shows both operationalist and inferentialist sentiments running together in at least one of Peirce's later versions of pragmat(ic)ism.

Regardless of whether we maintain a dual reading of the pragmatic maxim, there is yet another significant indication of tolerance if not acceptance of inferentialism in Peirce's later work. This occurs, namely, in a small number of references to "the development of concrete reasonableness" as a "still higher grade of clearness" beyond the three grades acknowledged in 1878a (see, for instance, Pfeifer 2011; Thompson 1953; Parker 1998). A fairly straightforward presentation of the first three grades of clearness, published in 1897, goes as follows:

> Now there are three grades of clearness in our apprehensions of the meanings of words. The first consists in the connexion of the word with familiar experience. ... The second grade consists in the abstract definition, depending upon an analysis of just what it is that makes the word applicable. ... The third grade of clearness consists in such a representation of the idea that fruitful reasoning can be made to turn upon it, and that it can be applied to the resolution of difficult practical problems. (Peirce 1897, CP3:457)

This passage was introduced in an article designed to clarify the logical notion of *relation*. In other words, Peirce again intended to show how to apply the pragmatic maxim, this time to clarify a particularly fundamental notion in logic and mathematics. We need not go into those details here, but we do want to take stock of the formulation of the pragmatic maxim—now in terms of providing a definition of a word such that "fruitful reasoning can be made to turn upon it" and otherwise such that it is applicable to solving "difficult practical problems." This is relatively easy to comprehend when compared to the original formulation twenty years prior, whether or not the two formulations say the same thing. Particularly noteworthy is the attention given to engendering fruitful reasoning.

There are other contexts in his later work where Peirce's focus with regard to saying what pragmatism is seems to be more on *reasoning* and *reasonableness*. In particular, the following (shortened but still longish) passage is from a 1905 manuscript where Peirce is recounting the origins of pragmatism.

> But pragmatism does not undertake to say in what the meanings of all signs consist, but merely to lay down a method of determining the meanings of intellectual concepts, that is, of those upon which reasonings may turn. Now all reasoning that is not utterly vague, all that ought to figure in a philosophical discussion involves, and turns upon, precise necessary reasoning. Such reasoning is included in the sphere of mathematics, as modern mathematicians conceive their science. ... The reasoning of mathematics is now well understood. It consists in forming an image of the conditions of the problem, associated with which are certain general permissions to modify the image, as well as certain general assumptions that certain things are impossible. Under the permissions, certain experiments are performed upon the image, and the assumed impossibilities involve their always resulting in the same general way. The superior certainty of the mathematician's results, as compared, for example, with those of the chemist, are due to two circumstances. First, the mathematician's experiments being conducted in the imagination upon objects of his own creation, cost next to nothing; while those of the chemist cost dear. Secondly, the assurance of the mathematician is due to his reasoning only concerning hypothetical conditions, so that his results have the generality of his conditions; while the chemist's experiments relating to what will happen as a matter of fact are always open to the doubt whether unknown conditions may not alter. ... Such reasonings and all reasonings turn upon the idea that if one exerts certain kinds of volition, one will undergo in return certain compulsory perceptions. Now this sort of consideration, namely, that certain lines of conduct will entail certain kinds of inevitable experiences is what is called a "practical consideration." Hence is justified the maxim, belief in which constitutes pragmatism; namely,
>
> *In order to ascertain the meaning of an intellectual conception one should consider what practical consequences might conceivably result by necessity from the truth of that conception; and the sum of these consequences will constitute the entire meaning of the conception.* (Peirce 1905c, CP5:8–9)

This is again a rather long quote, but it is important to examine Peirce's discussion here of "precise necessary reasoning" in mathematics and chemistry, not to mention the clarification of what is meant by the phrase 'practical considerations' and the subsequent reformulation (yet again) of the pragmatic maxim in such terms.

Note that the latter formulation is stated with respect to so-called intellectual conceptions where "sensible results" have been recast as conceivably necessary consequences of such conceptions being *true*. Out of context, this may sound as if logical consequences have taken the place of operational results in a new formulation of the maxim. His previous discussion of necessary reasoning and of mathematicians' experiments in the abstract may support such a reading. *But* look at his characterization here of a "practical consideration" as the notion that the exertion of specific volitions will result in respective "compulsory perceptions," or that certain kinds of conduct "will entail certain kinds of inevitable experiences." Peirce is *still* talking about the conceivably tangible results of conceivable courses of conduct (action, exertion of volition, etc.)—about *practical* consequences, not deductive consequences as such (viz., truths deduced from other assumed truths). He is doing this in a way that is tailored to fit the "intellectual conceptions" characteristic of mathematics as much as of any other field of inquiry.

It is relatively easy to accept the claim that mathematicians work by *reason*; but this should not be accepted for the wrong reasons, that is, because mathematicians focus only on relations among ideas (in the imagination) and not on matters of fact (in the world at large), so to speak. Mathematics, like any science, is experimental though its experiments are "conducted in the imagination upon objects of [the mathematician's] own creation" under purely "hypothetical conditions, so that his results have the generality of his conditions." Experimentation in chemistry is conducted rather in a physical laboratory of some sort with physical tools and materials under controlled conditions that nevertheless cannot be entirely controlled, with the generality of one's results being contingent therefore upon having controlled even for unforeseen conditions.

One point that Peirce is making here is that mathematics is not exclusively deductive in its methods, just as chemistry is not purely inductive in *its* methods. Rather, any such science will wield the full arsenal of logical methods of inference: abductive, deductive, and inductive. In mathematics, on this account, experimentation consists in proving theorems, and writing up a proof would be the equivalent of a laboratory report. In any case, the differences among various sciences are not in their logic, which is the same for all, but in their respective subject matters.

The more important point presently is that, for Peirce, experimentation is an essential part of *reason*. It is not something *extra* that is done to test the results of reasoning but is a *bona fide constituent* of reasoning.

> There is no reason why "thought," in what has just been said, should be taken in that narrow sense in which silence and darkness are favorable to thought. It should rather be understood as covering all rational life, so that an experiment shall be an operation of thought. (Peirce 1905a, EP2:337)

This does not say that operations of thought may be considered to be experiments. It says, rather, that experiments may be considered to be operations of thought! The chemist's mixing two liquids in a test tube to see if there will be a precipitate is included in his or her reasoning, just as the geometer's setting out and subsequent manipulation of a diagram with compass and straightedge is part of his or her reasoning. This points to what Peirce may have meant by *concrete reasonableness*, namely, reasonableness that is cultivated by way of effectively exploiting the full range of logical methods of inference.

This is a notable insight on Peirce's part. But at least one problem remains unresolved. Up to this point, the increasing emphasis that is put on reasoning in Peirce's later characterizations of pragmatism has been presented (quite fairly, judging by the passages quoted) as a refinement of the original statement of the pragmatic maxim, including the supposition that there are three grades of clarity.

One of the quotes above is from 1897. The other is from 1905. In 1902, in a dictionary entry where he is hesitant to endorse James's characterizations of pragmatism in *The Will to Believe* (1897) and *Philosophical Conceptions and Practical Results* (1898), Peirce attributes an even more distinctive role to reasoning in characterizing what pragmatism is:

> If it be admitted, on the contrary, that action wants an end, and that that end must be something of a general description, then the spirit of the maxim itself, which is that we must look to the upshot of our concepts in order rightly to apprehend them, would direct us toward something different from practical facts, namely, to general ideas, as the true interpreters of our thought. Nevertheless, the maxim has approved itself to the writer, after many years of trial, as of great utility in leading to a relatively high grade of clearness of thought. He would venture to suggest that it should always be put into practice with conscientious thoroughness, but that, when that has been done, and not before, *a still higher grade of clearness of thought* can be attained by remembering that the only ultimate good which the practical facts to which it directs attention can subserve is *to further the development of concrete reasonableness*; so that the meaning of the concept does not lie in any individual reactions at all, but in the manner in which those reactions contribute to that development. (Peirce 1902b, CP5:3; emphasis added)

One might argue that the "higher grade of clearness of thought" that is mentioned here is a higher grade of the third grade of clearness originally proposed in 1878. Thus it was already covered (though obscurely) by the original statement of the pragmatic maxim. A better thesis, one might claim, is that Peirce's later reformulations of the maxim were due to a nascent and growing appreciation of a Jamesian inferentialism—not that it is at odds with Peirce's operationalist sentiments but that (1) both are subsumed by what is meant by *reasonableness* and that (2) this elaboration of what is meant by "practical considerations" (as it were) calls for distinguishing a fourth grade of clearness of thought (Thompson 1953; Parker 1998; Pfeifer 2011). Specifically, the third grade of clearness would be identified with operational concreteness, while the fourth grade of clearness would be associated with "conscientious [inferential] thoroughness." The former is our only "user guide" for relevant experimental tools and techniques; and the latter provides the only means for exploring and determining what exactly should be tried and tested.

Thus the idea of "furthering concrete reasonableness" as "the highest of all aims" (see Peirce 1902a, CP2:34n2) nicely amalgamates inferentialist and operationalist aspects of pragmatism, as follows:

- *concreteness* would be achieved by operationally grounding one's grasp of a given subject matter (that is, by operationally defining one's terms so as to enable the testing of hypotheses experimentally in accordance with those operational specifications); and
- *reasonableness* would be gauged by the combined coherence of abductive, deductive, and inductive methods of inference addressed to that subject matter (including statistical inference requiring careful experimentation, broadly conceived).

On this account, we could distinguish four grades of clarity of thought as follows:

- $Clear_1$: *familiar* (Peirce 1878a, EP1:124–125).
- $Clear_2$: *precisely defined* in abstract terms all of which are $clear_1$ (Peirce 1878a, EP1:125; Peirce 1897, CP3:457).
- $Clear_3$: *operationally defined* in the sense of chapter 3 above (especially page 30, citing Peirce 1878a, EP1:127–132) perhaps as the basis for understanding what is meant by "fruitful reasoning" as applicable "to the resolution of difficult practical problems" (Peirce 1897, CP3:457).
- $Clear_4$: *thoroughly if not globally reasonable* in concrete terms, i.e., incorporated consistently into one's stock of beliefs so as to be inferentially traceable (one way or another) to ideas and opinions which are $clear_3$.

In this light, we could regard operationalism and inferentialism as two different but equally necessary aspects of pragmatism, whether or not it really matters in the end. The preceding results purport to show that there is a real distinction to be made which calls in turn for distinguishing four grades of clearness of thought rather than three.

At the same time, it would appear that pragmatism for the most part has come to be understood almost entirely in terms of an inferentialist reading of the original pragmatic maxim, both by those who accept and promote some form of pragmatism and by those who reject and would rather ignore it. In that case, we could afford to better understand the operationalist reading, which will be the main focus of subsequent chapters.

Before proceeding further, it may help to further clarify what is at issue regarding the alleged distinction between inferentialism and operationalism. The following examples highlight inferentialism at work in the recent past where it might otherwise not have been noticed. There are other such examples, but these should suffice for the present.

A. A good example of the predominance of an inferentialist conception of pragmatism (without going into details) is Haack's "foundherentist" epistemology—a "broadly Peircean" "double-aspect" epistemology "offering a new explication of epistemic justification ... allowing both for pervasive mutual support among beliefs and for the contribution of experience to empirical justification" (Haack 1993, 1–2). The quasi-coherentist aspect of this view easily and explicitly accommodates inferentialist concerns (135, 208). Otherwise, Haack's way of dealing with the role of experience in justification, while not incompatible with an operationalist reading of the pragmatic maxim, need be regarded as nothing more than an improved version of Carnap's sensationist empiricism. It provides a "conception of supportiveness of evidence [that is superior to] the more usual notion of inductive validity" (135); but the details of her "evidentialism" (for instance, her so-called Petrocelli Principle) fall wholly within the purview of an inferentialist account of empirical evidence (82, 217, 219). Haack goes as far as one might go in promoting the role of perceptual evidence and "experiential anchoring" in the justification of beliefs (139, 209, 213, 218), even including a discussion of Gibson's ecological psychology (4, 113–114, 220; see chapter 7 below), without explicitly endorsing any recognizable form of operationalism. It would not be hard at all to push foundherentist epistemology in operationalist directions; yet the quasi-foundationalist aspect of foundherentism in its present form is more easily regarded as a Jamesian/Carnapian empiricism than as a full-fledged Peircean operationalism. The reason for this, more likely than not, is that operationalist pragmatism has simply not been on Haack's or anyone else's radar screen. What exactly is operationalism, after all? In particular, what difference would it make to Haack's detailed explication of the notion of "supportive evidence"? We cannot answer the latter question here, depending as it does on an answer to the first question. What we can and will do, though, is move in the direction of answering the first question.

B. A second example of the lure of inferentialism in the science of meaning, this time with regard to so-called mathematical logic, is in the concluding section of Barwise's introductory entry in the collection *Model-Theoretic Logics*, edited by Barwise and Feferman (1985). Barwise examines the very notion of *logic* itself and, minimally, rejects the view that logic is just first-order logic. (Peirce would reject the view that logic is just deductive logic, not to mention first-order deductive logic in particular; but that is not to the point here.) In the concluding section of this piece, Barwise surveys some topics that are *not* covered in the book that he is introducing but which point to the need for broader conceptions of logic. What he has to say in this regard at first sounds promising if one wants to promote an operationalist conception of meaning:

> The semantics of computer languages, and the differences that emerge in that work from more traditional model theory, points to a shortcoming in the latter, namely,

> its failure to come to grips with activity, as opposed to objects and static relations between them. This same shortcoming causes problems with traditional attempts to apply model theory to human languages, another topic not treated here. (Barwise 1985, 22)

The conception of activity here is nevertheless restricted, in good inferentialist form, to activities and effects of using language and to *inference* itself as a kind of activity:

> Traditional model theory focuses on truth (and satisfaction) of sentences, and so leaves out the use of language to [e]ffect change. This is a shortcoming that has been emphasized by Austin [e.g., 1950] and other writers on natural language in the tradition of "speech act" theory. This power of language to effect change (in the so-called "side-effects") is one of the things that makes the semantics of computer languages strikingly different.
> Another area where work on computer and human languages makes the traditional work in logic appear too static is in the treatment of inference. Inference, whether by man or machine, is an activity, a process of extracting information, whereas the tradition attempts to reduce inference to objects (proofs, strings of symbols). (Barwise 1985, 22)

Pointing to these kinds of shortcomings in traditional semantics when extrapolated broadly, beyond the formalization of mathematics to programming languages and natural human languages, works in favor of an inferentialist reading of the pragmatic maxim. So much the better for pragmatism. On the other hand, there is no apparent tendency in these remarks to consider activities of, say, perception, measurement, or experimentation when addressing the failure of traditional semantics "to come to grips with activity."

C. Though John Dewey (pragmatist extraordinaire) has been given scant attention here, there are some useful points worth mentioning regarding his apparent endorsement of operationalist ideas in the late 1920s and throughout the 1930s.

First, it is worthwhile to recall Dewey's distinction between *observed facts of a case* (as aspects of a problem at hand) and *proposed ideas* (indicating possible solutions to that problem), and his emphasizing "the operational character" of each of these "functional divisions in the work of inquiry." The specific reference here is to section V of chapter 6 of *Logic: The Theory of Inquiry* (1938b, LW12:116). The title of that section of the chapter is "The Operational Character of Facts-Meanings." One might reasonably expect to find an explicit endorsement of Peirce's operationalism here. Instead, what we find comes closer to being an implicit *identification* of operationalism and inferentialism.

> Observed facts in their office of locating and describing the problem are existential; ideational subject-matter is non-existential. How, then, do they cooperate with each other in the resolution of an existential situation? The problem is insoluble save as it is recognized that both observed facts and entertained ideas are operational. Ideas are operational in that they instigate and direct further operations of observation; they

are proposals and plans for acting upon existing conditions to bring new facts to light and to organize all the selected facts into a coherent whole.

What is meant by calling facts operational? Upon the negative side what is meant is that they are not self-sufficient and complete in themselves. They are selected and described, as we have seen, for a purpose, namely statement of the problem involved in such a way that its material both indicates a meaning relevant to resolution of the difficulty and serves to test its worth and validity. In regulated inquiry facts are selected and arranged with the express intent of fulfilling this office. They are not merely *results* of operations of observation which are executed with the aid of bodily organs and auxiliary instruments of art, but they are the particular facts and kinds of facts that will link up with one another in the definite ways that are required to produce a definite end. Those not found to connect with others in furtherance of this end are dropped and others are sought for. Being functional, they are necessarily operational. Their function is to serve as evidence and their evidential quality is judged on the basis of their capacity to form an ordered whole in response to operations prescribed by the ideas they occasion and support. If "the facts of the case" were final and complete in themselves, if they did not have a special operative force in resolution of the problematic situation, they could not serve as evidence. (Dewey 1938b, LW12:116–117)

The emphasis here is not on the operational character of facts and ideas but rather on their inferential qua *functional* character—that is, in a Jamesian sense of their inferential role in furthering the course of some respective inquiry. Consider each of the two quoted paragraphs in turn.

In the first paragraph, we find that the function of *ideas* is to "instigate and direct further operations of observation ... to bring new facts to light and to organize all the selected facts into a coherent whole" such that what they *are* by virtue of this functionality is "proposals and plans for acting upon existing conditions." That is, they are what they are by virtue of how they function in inquiry. They are explanatory hypotheses (proposals) that call for new kinds of evidence. They are *operational*, we might say, because their *function*, in part, is to guide further observational activities. On the other hand, the point that observation by itself is literally operational (in the sense of an observer's "acting upon existing conditions" in order to obtain new data) is obscured by the greater emphasis given to the functional role of "bring[ing] new facts to light and [organizing] all the selected facts into [an inferentially] coherent whole."

In the second paragraph, in characterizing *facts* as operational, Dewey is more explicit about (mis)characterizing their operational character in terms of their inferential character. Most of this paragraph discusses the inferential function of facts as evidence. The paragraph may be summarized as an argument to show that facts are functional because they are operational and that they are operational because they are functional—where this functionality lies specifically in the inferential role played by facts as *evidence* for or against some respective proposal. Of course, once again, this is not anything that a sensationist empiricist could not embrace. There is just one clause in this second paragraph indicating that Dewey does not quite fit the sensationist-empiricist mold. Specifically, the denial that facts are "merely *results* of operations of observation which are executed with the aid of bodily organs and auxiliary instruments of art" actually affirms that they *are* such results of observational activities, though they are more than that as well. In the present view, it is this clause that explains why facts are operational in character whereas the bulk of what Dewey has to say here explains why they are inferential in character.

The point here is that, despite its title (which should perhaps be "The Inferential Character of Facts-Meanings"), section V of chapter 6 of Dewey's *Logic* is not the place to look for operationalist themes in Dewey's brand of pragmatism. An operationalist stance is there, but not in the way that is clearly enough distinguished from inferentialism.

A more robust endorsement of operationalism is to be found rather in *The Quest for Certainty* (1929, LW4:88–92) where Dewey cites P. W. Bridgman and A. S. Eddington and explicitly acknowledges Peirce as an earlier proponent of the operationalist stance these physicists were promoting in the later 1920s:

> The position of present science on [the nature and office of ideas in reflective inquiry] has been stated as follows: "To find the length of an object, we have to perform certain physical operations. The concept of length is therefore fixed when the operations by which length is measured are fixed; that is, the concept of length involves as much as and nothing more than the set of operations by which length is determined. In general, we mean by any concept nothing more than a set of operations; the *concept is synonymous with the corresponding set of operations*" [Bridgman 1927, 5]. The same idea is repeated by Eddington in his Gifford Lectures. His statement is as follows: "The vocabulary of the physicist comprises a number of words such as length, angle, velocity, force, potential, current, etc., which we call 'physical quantities'. It is now recognised that these should be *defined* according to the way in which we recognise them when actually confronted with them, and not according to the metaphysical significance which we may have anticipated for them. In the old textbooks mass was defined as 'quantity of matter'; but when it came to an actual determination of mass, an experimental method was prescribed which had no bearing on this definition" [Eddington 1928, 254–255]. (Dewey 1929, LW4:89–90)

These are two classic statements of 1920s operationalism from two leading physicists at the time. Bridgman (1882–1961) was an innovative experimental physicist (winning the Nobel Prize in Physics in 1946 for his work on the physics of high pressures) who wrote extensively on the nature of scientific method and the philosophy of science in general (for example, 1927; 1936; 1938; 1950; 1959). He effectively coined the terms 'operational definition' and 'operational analysis'. Eddington (1882–1944) was an astrophysicist and philosopher of science well known for his exposition of Einstein's theories of special and general relativity. His expedition to the island of Príncipe off the west coast of equatorial Africa to observe the solar eclipse of 29 May 1919 provided one of the earliest tests of the light-bending predictions of general relativity theory. Both Bridgman and Eddington were accomplished "laboratory-men," as Peirce would have put it (1905a, EP2:332), who at the same time understood the philosophical significance of what they were saying.

Dewey includes a long footnote following the quote by Eddington that displays a full appreciation of the import of operationalism as such, particularly as it relates to Peirce's statement of the pragmatic maxim in 1878:

> It is implied in the quotation that concepts are recognized by means of the experimental operations by which they are determined; that is, operations define and test the validity of the meanings by which we state natural happenings. This implication is made explicit a few sentences further along when in speaking of EinsteinMr. Eddington says his theory "insists that each physical quantity should be defined as the result of certain operations of measurement and calculation." The principle is anticipated in Peirce's essay on "How to Make Our Ideas Clear" published as far back as 1878—now reprinted in a volume of essays, edited by Morris R. Cohen, and entitled *Chance, Love, and Logic* [Peirce 1923]. Peirce states that the sole meaning of the idea of an object consists of the consequences which result when the object is acted upon in a particular way. The principle is one element in the pragmatism of James. The idea is also akin to the "instrumental" theory of conceptions, according to which they are intellectual instruments for directing our activities in relation to existence. The principle of "extensive abstraction"[3] as a mode of defining things [in terms of *events* if not *processes*?] is similar in import. On account of ambiguities in the notion of pragmatism—although its logical import is identical—I shall follow Bridgman in speaking of "operational thinking." (Dewey 1929, LW4:90n2)

Surprisingly, Dewey's mentioning his own "instrumental" theory of ideas as "intellectual instruments for directing our activities in relation to existence" at this point runs together in a somewhat confused way the inferential nature of ideas as *intellectual instruments* and the operational nature of *activities in relation to existence*. It would appear that Dewey might not have been aware of the ambiguity in his own rendition of the notion of pragmatism. Yet, in what follows next, he gets right to the point of stating and explaining the superiority of operationalist pragmatism over sensationist empiricism:

> The adoption of this point of view with respect to the meaning and content of thinking, and as to the validity or soundness of the ideas by means of which we understand natural events, makes possible what has been lacking throughout the history of thought, a genuinely experimental empiricism. The phrase "experimental empiricism" sounds redundant. It ought to be so in fact, since the adjective and the noun should have the same significance, so that nothing is gained by using the two terms. But historically such is not the case. For, historically, empirical philosophies have been framed in terms of sensations or sense data. These have been said to be the

---

[3] Presumably this is a passing reference to Whitehead's notion of *extensive abstraction*—for instance, see Whitehead 1920, chapter 4, 74–98.

material out of which ideas are framed and by agreement with which they are to be tested. Sensory qualities are the antecedent models with which ideas must agree if they are to be sound or "proved." These doctrines have always evoked an abundance of criticisms. But the criticisms have taken the form of depreciating the capacity of "experience" to provide the source and test of our fundamentally important ideas in either knowledge or morals. They have used the weaknesses of sensational empiricism to reinforce the notion that ideas are framed by reason apart from any experience whatsoever; to support what is known in the vocabulary of philosophical systems as an *a priori* rationalism. (Dewey 1929, LW4:90–91)

That is to say, there are serious deficiencies in sensationist empiricism; but until Peirce, the only reaction to those deficiencies was an equally deficient appeal to *a priori* rationalism. It is thought in many quarters that Kant resolved this drawn-out and excessively polarized debate in a synthesis of the two positions that yielded a unified view of rational experience. Peirce and others acknowledged the need for some such resolution but did not accept Kant's particular way of trying to achieve it. Peirce's way of going about it, overall, is also perhaps suspect; but minimally, by Dewey's lights, Peirce's operationalism cut the Gordian knot of modern epistemology:

From the standpoint of the operational definition and tests of ideas, ideas have an empirical origin and status. But it is that of acts performed, acts in the literal and existential sense of the word, deeds done, not reception of sensations forced on us from without. Sensory qualities are important. But they are intellectually significant only as consequences of acts intentionally performed. A color seen at a particular locus in a spectral band is, for example, of immense intellectual importance in chemistry and in astro-physics. But *merely* as seen, as a bare sensory quality, it is the same for the clodhopper and the scientist; in either case, it is the product of a direct sensory excitation; it is just and only another color the eye has happened upon. To suppose that its cognitive value can be eked out or supplied by associating it with other sensory qualities of the same nature as itself, is like supposing that by putting a pile of sand in the eye we can get rid of the irritation caused by a single grain. To suppose, on the other hand, that we must appeal to a synthetic activity of an independent thought to give the quality meaning in and for knowledge, is like supposing that by thinking in our heads we can convert a pile of bricks into a building. Thinking, carried on inside the head, can make some headway in forming the *plan* of a building. But it takes actual operations to which the plan, as the fruit of thought, gives instrumental guidance to make a building out of separate bricks, or to transform an isolated sensory quality into a significant clew to knowledge of nature.

Sensory qualities experienced through vision have their cognitive status and office, not (as sensationalist empiricism holds) in and of themselves in isolation, or as merely forced upon attention, but because they are the consequences of definite and intentionally performed operations. Only in connection with the intent, or idea, of these operations do they amount to anything, either as disclosing any fact or giving test and proof of any theory. The rationalist school was right in as far as it insisted that sensory qualities are significant for knowledge only when connected by means of ideas. But they were wrong in locating the connecting ideas in intellect apart from experience. Connection is instituted through operations which define ideas, and operations are as much matters of experience as are sensory qualities. (Dewey 1929, LW4:91–92)

This emphasis on "intentionally performed operations" is no small matter, apparently. Dewey ranks this other-than-Kantian operationalist synthesis of empiricist and rationalist sentiments as one of the greater "feats of intellectual history":

> It is not too much to say, therefore, that for the first time there is made possible an empirical theory of ideas free from the burdens imposed alike by sensationalism and *a priori* rationalism. This accomplishment is, I make bold to say, one of three or four outstanding feats of intellectual history. For it emancipates us from the supposed need of always harking back to what has already been given, something had by alleged direct or immediate knowledge in the past, for the test of the value of ideas. A definition of the nature of ideas in terms of operations to be performed and the test of the validity of the ideas by the *consequences* of these operations establishes connectivity within concrete experience. At the same time, by emancipation of thinking from the necessity of testing its conclusions solely by reference to antecedent existence it makes clear the originative possibilities of thinking. (Dewey 1929, LW4:92)

Despite Dewey's proclivity to cast Peirce's operationalism against an inferentialist background, the preceding account demonstrates Dewey's overall grasp of the broader import of pragmatism.

It is perhaps noteworthy that a "supplementary essay" by Dewey was included in the volume of Peirce's essays (Peirce 1923) that Dewey cited in his footnote quoted above. This was a reprint of an article by Dewey that had been published in 1916. For many, the respective volume of Peirce's essays was perhaps the best if not only means of access to Peirce's writings before the *Collected Papers* began to appear in the 1930s. In any case, Dewey's essay reveals that one could in 1916 already see that Peirce and James were not quite on the same page so far as pragmatism was concerned. Admittedly, much of the present book only echoes what Dewey already stated almost a hundred years ago.

Given that James's inferentialist version of pragmatism has become the predominant view of what pragmatism is, it will be important to show in detail how an operationalist reading of the pragmatic maxim should actually work. Obviously that will be key to arguing that an operationalist reading of the maxim is every bit as relevant as an inferentialist reading would be to critically and constructively assessing the potential influence of pragmatism in matters of vital concern (in politics, law, economics, medicine, religion, etc.). We will use the rest of this book, though, to informally run through a number of topics and illustrations that help to explain further what the pragmatist stance is, mainly to motivate and contextualize any future formal development of an operationalist semantics.

In the next chapter, we will contrast a pragmatist reaction to classical empiricism with two twentieth-century analytic attitudes concerning the nature of empirical verification. Namely, to start, we will look briefly at Quine's *holistic* conception of verification that was developed in response to logical-positivist atomistic conceptions of verification. Quine claimed that this holistic stance was "a shift toward pragmatism" (1951), though at best it would have to be James's kind of pragmatism that he had in mind. The fact that Quine did not accommodate operationalist pragmatism is proven by his first-order extensionalism—the key difference being that Quine's primary emphasis on first-order "things" simply ignores Peirce's primary emphasis on actions and tangible (sensible) effects.

An atomistic conception of empirical verification was well developed in Carnap's work. It will pay therefore to take a look at Carnap's work in order to reconsider what exactly is wrong with an atomistic conception of verification. We will do this by amending Putnam's 1995 comparison of pragmatism and Carnap's brand of empiricism—the key difference being ultimately that Carnap neglected the *interactive* (or enactive) nature of observation and measurement. The moral here is that "enactivist" aspects of pragmatism—reflecting Peirce's operationalist conception of pragmatism—provide an alternative response to atomistic forms of empiricism that Quine's holism does not capture—the latter being more closely aligned rather with James's view of pragmatism.

In chapter 6, to bolster appreciation of the contrast between pragmatism and atomistic empiricism, we will survey a range of well-known examples of the so-called observer effect as evidence for a conception of observation and measurement as interactive rather than as the workings of a passive, detached spectator. This is interesting in its own right, though a related point to be stressed here is that ordinary sensory perception of objects in the world by an individual perceiver is similarly interactive. This point is consistent with the interactional views of perception one finds in ecological psychology (e.g., Gibson 1979; 1982; Turvey et al. 1981, etc.) and in *enactivist* approaches to the cognitive sciences more broadly. The latter issues are explored in chapter 7.

In chapter 8, to illustrate the contrast between Carnap's sensationist empiricism and operationalist pragmatism, we will examine a particular case of a proposed analysis of the methods and organization of the so-called settlement movement during the so-called Progressive Era in the United States. One might think that the settlement movement by its very nature was a *pragmatist* enterprise (see, for example, Tindall and Shi 2007, 812, and Trattner 1998, 170); but the analysis given by Simkhovitch (1906) is clearly an empiricist analysis. A critique of Simkhovitch's analysis allows us to highlight what pragmatism *is not* as a way of better understanding what it is. On a positive note, this particular example helps us to concretely distinguish two different conceptions of *action* that are key to understanding the distinction between operationalist and inferentialist pragmatism.

In chapter 9, to better illustrate operationalist aspects of pragmatism, a number of philosophically substantive applications of a pragmatist methodology will be presented. In particular, we will quickly review some of the examples already considered with particular emphasis on Peirce's operational definitions of the words 'reality' and 'truth'. We will then explore how to define the words 'knowledge', 'democracy', and 'justice' in a similar fashion.

Finally, chapter 10 includes a reaction to various competing conceptions of pragmatism that are often found these days in mass media publications addressing U.S. national politics. Very few if any of these common conceptions of pragmatism in political arenas do justice to *real* pragmatism as originally formulated by Peirce and James. This reveals not just an innocuous lack of consistency between academic and real-world vocabularies. For the record, journalists and politicians alike are in large part incorrect in their uses of the word 'pragmatism'. They should apply other labels in the sound bites and slogans they use to make the various points they want to make.

FIVE
Empiricism versus Pragmatism

Pragmatism was developed in large part as a reaction against modern rationalism. This is apparent in some of Peirce's earliest writings (1868a; 1868b) as well as in the *Popular Science Monthly* articles (especially 1878a). This is also a frequent theme in James's discussions of pragmatism and in his "radical empiricism" (the culprit sometimes being labeled by James as absolutism or intellectualism) (1907h; 1909a; 1912). Yet neither Peirce nor James could rightfully be said to be modern empiricists. Of course, few if any recent philosophers can rightfully be said to be modern empiricists, strictly speaking. But what then is the difference between empiricism and pragmatism? Was James a pragmatist or merely an empiricist? To help answer such questions, we need to contrast the *pragmatic* method for clarifying meanings with some "standard" semantic methods, represented here by the views of Quine and Carnap.

QUINE'S HOLISM

The idea that pragmatism in some sense offers an alternative to classical empiricism will not be news to anyone familiar with Quine's "Two Dogmas of Empiricism" (1951). In that article Quine concluded by espousing a kind of "empiricism without the dogmas"—the two dogmas being, first, belief in a hard-and-fast analytic/synthetic distinction and, second, the principle that "every meaningful statement is ... translatable into a statement (true or false) about immediate experience" (1953, 38). Quine's alternative, after carefully arguing for why we should reject these two dogmas, is his well-known "holistic" conception of verification:

> Taken collectively, science has its double dependence upon language and experience; but this duality is not significantly traceable into the statements of science taken one by one. ... [In] taking the statement as a unit we have drawn our grid too finely. The unit of empirical significance is the whole of science. ... The totality of our so-called knowledge or beliefs [from casual matters of fact to the laws of physics and pure mathematics] is a man-made fabric which impinges on experience only along the edges. Or, to change the figure, total science is like a field of force whose boundary conditions are experience. (Quine 1953, 42)

The idea here is that conflicts with peripheral experience require adjustments in the field as a whole, respecting, for instance, the inferential interconnections among various statements. Literally anything is subject to adjustment, including the principles of inference themselves. This view allegedly includes a shift toward pragmatism in the (unclear) sense that

> [e]ach man is given a scientific heritage plus a continuing barrage of sensory stimulation; and the considerations which guide him in warping his scientific heritage to fit his continuing sensory promptings are, where rational, pragmatic. ... [This] turns upon our vaguely pragmatic inclination to adjust one strand of the fabric of science rather than another in accommodating some particular recalcitrant experience. Conservatism figures in such choices, as does the quest for simplicity. (Quine 1953, 46)

It is not clear what is meant by the term 'pragmatic' here, given that one might just as well have used alternative terms like 'prudent' or 'practical'. It *is* clear, though, that this would be a coherentist version of pragmatism where one's beliefs are ultimately tied (but are not reducible) to the "continuing barrage" of what Quine has referred to elsewhere as "stimulations of sensory receptors" or "surface irritations" (1960; 1981). Namely, what is most or best believable is what is most or best *workable* in preserving and/or strengthening the overall fabric of one's beliefs.

James would surely appreciate these "fabric" and "force-field" metaphors. If Quine's holism is a form of pragmatism, it is pragmatism in James's sense of the term. It is just as clearly *not* pragmatism in Peirce's sense for at least two reasons—or for one reason that can be explained in two ways. The reason Quine's view is not pragmatist in an operationalist sense is simply that his view of sensory "experience" is not operationalist. On one hand, the characterization of our engagement with the world as a barrage of sensory excitations or surface irritations includes in some sense the "sensible effects" highlighted in the pragmatic maxim but without mention of any modes of conduct or practices or actions that might yield such effects. We simply are creatures with various banks of sensitive nerve endings, and the world impresses itself upon us by causing excitations or irritations across these otherwise passive peripheral sensory surfaces. (This is essentially an ivory-tower conception of experience.)

The absence of interactivity in the course of acquiring sensory inputs is also what distinguishes Carnap's empiricism from Peirce's—a point we will return to shortly. Carnap's work—at least the early work—does not reflect anything like Quine's robust type of holism; but Quine and Carnap are remarkably similar in how they regard the physiological mechanics of sensation. Before we turn to Carnap, though, there is a second way to argue that Quine's holistic view of verification is not operationalist.

Namely, Quine's "ontological relativity" notwithstanding, the fact that his views are not operationalist in character is evidenced by his thesis that ontological commitments should be cast solely in terms of formal first-order languages. Recall, for instance, Quine's famous dictum that "to be is to be the value of a variable" (1948; 1958; 1968). This is not itself a metaphysical claim though it places certain constraints on how to formulate metaphysical claims. It reflects a style or way of thinking and theorizing that is fundamentally oriented to possible "entities" or "things." It presumes that the language of metaphysics is translatable (somehow) into a first-order language; and, of course, Tarski showed us how to provide an extensional semantics for such languages. Quine's dictum articulates the working principle that ontological commitments enter this semantic picture only in the specification of a "domain of discourse" (a collection of objects) over which the first-order quantifiers range. This kind of ontology is oriented to *things*. If we want to talk in this way about sets, events, processes, actions, times, mental states, phenomena, properties, relations, universals, or abstract entities of any kind, then so be it; but we are to treat them as first-order *things*. This view is therefore metaphysically promiscuous; yet *formally*, it is a kind of nominalism in that it presses any first-class reality into the mold of first-order thing-hood.

There are reasons in support of this view, and some of them may be good reasons. But a first-order language provides neither the best nor last word on what we should take as basic metaphysical categories. For instance, with operationalist pragmatism in mind, we might instead devise a formal language that takes action-types (types of operations) as primitive, i.e., associating (and thus sorting) variables with respective action-types so as to range over possible respective "sensible results" of acting in those ways. A pragmatist alternative to Quine's dictum would thus change the focus, saying something to the effect that "to be a possible effect of a possible action is to be the value of a variable." In this case, variables associated with particular ways of acting would range over respective ranges of possible outcomes, basic propositions would pertain to relations holding between such outcomes and/or ways of acting, and so forth. (Thinking along such lines should shed light, for instance, on Dewey's unusual conception of propositions in his 1938b *Logic: The Theory of Inquiry*.)

This may actually be too simple as stated, but it suggests a different orientation to formal analysis and thus to characterizing how ontological commitments are built into our forms of discourse. And it is not a new idea. It is essentially the idea of "sorting" variables by reference not to kinds of things but to types of actions and their immediate effects. This is exemplified by an operationalist account of the language(s) of mathematical physics where the sorting of variables—$\vec{x}, t, E, m, \vec{v}, \vec{p}$, etc.—is a routine practical matter drawing on the idea that such variables range respectively over possible quantitative values for respective physical properties or relations, a sufficient number of these being variables that range over numerical *outcomes* (with distinctive, characteristic "units") that are the possible results of performing appropriate kinds of measurement operations. Except in an ad hoc manner, this focus on operations and outcomes (actions and results) is hardly typical of a standard first-order semantics, including a standard thing-oriented many-sorted semantics.

The point here is that operationalist pragmatism, no more and no less than Quine's formal nominalism, puts constraints on the ontological commitments of a given discourse—but not by stipulating *what* to take as fundamental or as given but by stipulating *how* to characterize formal semantic grounds for that discourse. According to Quine's formal "first-order-logical" nominalism, languages of science take entities or things as the semantic basis for devising theories and models of how the world works. Namely, whatever is ontologically fundamental must be characterizable in terms of things serving as values of first-order variables. For an operationalist pragmatist, on the other hand, a scientific language would instead take types of actions and their respective effects as a semantic basis for devising theories and models of how the world works. This captures what Peirce meant, I want to claim, by asserting that conceivable effects of conceivable actions must ground our fundamental terminology for formulating and clarifying our ideas. This, I think, constitutes a fairly precise statement of the pragmatic maxim, at least in an operationalist sense.

We thus have two reasons to think that Quine's holistic conception of empirical verification is not operationalist and thus not pragmatist in Peirce's sense. First, Quine conceives of sensation as being passive in nature, and second, his first-order extensionalism compels him to think about the world as made up of *things*—a formally static orientation toward metaphysics that does not accommodate operationalism (unless, once again, it would be by way of an ad hoc treatment of operations and/or their possible results as "things"). The first of these two reasons warrants further investigation here (the second being put on hold for now). Specifically, we will turn now to look at Carnap's similar conception of sensory experience as passive—that is, as lacking an element of interaction—in order to see what exactly is wrong with it.

Carnap's Empiricism

Quine's holistic version of empirical verification, as stated above, was formulated in response to logical-positivist atomistic conceptions of verification, including the reductionist principle that "every meaningful statement is ... translatable into a statement (true or false) about immediate experience" (Quine 1953, 38). We have looked at two ways that one could argue that Quine's pragmatism is at most an inferentialist form of pragmatism, lacking certain necessary features of operationalist pragmatism. This absence of operationalist elements in Quine's holism gives evidence of a particular view of "sensory input" that he shared with Carnap and which, in large part, helps to explain a major difference between pragmatism and classical empiricism. We should look at this carefully. Putnam's discussion of Carnap's empiricism in *Pragmatism: An Open Question* (1995) is helpful here.

In particular, Putnam (1995, 69–71) identifies some interesting differences between the views of Peirce and Dewey and the views of Carnap on the nature of "inquiry," making it clear that Carnap's particular kind of grammatical formalism enforced certain methodological if not ontological commitments that are contrary to those of pragmatism. These constraints were "empiricist" rather than nominalist. Whether or not Carnap shared Quine's formal nominalism, though, is not the issue. The issue, rather, is whether Carnap's verificationist leanings might in some way promote operationalist pragmatism. One could safely wager that many proponents of pragmatism over the years have steered away from operationalist themes precisely because it too easily appears to move one into tighter alignment with Carnap's reductionist version of verificationism. That worry is misplaced. Having been immersed in early-twentieth-century European verificationist doctrine, Carnap even in his later work focused exclusively on "sensory effects" (evidence, etc.) and failed to accommodate modes of activity by which such effects are produced. The problem here is that essential features of a pragmatist stance are entirely missing from Carnap's views. Carnap's conception of evidence had the empiricist elements but lacked the operationalist elements of operationalist pragmatism. On this score, Carnap and Quine are largely in agreement.

Of course, whether we agree with him or not, Carnap's views are so familiar to us that it may be hard to get some perspective on this difference with operationalist pragmatism. Putnam unfortunately does not quite get to the heart of the matter.

Putnam's contrast between pragmatism and Carnap's kind of empiricism is based, first, on the odd fact that the later Carnap's major work on inductive inference (1950; 1952) contains almost no reference to experimentation. Theories, on Carnap's view, are confirmed by *evidence* (in the form of observation sentences), but Carnap gives no attention to and thus makes no allowances for distinguishing *how* such evidence may be obtained, whether by passive observation or by active intervention, whether "as the result of intelligently directed experimentation, or [because] it just happens to be available. ... [T]he question, whether one has actually tried to *falsify* the hypotheses that have been 'highly confirmed' is not a question that can be asked or answered *in* the languages Carnap constructed."

Secondly, the "methodological solipsism" of Carnap's earlier work (1928) is applicable to this later work in the sense that it is immaterial whether observation is cooperative or not. Thus, in Carnap's view, an observer is basically "a single isolated spectator who makes observations through a one-way mirror and writes down observation sentences." Assessing theories on this picture "is then simply a matter of using an algorithm to determine whether a sentence has a mathematical relation to another sentence (the conjunction of the observation sentences the observer has written down)." Scientific method will thus have been reduced to a method of computation (Putnam 1995, 69–71). In this sense, ironically, Carnap's "empiricism," like James's, is oddly rationalistic.

On the other hand, for pragmatists like Peirce and Dewey, inquiry is both an active manipulation of the environment and a cooperative social enterprise. The distinction between these two aspects of Peirce's and Dewey's view of inquiry is not inconsistent with our double-aspect rendering of the pragmatic maxim; but it is a different distinction. Its two components are the opposite of the two components of Carnap's view that Putnam highlights—a spectator conception of observation, and methodological solipsism.

Operationalist pragmatism is specifically designed to challenge the spectator conception of observation (whether the observer is an isolated individual or a community). Putnam may seem to address this issue in his references to active versus passive observation, and in his emphasis on "human interaction with an environment ... the active intervention, the active manipulation of the environment"; but these references are ambiguous in just the way that the pragmatic maxim itself is ambiguous. On one hand, there is the point that observation itself is active—looking in order to see; listening in order to hear; probing in order to detect; performing actions of some appropriate sort just to be able to register impressions; sampling a domain just to be able to note differences and similarities; varying one's perspective just to be able to pinpoint constancies in a landscape. On the other hand, there is the point that observations (once obtained) may be *used* to confirm or disconfirm hypotheses, to weaken or shore up existing beliefs, etc. This involves a different kind of action, a different kind of intervention, in which, for example, one designs, sets up, and runs experiments specifically in order to *test* particular hypotheses. The second kind of action here is not in running the experiment per se but in the use of the results to test some claim. One makes possible certain observations whose results may then be used in some way. We have, then, a difference between *making* observations (acquiring evidence) versus *using* those observations (using the evidence), where it is important to see that the first of these is itself a kind of active intervention even if it "just happens" to occur (and where the method of acquisition has as much to say about what the evidence *is* as does the way that it is used).

Putnam's critique of Carnap is not as thoroughgoing as it could have been because he misses this distinction. He immediately turns to inferentialist concerns when he connects the component of "active intervention" with *fallibilism*. As he puts it, Carnap was a fallibilist in the sense of agreeing that a presently (non-dis)confirmed theory may be disconfirmed by later observations; but the pragmatists had a stronger conception of fallibilism. "Before Karl Popper was even born, Peirce [for example, 1903e, CP5.599] emphasized that very often ideas will not be falsified unless we actively seek falsifying experiences. Ideas must be put under strain, if they are to prove their worth" (Putnam 1995, 71).

The latter says only that we must purposely experiment to try to falsify hypotheses, to see how well they *work* within a given theory or system of beliefs, as it were. This entails nothing one way or another about the (inter)active nature of observation itself, whether pursued for falsification purposes or not. Putnam is thus dealing with inferentialist concerns in a way that is not inconsistent with a conception of perception as passive reception of impressions (irritations of purely receptive nerve endings, etc.). On such an account, one may purposely put oneself in a position to passively receive certain kinds of impressions. It is just a matter of how and where the isolated spectator places the one-way mirror. Thus we will not have dealt particularly well with the "spectator" aspect of Carnap's kind of empiricism simply by emphasizing experimentation and verificationist themes. Quine's conception of sensory experience has the same problem. We have seen that this was James's problem as well.

The business of testing (straining, attempting to falsify) given hypotheses in problem-solving contexts is thus largely a matter for inferentialist pragmatism. A *verificationist* emphasis on experimentation is focused on assessing the systemic workability of various sentences among themselves, in various forms of abstract hypotheses, observation sentences, or what have you. The fact that the very acquisition of evidence requires active presence in the world, on the other hand, is an operationalist concern. An *operationalist* emphasis on grounding conceptual and theoretical schemes in active measurement procedures is focused rather on linking concepts concretely to registerable outcomes of distinctive observation activities. Putnam does not appear fully to appreciate this distinction. His notion of "active intervention" accommodates the inferentialist aspects of pragmatism but not its operationalist aspects.

Putnam proceeds to discuss other themes that are closely connected with inferentialist pragmatism, emphasizing in particular the cooperative nature of inquiry as answerable to "principles of discourse ethics" and to contextually interpretable normative maxims in place of merely formal strictures of computational algorithms. For such reasons, scientific inquiry, on a pragmatist account, does not reduce to the mechanical computations of a solipsistic spectator. "Both for its full development and for its full application to human problems, science requires the *democratization of inquiry*" (Putnam 1995, 73). Brandom (1994; 2000; 2008) has developed similar themes at great length in recent years. Also see chapter 9 below.

While Putnam's contrast between pragmatist and Carnapian views of inquiry is insightful, his discussion focuses exclusively on inferentialist themes of falsification and such when characterizing the active aspect of inquiry—as if there were not two versions of the pragmatic maxim. The fact that Putnam could so easily allow operationalist concerns to be obscured by inferentialist concerns is in fact a tribute to the force of the mathematical formalizations that Carnap and others were able to impress upon analytic philosophy early in the twentieth century.

On the contrary, both versions of pragmatism, I would claim, are equally important to the project of cutting through the mathematical jungle that has grown out of the soil of passive sensationist empiricism, cultivated throughout the middle decades of the twentieth century through the work of Carnap, Tarski, Quine, and others. Putnam may not have given operationalist pragmatism its due, but his discussion nicely facilitates identification of some key differences between an action-based pragmatist semantics and a passive-empiricist Carnapian semantics. At bottom, on the former account, we need to be more explicit than Carnap was about the nature and constitutive role of observers' actions in the acquisition of evidence.

Before we look at a concrete case where Carnapian empiricism has gotten in the way of understanding a kind of inquiry that is better understood in pragmatist terms, the next chapter will briefly survey a number of well-known types of measurement whose "interactive" character is more or less obvious. It is these kinds of examples we should keep in mind as we try to revise our intuitions about experimentation, observation, measurement, "evidence," and so forth along pragmatist rather than empiricist lines.

SIX

Measurement and the Observer Effect

We will next do two things. First, in this chapter, we will survey a list of examples of the so-called *observer effect* in various sciences, mainly to illustrate the interactive character of measurement and observation in the sciences—a feature of *evidence* that Carnap largely ignored. Secondly, in the following chapter, with these examples on the table, we will argue that ordinary perception is interactive in very much the same way. Perhaps the term 'argue' is too strong. We will rather survey an approach to the study of perception that promotes an "interactivist" view of it. This will be convincing at least to the extent that one is willing to acknowledge the consistency, scope, and explanatory fecundity of such a view.

The following discussion is supposed to help concretize the notion that animal perception is interactive (not just passively receptive) in fundamentally important ways. The point is that an operationalist reading of the pragmatic maxim is getting at something that is deeply rooted in our animal nature, not just promoting an operationalist methodology in professional science. Between these two poles lies much if not all of human cognitive activity. The obviously interactive nature of observation and measurement in the sciences should not be surprising if such activities are only extensions and refinements of ordinary perceptual capabilities. At the same time, the fact that ordinary perception is interactive may not be so apparent, given that sensory systems are traditionally conceived as passive channels for intake of information from the environment—or, to use a familiar analogy, as being like keyboards responsive to finger taps. (Even Peirce seems to have succumbed to this kind of view at times. Note, for example, his arguments against the existence of a Kantian faculty of intuition in 1868a, 14–17, claiming eventually that perception requires the application of supplementary conceptions.) A survey of various so-called *enactivist* conceptions of perception will support a view that perception is interactive—or, to use another familiar analogy, that it is more like the sweeping and tapping of a "white cane" as a tactile activity yielding information about the navigability of surrounding terrain.

An operationalist reading of the pragmatic maxim will not seem inappropriate in scientific disciplines where it is obvious that observed outcomes require interactive observational processes—wherever, more specifically, it is unreasonable on the surface to regard the observer merely as a passive and detached spectator. The theme of this chapter is that it is almost *never* appropriate to regard measurement and observation as passive and detached. Even when we can get away with doing that, it is because we can safely ignore the interactive nature of measurement and observation without incurring serious defects in the results.

A spectator conception of observation was of course built implicitly into modern Newtonian science—given, for example, that merely looking at moving billiard balls or planets *clearly* does not influence their motion. This conception of the detached observer fused nicely with respectively simplistic normative conceptions of objectivity and impartiality. Subsequent acknowledgment of the *observer effect*—acknowledgment that the act of observing can introduce changes to what is being observed—was initially hardly more than an acknowledgment of an unusual annoyance that complicated certain kinds of science relative to norms set by contemporary theoretical physics. To further complicate matters, the observer effect has too easily been regarded simply as a kind of observation bias, as if it were the kind of annoyance that with proper care may be corrected for if not eliminated.

On the contrary, the pragmatic maxim suggests that the observer effect is an "annoyance" only if we have failed to appreciate the interactive character of observation in the first place. Regarding ourselves as passively detached spectators is a rough approximation that is feasible within a relatively small range of our experience. It is a mistake, so the claim goes, to regard it as normal. Our conceptions of objectivity and impartiality will likewise have to be richer and more refined than what is suggested by a passively-detached-spectator conception of observation.

The following illustrations of the observer effect are well known (Wikipedia 2009). Each example may illustrate different facets of the observer-effect phenomenon, though no single example is necessarily more informative than any other. What is interesting here is the variety and ubiquity of examples. The fact that so many examples are so common supports the contention that a detached-spectator conception of observation is not normal.

In physics, observer effects (including so-called *probe effects*) are often the unintended results of using measuring instruments or techniques that unavoidably alter the state of the physical systems whose properties they are supposed to measure. This effect can be observed in many domains of physics, indicating that the example of using a ruler to measure the length of a smallish rigid object is not a typical kind of measurement. It would follow that physics on the whole (Newtonian or otherwise) is not so amenable to a spectator conception of observation after all.

For instance, in electronics, small amounts of capacitance, resistance, or inductance may be introduced into a bit of circuitry by attaching an oscilloscope or a multimeter (to measure voltage, current, *and* resistance) or some other probing device. Good measuring devices are supposed to have slight effects; but even slight effects may lead to unexpected changes (failures, fixes) when attached to sensitive circuitry.

In thermodynamics, a mercury thermometer must absorb thermal energy to record a temperature. Its presence therefore changes the energy state of the body whose temperature is being measured. This effect may or may not be negligible depending on the nature (relative size, thermal conductivity, etc.) of the measured body.

In meteorology, anemometers and weather vanes must absorb mechanical energy to record wind speed and direction. While the effects are usually negligible, relatively speaking, their presence changes the energy state of the atmosphere whose properties are being measured.

In materials science, three different notions of tensile strength are explicitly defined in terms of three different versions of the observer effect, namely, in terms of the possible results of destructive tests as applicable to specimens of a given material:

- *yield strength* is the stress necessary to produce a given inelastic strain in a material—the stress at which material strain changes from elastic deformation to plastic deformation, causing it to deform irreversibly (that is, the amount of force needed to bend a material to a point where it cannot return to its original shape);
- *ultimate strength* is the quantity of the utmost stress that a given unit area of a certain material is expected to bear without failing—the maximum stress a material can withstand when subjected to tension, compression, or shearing (i.e., the maximum stress on a stress-strain curve for that material); and
- *breaking strength* is the applied force required to rupture a specimen in a tension test under specified conditions—corresponding to the stress coordinate on the stress/strain curve at the point of rupture.

The observer effect is not an "annoyance" here. It is the basis rather for defining some key terms of the given discipline!

In particle physics, to be able to detect an electron visually (to be able to *see* it, as it were), photons would first have to interact with it. The interaction involving even a single photon would change the state (including the position or path) of that electron so significantly that for all intents and purposes we may expect not to be able to see an electron in any normal sense of the term. Less direct means of measurement (using diffraction gratings and photographic plates, for instance) will likewise affect electrons in the instance of their being detected, depending on the various ways in which such measuring devices are employed.

Along these same lines, the uncertainty principle in quantum mechanics has often been mistakenly conflated with the observer effect. This is largely due to the fact that the uncertainty principle can be characterized in terms of measurement, and measurement in quantum mechanics exhibits the observer effect in spades. Wave-function collapse is a key feature of measurement in the Copenhagen interpretation of quantum mechanics. Namely, after one has measured some "observable" feature of the quantum state of an experimental apparatus, the quantum state immediately changes in such a way that a second measurement of that feature (without re-initializing the system) would yield the same result as the first measurement. In contrast, multiple identical preparations and measurements of the quantum state of an experimental apparatus would usually be different (unlike measuring the length of a given two-by-four multiple times in succession with the same measuring tape). The expected result of such a measurement is described by a probability distribution specifying likelihoods of obtaining various possible macroscopic results. Thus, like tossing dice, a measurement process would appear to be random. (Compare this with the expectation that the likelihood of many different independent polls of a population of voters would vary somewhat around an actual election result but that any one act of polling voters should not by itself change the probability distribution. Polling the same sample of voters repeatedly, on the other hand, so as not to re-initialize the procedure, should be expected to yield the same result as before, all else being what it was at the time of the initial polling.) The more interesting point for now, though, is the conception of a measurement as a physical interaction, that is, as a physical interaction that moreover seems to result in relatively radical changes in the targeted system.

Turning from the microscopic to the telescopic, astronomy illustrates how the interactive character of observation in physics is constrained not only by the biological peculiarities of our sensory capabilities, or the designs of the instruments we use to extend and enhance those capabilities, but also by macroscopic physical realities that are equally beyond our control. These include law-like constraints such as the fact that our view of the large-scale universe, whether instrumentationally enhanced or not, is limited by the speed of light as the top speed by which information reaches us from distant regions of space. An observational effect (if not an instance of the observer effect per se) is that looking farther *out* in space goes hand-in-hand with looking farther *back* in time, so to speak. This feature of the evidence available to our eyes is a result of the fact that we as observers are moving at speeds slower than the speed of light relative to the respective observed objects. Arguably, this *is* an instance of the observer effect.

Closer to home, there are contingent constraints such as the fact that, while we seem to look passively at the night sky from a given vantage point, our observational platform resides on a spinning sphere that is itself moving along a trajectory encircling a nearby star (which is itself a piece of a galaxy that is both spinning and moving as an aggregate relative to other galaxies). It was not without some effort that we discovered that our take on the evidence available to our eyes is marked by complicated motions of our eyes (no matter how passively still we may make them relative to the planet's surface under our feet). The path of motion of Neptune may not be significantly altered by the functioning of our eyes as we look at it, but any visual evidence we may have of that motion is heavily dependent upon the dynamics of our own path of motion. Thus, there is an instance of the observer effect here attributable in part to the fact that our observational platform is spinning. There is an instance of the observer effect here in the sense that the act of observing by itself influences any evidence we have regarding what is being observed.

Einstein's operationalist version of special relativity theory (1916) undermines a spectator conception of observation by making it clear that determinations of apparently simple terrestrial quantities like temporal intervals and spatial lengths depend on the active use of clocks and measuring rods. We do not just passively note points in time or positions in space. Rather our determinations of places and times depend on the transfer of such information through space and across time by means of certain types of interactions using instruments with standardized spatial and temporal characteristics.

The examples, of course, do not stop with the physical sciences. In computer science, when testing the functionality of given software and/or the hardware on which it is run, an observer effect may occur as the result of observing a computational process while that process is running—so-called *event monitoring*. In particular, running both the observed and observing programs on the same CPU as a way of observing the performance of that CPU may lead to inaccurate results (since the observer program itself affects the CPU performance). Simply using a log file to track a process can slow that process. Viewing a log file or any other output file while a process is running may cause input/output errors if not stop the process altogether. In general, in code profiling and performance measurements, the insertion or removal of code instrumentation can cause disruptive delays or otherwise unpredictable behavior.

In psychology and in the social and behavioral sciences, so-called *reactivity* occurs when subjects change their behaviors as they become aware that they are being observed.

- A prime example of this is the *Hawthorne effect*, named after a study of possible correlations between lighting conditions and worker productivity in a factory setting. Apparently, the workers became aware of the study and subsequently altered their behaviors for that very reason.
- The *John Henry effect* is a special case of this general phenomenon that occurs when participants in a study alter their performance upon learning that they are in a control group.
- An *experimenter effect* can occur when experimenters inadvertently communicate their expectations to the subjects. Reactivity may occur in that subjects may purposely try either to comply with or to resist those expectations.

- A special case of the latter effect is the *Pygmalion effect*, which occurs when students alter their behavior to accommodate stereotypical teacher expectations.

These different versions of the observer effect threaten a study's internal validity if they are not adequately addressed in the initial design of the study. The fact that such threats can be deflected if handled properly (for example, by blinding or masking methods) is essential for the viability of any of the behavioral sciences.

Squarely facing up to these issues, contemporary cultural anthropology has successively honed a strategy of *participant observation* as a key research methodology. By most accounts this strategy can be successful if pursued correctly. There is no alternative, of course, if observation requires participatory interactions of some sort. Reactivity cannot be eliminated insofar as it is an integral part of the interactivity of observation. Rather it may be "controlled for" so that its influence on the evidence may be properly weighted and "factored out" when that is appropriate.

In medical research (whether in medical treatments or clinical studies), a *placebo effect* occurs when a subject's mere expectation concerning a medical intervention of some kind will by itself cause the subject's condition to change. The treatment may in fact have no intrinsic therapeutic value though it is administered as if it did. As opposed to "observer bias," this phenomenon involves the occurrence of concrete physiological effects due to a patient's expectations concerning a physical intervention versus effects due to the therapeutic value of the physical intervention as such. This kind of example of the observer effect in medical research is not unlike some forms of "reactivity" in social and behavioral sciences.

And so forth and so on. The point of this quick survey of examples of the observer effect, again, is to muster evidence against a passively-detached-spectator conception of observation and thus against Carnap's sensationist kind of empiricism. Measurement and observation are typically interactive. They are not typified by what you think you are doing when you look at your watch or what carpenters or tailors think they are doing when they meticulously confirm that their materials have certain spatial dimensions. The interactive and possibly fact-changing character of observation has to be taken into consideration as we try to understand an operationalist reading of the pragmatic maxim.

This point about the interactive and possibly fact-changing character of observation in the sciences bears directly on how we conceive of objectivity in the sciences (or in intelligent inquiry more broadly). We do not have to give up the notion of objectivity, but we do not get the latter for free simply by having detached or detachable observational capabilities. The latter, on this view, are essentially non-existent—namely, such capabilities are at best only approximate. Rather, objectivity is to be characterized, presumably, in terms of overall methodological considerations, including the fact that observation typically involves fact-changing interactions of an inquirer with a worldly subject matter of some sort.

This is a topic that by itself deserves extended attention, but that is not the direction we will take presently. The claim that observation is interactive (etc.) actually cuts more deeply than a study of scientific methodology might suggest. It applies not just to observation in the sciences (under deliberately controlled conditions, etc.) but also more broadly to the ordinary perceptual activities of live creatures intent on maintaining continued survival in a naturally and precariously dynamic world. The notion that perception itself is interactive is the topic to which we turn next.

SEVEN
Perception and Action

An operationalist reading of the pragmatic maxim would have us believe that our concepts will not be as clear as they might be if we cannot define them in terms of sensible results of activities in the world—or more accurately, in terms of conceivable sensible results of conceivable activities in the world. We have argued above (mostly by pointing to examples) that science in general, from this perspective, cannot honestly accommodate a passively-detached-spectator conception of observation. We will argue further that science also cannot allow even a passively-detached-spectator conception of *perception*. The point here is that much of the force of the pragmatic maxim lies in the fact that animal experience is deeply rooted in activity—all the way down—in which case, of course, those are going to be the kinds of considerations on which one ultimately depends to clarify one's thinking. There are no other viable options.

For what it is worth, the idea that perception is interactive is not just the Kantian idea that certain "categories of understanding" impose structure on a sensory manifold. Nor is it merely the legitimate inferentialist claim that observation is theory-laden. Nor is it the idea that perception is ampliative (which it is, no doubt). The point here is simply that perception in a fundamental way is *physically active* and that we need to better understand what it amounts to to say that.

'Enactivism' is a blanket label for a class of theoretical approaches in the cognitive sciences that promote the claim that ordinary perception is intrinsically interactive. Enactivism emphasizes the ways that live creatures (including human beings) *live* as organisms interacting in suitable ways with a changing environment. Enactivists of various stripes are not all on the same page in this regard, but presumably a fundamental emphasis on organism/environment interactions is common to any form of enactivism. That is, perceptual as well as higher forms of cognitive functionality are alleged to be rooted in such interactive capabilities.

This has broad implications for how we understand life, learning, experience, culture, and so on; and *that* can be problematic given that it is too easy to lose sight of the basis for those broad implications—the basis being the simple fact, namely, that perception and other fundamental life activities are just that: activities. Even among enactivists (for example, Hurley 1998; 2006) it has been too easy to emphasize functional aspects of perception and lose sight of its operational nature.

Enactivism (or at least the label) has been around for several decades, encompassing a wide range of work in a number of fields—see Noë 2004 (17) for a long list of references. The opening paragraph of chapter 1 of Noë's *Action in Perception* (2004) immediately gets to the point in describing an enactivist approach to perception:

> The main idea of this book is that perceiving is a way of acting. Perception is not something that happens to us, or in us. It is something we do. Think of a blind person tap-tapping his or her way around a cluttered space, perceiving that space by touch, not all at once, but through time, by skillful probing and movement. This is, or ought to be, our paradigm of what perceiving is. The world makes itself available to the perceiver through physical movement and interaction. In this book I argue that all perception is touch-like in this way: Perceptual experience acquires content thanks to our possession of bodily skills. *What we perceive* is determined by *what we do* (or what we know how to do); it is determined by what we are *ready* to do. In ways I try to make precise, we *enact* our perceptual experience; we act it out. (Noë 2004, 1)

We will not investigate Noë's position in detail, but the book from which the quote above was taken is worth reading to see how this idea of perception as a way of acting is developed and justified. See also section 6 of Noë 2006, a paper that addresses the problem of perceptual *consciousness* from an enactive-externalist perspective. Rowlands's "vehicle externalist" development of an enactivist conception of *representation* (2006) is also promising as a way of developing pragmatist themes in the philosophy of mind. This recent work by Noë, Rowlands, and others (including Clark 1993; 2001) followed earlier seminal work by Johnson and Lakoff dealing with embodied cognition (see, e.g., Lakoff and Johnson 1999). Johnson in particular connects his conception of *image schemata*—as regularly recurring embodied patterns of experience acquired during the course of early child development (1987)—with John Dewey's notion of experience (1934; 1938b) as well as with Eleanor Gibson's and Anne Pick's ecological account of child perceptual development (Gibson and Bergman 1954; Gibson and Walk 1960; Pick 1965; Gibson and Pick 2000).

Interestingly, an earlier form of enactivism related to childhood cognitive development can be found in Piaget's work (1936; 1945; 1954; 1976). In particular, consider the fundamental role of action in what Piaget calls the sensorimotor stage of epistemic development:

> Action ... is the necessary condition for the infant's achievement of the ecologically valid "correlations" that constitute the segmented and segregated objects of experience. Action and some input from the distance receptors provide the necessary and sufficient conditions for such progress—assuming now an intact nervous system.... These are the preliminaries that, in our view, set the stage for the sensory phase of [epistemic] development of which Piaget (1954) has written so brilliantly, a stage in which action and external experience are fused. He refers to the first part of senso-

rimotor intelligence as one in which things are "lived rather than thought." (Bruner 1966a, 16–17)

Bruner developed his own theory of cognitive growth that included three stages of development of representational capabilities: enactive, iconic, and symbolic. He describes enactive representation as follows:

> What is meant by representation? What does it mean to translate experience into a model of the world? Let me suggest that there are probably three ways in which human beings accomplish this feat. The first is through action. We know many things for which we have no imagery and no words, and they are very hard to teach to anybody by the use of either words or diagrams and pictures. ... We have come to talk about [this] first form of representation as *enactive*. ... In earliest childhood events and objects are defined in terms of the actions taken toward them. ... An object is what one does to it. (Bruner 1966b, 10–12)
>
> Toward the closing months of the first year of life ... the identification of objects seems to depend not so much on the nature of the objects encountered as on the actions evoked by them. ... For the infant, then, the actions evoked by stimulus events may serve in major part to "define" them. ... In later childhood this first technique of representation does not fully disappear. (Bruner 1966a, 12)

These statements speak for themselves, though it needs to be acknowledged that Piaget and Bruner promoted a weak kind of enactivism—weak in the sense that it was limited (in any substantial form) to the first year or so of life. On the other hand, Noë and others are promoting a kind of enactivism with respect to perception and cognition in general, not just at an early stage of epistemic or cognitive development.

Another notable example of enactivism in cognitive science that we will dwell on at greater length here is James J. Gibson's so-called *ecological psychology* (1950; 1966b; 1979). The details of his theory of perception, like any other theory of perception, are in some ways complicated; but the main ideas are relatively easy to grasp. Gibson's theory is essentially built around three fruitful ideas: the detection of invariants, the fixation of attunements, and perception of affordances. We will examine each of these notions in turn, looking first at invariants, then at affordances, and then at attunements.

INVARIANTS. Gibson by his own account was influenced early on by Koffka's gestalt psychology as well as by the "radical empiricism" of his teacher E. B. Holt (who, interestingly, was one of William James's psychology students at Harvard— cf. Heft 2001). A key inspiration for Gibson's unique and groundbreaking view of perception came from his work as director of the Army Air Force Motion Picture Research Unit in Aviation Psychology during World War II (Gibson 1967; Hochberg 1994). As part of this work, Gibson developed visual aptitude tests used to screen pilot applicants. He also worked on improving training methods for flying and landing airplanes, for real-time recognition of distant aircraft, and for aiming at moving targets from a moving platform. In the course of this work, he observed that more information could be drawn from moving pictures than from static ones (1967, 137–138). This observation focused Gibson's interest on visual perception in dynamic settings. He quickly came to the view that perceptual tasks associated with flying airplanes are typical—that perception, visual or otherwise, is essentially a process of active pickup of stimulus information in dynamic environments.

> Every photographer is aware that even a slight movement of his camera during exposure will shift the image on the film, for it ruins the picture. The same kind of shifting of the image on the retina occurs all the time during vision with the difference that vision is enriched rather than spoiled. (Gibson 1950, 117)

As he put it later, "optical transformations in time are the main carriers of information, not optical forms frozen in time" (Gibson 1967, 133). Rather than working like a still camera, *visual* perception in particular involves the detection of invariants in dynamically changing ambient optic arrays. This would include invariants of optical structure under changing illumination, invariants of optical structure under changes in the point of observation, invariants across successive sampling of the ambient optic array, local invariants under local disturbances of the ambient optic array, and so forth (1979, 310–311). More generally, in this view, perception in *any* of its modes is based on a process of accessing ambient fields of information and detecting ("extracting") invariants in the resulting flow of excitation, whether optical, acoustic, mechanical, or chemical.

A notable feature of this approach to perception is the emphasis on physics at terrestrial scales—the physics of distances and durations typical of animal locomotion, and of forces and materials typical of biological activities in terrestrial environments (Gibson 1966b, chap. 3; Reed 1982). The *variations* relative to which detectable invariants occur are in large part at macroscopic scales of bodily activity. This is the case for each of six perceptual systems (or five, depending on how you count the taste/smell system—see Gibson 1966b, 50):

- Invariants in changes of forces of gravity and acceleration (as detected by mechanoreceptors in vestibular organs) provide information regarding bodily orientation relative to the direction of gravity. They also provide information regarding events of being pushed—as in the beginnings and endings of movements of the body.
- Invariants in changes of vibrations in the air (as detected by mechanoreceptors in the cochlear organs coupled with the middle ear and auricle) provide information regarding the nature and location of "vibratory events."
- Invariants in changes of tissue deformation, muscle-fiber tension, and joint configuration (as detected by mechanoreceptors and perhaps thermoreceptors in the skin, joints, and muscles) provide information regarding bodily contact with the ground, mechanical encounters, object shapes, and material states like solidity and viscosity.

- Invariants in changes in the intake of air (as detected by chemoreceptors in the nasal cavity) provide information regarding the composition of the air and the nature of volatile substances.
- Invariants in transformations of ingested materials (as detected by chemo- and mechanicoreceptors in the oral cavity) provide information regarding the nutritive and biochemical value of those materials.
- Invariants in changes in variable aspects of structure in ambient light (as detected by photoreceptors in the ocular mechanism—the eyes, including intrinsic and extrinsic eye muscles coupled with the vestibular organs, the head, and the whole body) provide information regarding objects, animals, motions, events, places, or anything else that can be specified by the variables of optical structure.

All of these systems cooperate (e.g., the basic orienting system provides a frame of reference for the other perceptual systems), and information from different perceptual systems is often redundant (a surface that looks smooth may indeed feel smooth; a source of noise that sounds far away may indeed look far away). Interestingly, bodily perceptual organs are coupled with informational structures exterior to the body in such a manner that we may include the latter as components of what Gibson calls "perceptual systems." Perception is a combination of the activities of these different systems—activities of bodily orientation, listening and orienting to sounds, touching and bodily movement, sniffing and smelling, tasting and savoring, looking and visual exploration—such that perceptual attention, as a *resolution process*, is constituted by the activities of systems that include structures outside the body as much as they include organs and receptors inside the body (Everett 2013; Burke and Everett 2013).

Obviously this "ecological" view of perception conflicts with commonsense stimulus-response conceptions of an alleged relation between sensation, thought, and overt behavior (the standard empiricist view). Gibson put emphasis not on an alleged distinction between sensory systems versus motor systems or central versus peripheral neural processes but on what he called *muscle systems* and what Reed (1982) referred to as *action systems*.

> The neat and simple contrast between sense organs and motor organs is incorrect, and the convenient formula of the sensory-motor arc to represent the action of the nervous system is inadequate. There is an output to perceptual systems and an input from motor systems. The physiologist can properly distinguish between afferent and efferent, ingoing and outgoing pathways, but he really ought not to speak of "sensory" and "motor" pathways. Nevertheless there are muscles, and they combine in complex combinations to make muscle systems. (Gibson 1966b, 56–57)

Gibson thus distinguished a number of such systems—postural, orienting-investigating, locomotor, appetitive, performatory, expressive, semantic—where "some kind of awareness goes along with all of them, [though] not always perceptual awareness" (1966b, 57). The point, again, is that much of the activity—even "computational" activity—that constitutes awareness if not perceptual awareness takes place not solely at neuronal levels as such but on macroscopic scales of muscle systems working in terrestrial environments.

A better understanding of how retinal or inner-ear neurons operate would only further improve a Gibsonian theory of visual or auditory perception; but Gibson's emphasis on terrestrial physics derives from the principled claim that an explanation of the workings of perception in terms of the detection of invariants in changing ambient arrays of stimulus information at terrestrial scales is not *reducible* to any such account of the workings of neurons, whether singularly or in aggregate systems. Perceptual attention and phenomenal consciousness (if we can make sense of such things at all) occur wholly within perceptual systems whose biophysical infrastructure incorporates tightly coupled structures both external and internal to the body.

This indicates one sense in which Gibson's enactivist psychology is "ecological." It also indicates how and in what sense perception is *direct*. Perception takes place *within* the activities of perceptual systems—not as mere intake and preliminary manipulation of information that is then passed on to non-perceptual modules to be turned into some kind of conscious awareness of external objects. Objects as objects of perception *emerge* into awareness (become apparent) *in the midst of* activities that include (extend to, encompass) aspects of the environment external to neural systems. Neural activities are a necessary feature of this process, of course, but typically they are not sufficient (at least not for veridical perception). Obviously Gibson is not solving the hard problems of consciousness here, but he is telling us specifically *where* and perhaps vaguely *how* to look for it and where and how not to.

AFFORDANCES. There is, of course, a good deal more to Gibson's ecological psychology besides the detection of invariants as just recounted. Equally important is the notion of *affordances* as objects of perception (1977; 1979; 1982).

Gibson's characterization of affordances, as with invariants, is at odds with commonsense empiricism as reflected in the meta-metaphysical orientation of first-order languages (a la Carnap and Quine) to *things* and their sensible properties. Namely, it is alleged in this latter "first-order linguistic" view that one perceives individual objects out there in the world by means of sensory excitations at one's bodily surfaces. Little or no account is given of how sensations produce perceptions, yet somehow these sensory excitations indicate the apparent presence of certain properties inhering in the objects which are the respective sources of those excitations so that by means of these excitations the objects are thus perceived.

This view—still alive and allegedly well—is admittedly problematic on various grounds; but it is "obviously" a basic sketch of how perception works, no? Well, no. For some recent developments of such a view that might otherwise be thought to be enactivist in nature, see Prinz 2002; 2006. Likewise Rowlands 2006 (chap. 5) cites MacKay 1967 as a representative example of enactivism though MacKay's notion of sensorimotor coordination and so forth (see his Figures 1–3, for instance) comes down squarely on all fours as an empiricist spectator theory of perception.

On Gibson's account, we are obviously aware of "objects" in the world around us—rocks, clocks, chairs, bears—but the relationship between sensory excitation and awareness of objects in the world cannot work like commonsense empiricism says it does. For Gibson, the basic "raw elements" of perception are *invariant detections*, not sensory excitations. Nothing really registers "sensorially" (so to speak) except in the form of invariants in the flow of sensory excitations. Nothing else is trustworthy, as it were.

For example, even at a cellular level, the human visual system may be able to detect single photons though typically, under normal conditions, several (at least six or eight) photons are necessary for the human eye to register a flash of light. Perhaps single photons are drowned out by "noise in the system" so that several photons are needed just to overcome the noise. An alternative Gibsonian explanation would be that a single photon can affect electrochemical properties of a retinal cell and thus be singularly registered in some sense as a sensory excitation, but what really "turns the cell on" (as a sensory stimulus) will be multiple photons with the *same* (viz., invariant) energy level and direction of motion (presumably within some small degree of tolerance). Thus a kind of preliminary reliability measure would be naturally built into the system, given that there is no better way to gauge (comparatively) whether a single photon's worth of energy by itself is noise or not. Gibson is thus able to explain how even the most elementary "sensory stimulation" involves reactions only to invariant features of events (in this case, invariant directions and frequencies across a flow of retinal cell excitations, i.e., a stream of absorptions of electromagnetic energy).

In general, it should be possible to give some such invariant-detection explanation at every layer and level of analysis of the cascade of optical information throughout the visual system. We have invariant detection all the way up and all of the way down in this view.

After telling such a story, *what* then can we say is perceived in the course of all of the invariant detection utilizing muscle and perceptual systems? Somehow this is all relevant to our being aware of things in the world. A Gibsonian story sandwiches two crucial kinds of activity between the two standard empiricist notions of sensory excitation and object awareness. These are, namely, *invariant detection* (as discussed above) and *the perception of affordances*. Thus, in Gibson's view, there are at least four distinguishable orders or kinds of activity and achievement involved in any act of perception, as follows:

(1) excitation of sensory receptor cells and membranes;

(2) detection of invariants in the flow of such sensory excitations;
(3) perception of affordances; and
(4) awareness of things, events, etc., in the world.

Later entries in this list are built upon previous entries. Invariants (2) occur and are thus detectable in flows of sensory excitation (1). Not all awareness is strictly perceptual in nature; but contrary to the ways that metaphysical debates about objects and properties usually transpire, objects as we are aware of them (4) are cast here as systems of affordances (3) rather than simply as bundles of sensible qualities or properties.

So what about the affordances themselves? What are they, specifically in terms of detectable invariants and in terms of their associations with different kinds of objects? Making sense of this list crucially requires that we make sense of the notion of affordances.

Gibson traced the origin of the concept of affordances to gestalt psychological notions of valence, invitation, and demand, though he argued that these notions are not quite adequate (1979, 138–140). Instead, he characterized affordances as follows, relying on extensive lists of examples (which we will not reproduce here) to nail down what he means:

> The *affordances* of the environment are what it *offers* the animal, what it *provides* or *furnishes*. ... I mean by [the term *affordances*] something that refers to both the environment and the animal in a way that no existing term does. It implies the complementarity of the animal and the environment. (Gibson 1979, 127)
>
> Roughly, the affordances of things are what they furnish, for good or ill, that is, what they *afford* the observer. ... Not only objects but also substances, places, events, other animals, and [artifacts] have affordances. ... I assume that affordances are not simply phenomenal qualities of subjective experience (tertiary qualities, dynamic and physiognomic properties, etc.). I also assume that they are not simply the physical properties of things as now conceived by physical science. Instead, they are ecological, in the sense that they are properties of the environment relative to the animal. (Gibson 1982, 403–404)

An ecological (externalist) notion of an affordance is simple enough in such broad terms. Gibson repeatedly states, moreover, that affordances are directly perceived. More specifically, what we perceive when we attend to *things* (places, substances, surfaces, objects) are their affordances (1979, 134). This points to how awareness of objects (4) is constituted in terms of perceptions of affordances (3). Here is a series of informative statements along such lines:

> Orthodox psychology asserts that *we perceive ... objects insofar as we discriminate their properties or qualities*. ... [P]sychologists assume that objects are *composed*

of their qualities. But I now suggest that what we perceive when we look at objects are their affordances, not their qualities. (Gibson 1979, 134)

The perceiving of an affordance is not a process of perceiving a value-free physical object to which meaning is somehow added in a way that no one has been able to agree upon; it is a process of perceiving a value-rich ecological object.... Physics may be value-free, but ecology is not. (Gibson 1979, 140)

There has been a great gulf in psychological thought between the perception of *space and objects* on the one hand and the perception of *meaning* on the other. But when space and objects are defined in terms of the opaque solid geometry of surface layout, and when meaning is defined in terms of the affordances of [things], these problems are seen to be linked.... The meaning or value of a thing consists of what it affords. Note the implication of this proposed definition. What a thing affords a particular observer (or species of observer) points to the organism, the *subject*. The shape and size and composition and rigidity of a thing, however, point to its physical existence, the *object*. But these determine what it affords the observer. The affordance points both ways. What a thing *is* and what it *means* are not separate.... The perception of what a thing is and the perception of what it means are not separate, either.... Thus we no longer have to assume that, first, there is a sensation-based perception of a thing and that, second, there is the accrual of meaning to the primary percept (the "enrichment" theory of perception...). The available information for the perception of a certain [thing] is the same information as for the perception of what it affords. (Gibson 1982, 407–408)

A key claim here is that *what a thing's affordances are* and *what the thing is* are not separate. It is in this sense that whole objects are to be thought of as systematic combinations not of mere properties but of affordances. For this to make sense, we still have to be able to say more specifically what affordances are—to say more clearly what is meant by the word 'affordance'.

At this point we should not fail to appreciate the distinction between ecological psychology (a) as augmenting the conception of belief on which a pragmatist conception of meaning is based, and (b) as a body of scientific theory whose basic terminology calls for the kind of clarification$_{3,4}$ that is required of any science. Attempting to clarify$_{3,4}$ the term 'affordance' in effect turns the pragmatist methodology back on itself. This is virtuously circular. A pragmatist conception of meaning *should* ultimately be applicable to the terms in which that conception is presented.

(a) Gibson's ecological psychology can augment Peirce's characterization of the "fixation of belief" by casting the latter as a special case of a more general notion of the "fixation" of invariants. Philip Wiener lends support to such a point when he remarks that Peirce's doubt/belief conception of inquiry was essentially a specific application of the "evolutionary idea of natural selection [etc.]":

Peirce's problem was to convert the evolutionary idea of natural selection and the survival of the fittest among biological species into the idea of an evolution of the mind by means of a logical competition among thoughts which eliminates those not fit to stand for the truth fated to be discovered by those who investigate. The methods of authority, tradition, and tenacity compete with that of science to fix belief in every walk of life. The exact sciences were evolving to a stage where the rules for the efficient discovery of laws were beginning to take shape. In psychology, history, law, as well as in metaphysics, a growing consciousness of method was apparent to Peirce, and the living manifestations of this "growth of concrete reasonableness" were found by him in the thinking of the distinguished associates upon whom he conferred membership in his Metaphysical Club.... Peirce was more conscious than any of his contemporaries of the historical significance of the discussions by his group of the major ideas of the time, particularly the idea of evolution, or, more accurately, *evolutionism*, which is the generic name for the flock of generalizations that invaded every province of thought with the gradual acceptance of the Darwinian theory of evolution, much debated in the two or three decades after 1859. (Wiener 1946, 225–226)

Concretely, the "fixation" of biological species by way of "natural selection" can be regarded as a tentative establishment of invariants in a "flow" of begettings and birthings in different dynamic environments. We will not trace the development of Peirce's evolutionary cosmology here, but he even characterized "laws of nature" (literally) in a similar way as evolutionary invariants (see, e.g., EP1:285–371). We do want to highlight, though, how Gibson's conception of the detection of invariants provides a general terminology that extends across discussions of natural laws, biological species, fixed beliefs, perceivable affordances, and sensory stimuli alike. There is a common theme in all of these discussions, namely, that each involves in its own fashion the *fixation* of invariants in the midst of some ongoing variation. (This indicates even the generic pattern of the *execution of an operation* involving the emergence of some tangible effect as the result of some specific type of activity.) This is a general pattern of which the doubt/belief depiction of inquiry is just one instantiation.

Generally speaking, an invariant, while a constancy of some sort, is *static* only in the sense of being a *stable* way of acting. The variation out of which an invariant emerges does not thereby *stop* but rather adopts some type of holding pattern or routine, so to speak. This is not an implausible way of characterizing biological species. Also recall Peirce's claim that the formation of a belief (in the course of inquiry) is the establishment of a habit, and the latter consists of one or more rules of action (see pages 10–11 above). Such rules are not "laws of nature" in a strict sense but they do reflect established (evolved, learned, stabilized) patterns of behavior (routines) of the bearer of those respective habits.

Gibson's treatment of sensation and perception displays similar patterns of lower-order and higher-order "fixation" activities. This pattern is evident, for instance, in his descriptions of five or six types of perceptual systems (see page 83 above). We may infer that the general conception of invariant detection encompasses Peirce's more specific notion of inquiry (as belief fixation). This conclusion provides the means for clarifying Gibson's notion of *affordances*.

(*b*) Highlighting their functional role in constituting what *things* (objects) *are* for a given animal already tells us something about what affordances are. At the same time, Gibson also essentially explains what affordances are "operationally" in terms of abilities to detect invariants (2) in flows (variations) of sensory excitation (1). Namely, an affordance is alleged *to be* (or *to be specified by*) a kind of *higher-order invariant* involving combinations of lower-order invariants in flows of sensory excitation. Of course, affordances as such are not "conceptions"; but the conception of *affordances* is a conception and thus, it is hoped, should be clearly$_3$ definable.

For such an operational definition, it should be clear that the respective elementary operations would consist in producing (creating, promoting) appropriate flows of sensory excitations, where detections (extractions, registerings) of invariants in such flows would be the respective tangible results of such activities. While not yet a definition of the term 'affordance', this specifies an operational basis for such a definition. So what might that definition be?

Gibson's various characterizations of affordances are worth considering at this point. In his lists of examples, Gibson sometimes somewhat cryptically refers to affordances themselves as invariants (e.g., Gibson 1979, 18–19, 21). At times he is quite explicit:

> There is much evidence to show that the infant does not begin by first discriminating the qualities of objects and then learning the combinations of qualities that specify them. Phenomenal objects are not built up of qualities; it is the other way around. The affordance of an object is what the infant begins by noticing. The meaning is observed before the substance and surface, the color and form, are seen as such. An affordance is an invariant combination of variables, and one might guess that it is easier to perceive such an invariant unit than it is to perceive all the variables separately. (Gibson 1979, 134–135)

Again, the key statement here (for present purposes) is that "an affordance is an invariant combination of variables." That these are *higher-order* invariants of some sort is due to the fact that the so-called variables whose so-called combination constitutes the affordance are variables each of which is associated with a comparatively lower-order ability to detect invariants in some flow of sensory excitation. In other words, the possible "values" of these variables are detectable invariants of some specific (lower-order) sort.

An affordance, meanwhile, is said to be determined by a law-like relation—a constancy of some sort—among some respective collection of such lower-order variables. A longer passage, below, develops this latter point. The entire passage (about three paragraphs) is included here in hopes of minimizing the chance of losing sight of the key statements about affordances as (being specified by) "invariants of invariants"—in order to be abundantly if not redundantly clear that the characterization of affordances as being specified by "invariant combinations of invariants" is just how Gibson characterizes them:

> The central question for the theory of affordances is not whether they exist and are real but whether information is available in ambient light for perceiving them. ... The skeptic understands the stimulus variables that specify the dimensions of visual sensation; he knows from psychophysics that brightness corresponds to intensity and color to wavelength of light. He may concede the invariants of structured stimulation that specify surfaces and how they are laid out and what they are made of. But he may boggle at invariant combinations of invariants that specify the affordances of the environment for an observer. The skeptic familiar with the experimental control of stimulus variables has enough trouble understanding the invariant variables I have been proposing without being asked to accept invariants of invariants.
>
> Nevertheless, a unique combination of invariants, a *compound* invariant, is just another invariant. It is a unit, and the components do not *have* to be combined or associated. Only if percepts were combinations of sensations would they have to be associated. Even in the classical terminology, it could be argued that when a number of stimuli are completely covariant, when they *always* go together, they constitute a single "stimulus." If the visual system is capable of extracting invariants from a changing optic array, there is no reason why it should not extract invariants that seem to us highly complex.
>
> The trouble with the assumption that high-order optical invariants specify high-order affordances is that experimenters, accustomed to working in the laboratory with low-order stimulus variables, cannot think of a way to *measure* them. How can they hope to isolate and control an invariant of optical structure so as to apply it to an observer if they cannot quantify it? The answer comes in two parts, I think. First, they should not hope to *apply* an invariant to an observer, only to make it available, for it is not a stimulus. And, second, they do not have to quantify an invariant, to apply numbers to it, but only to give it an exact mathematical description so that other experimenters can make it available to *their* observers. The virtue of the psychophysical experiment is simply that it is disciplined, not that it relates the psychical to the physical by a metric formula. (Gibson 1979, 140–141)

We see here that affordances as such involve higher-order invariants. Namely, they are specified by "invariants of invariants," by "unique combinations of invariants," by "compound invariants," by invariants that are "highly complex." In this sense, affordances are something other than just collections or sets of invariants, though they are supposed to be subject to *some* kind of "exact mathematical description."

An interesting twist in the characterization of affordances appears in these latter paragraphs that should be highlighted. The earlier quote on page 90 includes the statement that "an affordance is an invariant combination of variables" (whatever that is supposed to mean). But, in the longer quotation above, "invariant combinations of invariants" are said to "specify affordances" (of the environment, for an observer). This may seem like a difference that makes no difference, but it raises a question of whether affordances *are* higher-order invariants or whether they are *specified by* higher-order invariants. If they are specified by the higher-order invariants, then one would expect that they are something other than the higher-order invariants themselves. In the latter sense, a given higher-order invariant, if expressible (e.g., if exactly mathematically describable) as a law-like relation among lower-order variables, might *specify* numerous affordances rather than simply *be* a single affordance. We should explore this distinction further.

One thing to note, first of all, is the degree to which these statements echo James's *radical empiricism*. As previously noted, this should be no surprise given that Gibson studied with E. B. Holt at Princeton, who in turn had studied with William James at Harvard (see Heft 2001). In fact Gibson cites James in this regard, recalling James's assertion that visual lines and other visual shapes are themselves simple data rather than collections of point sensations (Gibson 1950, 15). A key feature of James's radical empiricism is the claim that "the relations between things, conjunctive as well as disjunctive, are just as much matters of direct particular experience, neither more so nor less so, than the things themselves," along with the claim that "the parts of experience hold together from next to next by relations that are themselves parts of experience. The directly apprehended universe needs, in short, no extraneous trans-empirical connective support, but possesses in its own right a concatenated or continuous structure" (James 1909a; 1912). Gibson's notions of invariants of invariants or of combinations of invariants reflect a similar attitude about their being "matters of direct particular experience." In this regard, radical empiricism is "radical" not in the sense of being dogmatic or bullheaded but in the sense that it acknowledges a *wider range* of what is subject to direct experience beyond so-called *atomic* sensory stimulation. Not everything that is experienced is reducible to merely atomic sensory stimuli. Apparently it is "radical" to say that relations among sensory stimuli may themselves be directly experienced as simple data.

Nevertheless, when Gibson says that an affordance qua invariant is not a stimulus in the traditional stimulus-response sense (though it is directly perceived and thus in some sense *is* a stimulus), that tells us something about what it is not, not what it is. Some further cryptic remarks from notes published posthumously continue in the same vein:

> Affordances are invariant combinations of properties of things (properties at the ecological level) *taken with reference to* a species of an individual. I now add: with reference to its *needs* (biological and social) as well as to its action-systems and its anatomy. The affordances for behavior and the behaving animal are *complementary*.
> Affordances are perceived, i.e., attended to.
> Affordances do not *cause* behavior but constrain or control it.
> Needs control the perception of affordances (selective attention) and also initiate acts.
> Acts are *not* responses to stimuli, and percepts are not responses to stimuli. An observer is not "bombarded" by stimuli. He extracts invariants from a flow of stimu-

lation.

Affordances, and the stimulus information to specify affordances, are neither subjective nor objective but transcend this dichotomy.

The actor/perceiver and the environment are *complementary*.

An affordance is not the outcome of a perceptual process, as a "meaning" is supposed to be. (Gibson 1982, 410–411)

According to such remarks, affordances are said to be invariant combinations of ecological-level properties (for a species) "with reference to its needs," its action-systems, and its anatomy. Note also the remark that affordances do not "cause" behavior but rather constrain it. How can we make sense of these and other statements that are supposed to tell us, in some clear and general fashion, what affordances are?

ATTUNEMENTS. To answer the latter question, we need to acknowledge a third fundamental technical notion (in addition to the notions of *invariants* and *affordances*) that has currency among many proponents of ecological psychology, that was promoted by Gibson beginning in the 1960s, and that is essential, on the present account, to characterizing *in general* what affordances are. This is, namely, the notion of *attunement*. Initially, we may think of an attunement as a complementary melding of stable interactions between organisms and their environments (between environments and their constituent organisms)—as if the interactivity among environments and organisms were capable of various dynamic regularities and thus were to develop various "natural frequencies" to which various perceptual systems (as "resonators") may become adapted. Gibson derived this idea (at least in part) from some remarks by Karl Lashley (1950) in regard to some summary conclusions concerning his (Lashley's) attempts "to discover the physiological basis of memory":

All theories of learning by association presuppose some kind of central enrichment of an impoverished input to the nervous system. The supplementation, no matter how conceived, is supposed to depend on memory, that is, on some cumulative carryover of the past into the present. It may be conceived either as an accumulation of nervous bonds or connections, or of images or engrams, but at any rate an accumulation of traces in some sense of the term.

Lashley sought to discover the physiological basis of memory during a long career of investigation. But he had to conclude in the end that "it is not possible to demonstrate the localization of a memory trace anywhere within the nervous system" (1950, 477). The "search for the engram," as he put it, had failed. (Gibson 1966b, 275)

At the very end of the paper, however, Lashley sounded another note. He suggested that "the learning process must consist of the attunement of the elements of a complex system in such a way that a particular combination or pattern of cells responds more readily than before the experience" (1950, 479). ... If learning is a kind of *resonance* in the nervous system, a tuning of the system to certain inputs, then it is

> not any sort of storage of engrams or deposits of traces. ... [This suggests] an astonishing hypothesis, that learning does not necessarily depend on memory as it has always been conceived. ... (Gibson 1966a, 172)
>
> This hypothesis of tuning or resonance implies something quite different from the accumulation of traces. When it is combined with the hypothesis of information pickup, it suggests a surprising possibility—that learning does not depend on memory at all, at least not on the re-arousal of traces or the remembering of the past. (Gibson 1966b, 275)
>
> Perhaps, as Lashley suggested, the brain resonates to whatever is invariant under transformation and becomes increasingly attuned to it with recurrence over time. If so, perception and learning could be accounted for without any assumption of memory considered as an accumulation of traces. The brain would be a self-tuning resonator, not a storehouse. (Gibson 1966a, 174)

These remarks come from two sources, both published in the same year and both addressed to the issue of temporal order in perception and memory. They touch on several useful notions that Gibson develops more extensively elsewhere.

For instance, despite what is explicitly stated in the previous quotes, *resonance* as such (whether we regard it metaphorically or literally) is not an accomplishment of the brain alone but involves muscle systems working in terrestrial environments and, thus, (at least) the nervous system as a whole (Gibson 1966b, 5; Heft 2001, 366). "Instead of postulating that the brain constructs information from the input of [sensory nerves], we can suppose that the centers of the nervous [and muscle] system[s], including the brain, resonate to information" (Gibson 1966b, 267). An account of how nervous and muscle systems *resonate to information*, then, is supposed to explain (rather than presuppose) so-called recognition and remembering, not to mention perception of affordances (Gibson 1966b, 147).

The notion of "resonance" as utilized here is largely if not entirely metaphorical. That by itself is not a problem insofar as it is only an alternative to the popular metaphor likening the retina to photographic film. The substantive question here regards how exactly the resonance metaphor is supposed to get us anywhere.

Technically, we might think of systems identified with the organism (e.g., combined nervous and muscle systems) as *resonators* that, so to speak, "naturally oscillate" with greater amplitude at *some* frequencies (their resonant or natural frequencies) than at other frequencies—in reaction, say, to the resonant or natural frequencies of systems identified with the environment (e.g., mechanical, electromagnetic, acoustic, chemical, etc.). Resonance in this sense occurs in the form of *sympathetic resonance* whereby an otherwise passive organism system responds to harmonically compatible environmental activities. Though Gibson sometimes seems to promote this kind of picture when he talks loosely about the brain resonating to information in the environment (e.g., 1966b, 260, 267, 271), this is not what we want insofar as it merely reconstructs the philosophically deadly kind of body/world (inner/outer) duality that we would rather avoid.

The resonance metaphor is better depicted as follows. Literally, in response to a complex excitation, any vibrating object will fairly quickly come to vibrate at its resonant frequencies, essentially ignoring other frequencies present in that excitation. Consider, for instance, a so-called simple pendulum—a massless string of fixed length with an otherwise freely-moveable point mass attached at one end and with the other end anchored at a pivot point, all in a uniform gravitational field. It is important to regard the gravitational field and the anchor point—being solidly motionless relative to the gravitational field—as essential constituents of the pendulum, not just the weighted string alone. So what happens when you swat the point mass? Its initial motion will typically be complex, depending on the magnitude and direction of the force of the swat; but quite soon the mass will settle into swinging back and forth at *the pendulum*'s natural frequency in some respective orientation. The swat will have introduced a relatively arbitrary complex excitation of the pendulum as a whole, but the pendulum, as a harmonic oscillator, ultimately responds by oscillating at its natural frequency.

This simple example illustrates the notion of resonance we want to draw on. Namely, we have a complex system eventually behaving in a way that "resonates" according to its own fixed structure. The *swat* comes out of the blue, but the pendulum system as a whole, if still intact, responds in a way characteristic of its established overall construction.

We want to distinguish, then, two kinds of "fixation" of invariants with regard to this particular illustration. First, there is an initial irregular motion that eventually achieves or adopts a regular oscillation in line with the pendulum's fixed natural frequency. Resonance in this sense is a kind of invariant (Gibson 1966b, 271), and achieving resonance may be regarded as a kind of fixation. Second, there is the prior "fixation" of that natural frequency itself. That is, the pendulum's natural frequency will have been *fixed* as a result of altering, e.g., the string's length or the magnitude of the gravitational force.

A simple pendulum by itself does not illustrate this second kind of fixation insofar as the pendulum's construction is essentially done arbitrarily. Instead, consider a pendulum clock. In this case, a pendulum (coupled with an "anchor" and an "escapement gear") is used to regulate the rate at which the energy source for the clock is released to move the gear trains of the clock. Toward its lower end, the pendulum will have a weight whose position can be moved up and down the rod to adjust the effective length of the pendulum (i.e., the distance between the pendulum's upper pivot point and its lower center of mass). Such adjustments will directly alter the pendulum's natural frequency and thus the rate at which the energy source for the clock is released to move the gear trains of the clock. The hands of the clock will move more quickly or more slowly depending on whether the weight is moved up or down the rod.

So, after making sure that the clock is powered up (the hanging weights are raised, the mainsprings are wound, the batteries are charged, etc.), one may give the weight at the lower end of the pendulum a slight tap to get it moving. A tap is a more or less *gentle* swat of the pendulum as mentioned previously; and, again, it is an excitation out of the blue that, if strong enough, results eventually in the pendulum's oscillating at its present resonant frequency (with a small additional boost from the escapement arrangement to counteract damping forces). The initial velocity of the weight at its initial position (when tapped) may be inconsistent with its velocity at that position while oscillating at the pendulum's resonant frequency, but eventually the weight's velocity at that or any other position that it assumes will be consistent with the pendulum's resonant frequency. The clock will by that point be "ticking" at a regular rate. This is the first kind of invariant fixation mentioned earlier.

One will also want to synchronize the movement of the hands of the clock with those of other clocks, whatever the standard may be. It will probably take a number of increasingly refined adjustments with follow-up comparisons of results to determine where "exactly" the weight should be positioned so that the clock is properly synchronized. That adjustment process—*tuning* the clock—is a process of fixation. It is a process of securely adjusting the constitution of the clock so that the movements of its hands (etc.) are synchronized with those of other clocks. Eventually the pendulum clock will have become properly tuned—*attuned*—to the "regular passage of time" as measured by some standard clock. This is the second kind of invariant fixation mentioned earlier.

We should not push this metaphor too far. The main point here is to distinguish lower-order and higher-order fixations of invariants. Lower-order invariant fixation is a matter of a dynamic system settling into one of perhaps many possible pre-established stable patterns of behavior in response to some perturbation or disturbance (e.g., the swat of a stick, the tap of a finger). Higher-order invariant fixation is a matter rather of the adjustment (tuning, attunement) of a dynamic system so as to establish that range of possible stable patterns of behavior. The impetus in this case is also a disturbance of some kind—a higher-order disturbance due, namely, to a lack of fulfillment of a *need* or purpose of some sort.

A pendulum clock, which by itself has no needs, will have become attuned to *standard clock time* because of its builder's or owner's intention that it function consistently with other clocks. Gibson's thesis—essentially a Darwinian thesis—is that living creatures, unlike pendulum clocks, are *self-tuning* dynamic systems (1966b, 271). First, they are inclined to resonate in synchrony with their own natural frequencies; but, second, they also continually *tune* their own natural frequencies by incremental adaptation (resolution, evolution, learning), establishing *stable* organism/environment configurations (and consequent natural frequencies) that answer to larger needs—from basic survival needs to more luxuriant needs to securely augment one's well-being.

As if echoing Peirce, Gibson describes each of these kinds of fixation as a kind of *clarification*, lower-order fixation being constrained by affordances determined by established attunements qua higher-order fixations. We find various statements like the following regarding lower-order fixations:

> How are the exploratory shifts of [visual] fixation guided or controlled? What causes the eyes to move in one direction rather than another, and to stop at one part of the [ambient optic] array instead of another? The answer can only be that interesting structures in the array, and interesting bits of structure, particularly motions, *draw* the foveas toward them. Once it is admitted that the variables of optical structure contain information or meaning, [that is,] that they specify what their sources afford, this hypothesis becomes reasonable. Certain loci in the array contain more information than others. The peripheral retina registers such a locus, the brain resonates vaguely, and the eye is turned. Subjectively we say that something "catches" our attention. Then the orienting reactions begin and continue until the retino-neuro-muscular system achieves a state of "clearness," and the brain resonates precisely. The focusing of the lens is just such a process and it, of course, accompanies fixation. (Gibson 1966b, 260; see also 147, 271, 304)

> The body explores the surrounding environment by locomotion; the head explores the ambient array by turning; and the eyes explore the two samples of the array, the fields of view, by eye movements. These might be called *exploratory adjustments*. At the lower levels, eyelid, lens, pupil, and retinal cells make what might be called *optimizing adjustments*. Both the global structure and the fine structure of an array constitute information. The observer needs to look around, to look at, to focus sharply, and to neglect the amount of light. Perception needs to be both comprehensive and clear. The visual system *hunts* for comprehension and clarity. It does not rest until the invariants are extracted. Exploring and optimizing seem to be the function of the system. (Gibson 1979, 219)

This lower-order visual fixation (a kind of self-tuning) occurs spontaneously. "Bits of structure" in the ambient optic array are informative not just because they are structured as such but because they specify affordances (for the perceiver) of the reflective sources of that optical structure—and such affordances for the perceiver in that environment are what they are only because of attunements (higher-order self-tunings) that reflect how the perceiver and the given environment are coupled. In much the way that a pendulum will spontaneously settle into oscillating with its natural frequency, a perceptual system (by sampling, gradient descent, etc.) will spontaneously seek and locate points of resonant *clarity*. The latter constitute points of *sensitivity* that, by way of self-reinforcement, involve a kind of least effort and maximal intensity, as if reaching "some optimal state of equilibrium" (1966b, 271). Interestingly, Gibson uses the latter kind of language to characterize the *learning* of such sensitivities in the first place:

> When *patterns* of intensity, frequency, or separation are presented to an observer, learning is the rule, for patterns may carry information. A great number of psychophysical experiments have shown decreasing errors in discriminating, estimating, detecting, and recognizing, even when the observer is kept in ignorance of his errors. ... [T]he observer learns to look for the critical features, to listen for the distinctive

variations, to smell or taste the characteristics of substances (perfumes or wind) and to finger the textures of things (wool or silk).... [We] now consider this an education of attention to the information in available stimulation. ...

[T]he mechanisms for this learning are becoming clearer. The process is one of learning what to attend to, both overtly and covertly. For the perception of objects, it is the detection of distinctive features and the abstraction of general properties. This almost always involves the detection of invariants under changing stimulation. ...

Psychologists have become accustomed to thinking of an association as something that is formed between two sensory impressions or between a sensory impression and a response.... Let us consider, however, the *fact* of ecological associations, as distinguished from the *formation* of associations. The result of this fact is an invariance of stimulus combinations.... To the extent that a fire *always* conjoins an optical flame with an acoustic sound, a cutaneous warmth, and a volatile odor, the combination is invariant and constitutes a stimulus of higher order; more exactly, each component contains the same stimulus information. ... The act of perceiving a fire ..., then, might just as well be considered the pickup of the associated variables of information [rather than] the associating of sensory data. Two things are necessary: the dimensions of quality must have been differentiated, and the invariant combinations of quality must have been detected. The formation of associations is not necessary.

... [Stimulus-response theory] takes no account of stimulus *information*. In perception theory, at least in the kind being advocated, the response of interest is that to the association, not to [any] of the stimuli alone. In short, learning *by* association becomes the learning *of* associations. (Gibson 1966b, 270–273)

The puzzle of constant perception despite varying sensations disappears and a new question arises, [namely] how the invariant information is extracted. Perceptual development and perceptual learning are seen as a process of distinguishing the features of a rich input, not of enriching the data of a bare and meaningless input. A perceptual system hunts for a state of what we call "clarity." Whatever this state is physiologically, it has probably governed the evolution of perception in the species, the maturation of perception in the young, and the learning of perception in the adult. (Gibson 1966b, 320)

Some key statements here are (a) that associations among kinds of stimuli are learned, constrained by a general impetus to attend to what needs to be attended to; (b) that learning these associations is the result of hunting for dynamic clarity; and (c) that such associations are invariant and, in their own right, constitute higher-order stimuli such that each lower-order component of a learned association provides access to the same higher-order information.

Detecting any of the lower-order features of a fire, e.g., merely seeing a flame or merely hearing a distinctive sound, permits the perception of the other component affordances of fire by virtue of one's having "learned"—one's being attuned to—the invariant association of those lower-order features. Such learning is in its own fashion a fixation process: an education of attention—an attunement—to associations of stimuli. It consists not in forming associations among bare data (as advocated by the enrichment theory of perception) but rather in detecting and clarifying existent associations among various distinguishable kinds of stimuli.

This process typically is not particularly simple. Gibson resolves this "development of learning to perceive" into several constituent types of development (1966b, 283–286). We need not pursue this further except perhaps to note that the initial emphasis is on *differentiating* ranges of possible stimuli (as possible tangible results of various modes of sensory activity) in order then to be able to pay attention to their possible covariation. Learning the affordances (viz. values, meanings) of objects is "based entirely on the education of [one's] attention to the subtleties of invariant stimulus information" (285). This is Gibson's theoretical alternative to a conception of "associating, organizing, remembering, recognizing, expecting, and naming" and other "familiar psychological processes" as "operations of the mind upon the deliverances of sense" (1966b, 283). Pavlov's dogs did not *form* associations between bell sounds and food but rather detected and became habituated to the constant association of such stimuli that was imposed within their artificial environment (1966b, 272). If we want to capture this deeper kind of perceptual development in a word, that word would be 'attunement' (see Heft 2001, 366).

The word 'attunement' is ambiguous, though, in at least the following sense. It may refer to a process of *becoming* attuned, or it may refer to a process of *being* attuned. The former notion of attunement is akin to *habituation* while the latter may be likened to an established *habit*. The former is like the *fixing* of belief while the latter is analogous to a *fixed* belief. The term 'fixation' is itself ambiguous in the same way. In any case, attunement and fixation in the latter senses are supposed to be (for Gibson and for Peirce, respectively) what makes perception quick and efficient.

Fixing (establishing, learning, achieving, developing) a particular mutual organism/environment attunement is not unlike the establishment of a "law of nature" or "rule of action" in the sense that it reflects the establishment of particular regularities of dependency (correlation, covariance, etc.) among specific variables of some sort (e.g., variables associated with various more basic invariant-extraction action-types). The fixation of a belief and the fixation of an attunement are of course different in that the former involves elements of thought and inquiry while the latter need not involve such elements; but both share a common pattern as *fixation* processes.

The notion of affordances can then be explicated in terms of the notion of attunements:

> [T]he central tenet of the ecological approach is the complementarity of the animal and the environment. An "affordance" refers to the fit between an animal's capabilities and the environmental supports and opportunities (both good and bad) that make possible a given activity. ... Fundamentally, the realization of an affordance requires that animal and environment be adapted for one another. ... Some affordances may

be easily learned; others may require much exploration, practice, and time.... Even a universal affordance for humans, such as the graspability of an object of a given size and location, shows developmental changes that involve learning. (Gibson and Pick 2000, 15–17)

The notion here of animal/environment *fit* is just the notion of attunement. *Fitness* is an achievement, being the result of adaptation, of development, of learning, of becoming fit. Various kinds of fit between an organism and its environment, as invariants, in this sense reflect dynamic regularities of various sorts among bodily capabilities and environmental supports.

Natural "laws" are supposed to exemplify such regularities if only approximately. The notion of *attunement* extends this idea so as to encompass regularities in the dynamics of organism/environment systems, not excluding the idea that such regularities are subject to evolutionary pressures (Peirce 1884; 1901). What laws of nature *are* and how they come about (if it is not the case that they just *are* once and for all) is a difficult question, but what organism/environment attunements are (once developed, if not how they develop) is to be understood in essentially the same way. The achievement of a specific attunement is a matter of an organism/environment system incorporating a respective law-like regularity—an invariant in its own right—into its life activities. The latter, of course, sounds very much like a conception of the establishment of a *habit* (Gibson 1966b, 308–309). Habits in this sense (as constitutive organism/environment attunements) are what *specify* affordances (Heft 2001, 184–185).

Interestingly, the results of such fixation processes might be mathematically "formulated" in much the same way that laws of nature may be formulated. The quick and efficient character of perceiving should in this sense be law-like, given certain invariant relations among respective stimulus variables. A resulting attunement when mathematically described in this way illustrates especially well how attunements *specify* affordances. In short, *attunements* (as achievements) are invariants of invariants, i.e., "invariant combinations of invariants," which *specify affordances* in just the way that law-like relations *predict* values for certain variables given specific values for respectively related variables (Gibson 1966b, 280).

Various proposals regarding the general nature of such mathematical formulations have been floated over the years (e.g., Shaw and Turvey 1981; Turvey et al. 1981). The proposal to be promoted here may or may not be new, but it is surely in line with Gibson's statements above. Specifically, following up on an earlier proposal that a pragmatist formalism might work with sorted variables ranging over possible types of sensible results associated with respective types of action (versus Quine's first-order formal nominalism; see page 67 above), one could begin at some functionally basic level with invariant-detection abilities as action-types (involving, e.g., flows of respective types of sensory excitation) and associate variables with each such action-type that range respectively over a set of possible invariant-types (e.g., invariants in some respective flow of sensory excitation) as possible "tangible results." The law-like relations that specify affordances may then be modeled mathematically by means of relations among these lower-order stimulus variables. Namely, if such lower-order stimulus variables can serve as the basis for describing a kind of "syntax" and thus "grammar" of sensory stimulation, we ought to be able to specify *models* for such grammars as a way of modeling *attunements* which in turn specify what affordances are. Thus one would expect that it is possible to give "an exact mathematical description" of at least some attunements in the form of (sets of) models for grammars of sensory stimulation.

What more can be said about how this might work? First, to reiterate a previous point, notice that the regularities under discussion characterize (belong to, constrain the behavior of) an organism/environment as a whole. As such, generally speaking, habits (and thus the live creature, as a system of habits) may extend as much into an environment as into a respective organism, with some variability in either direction. For this reason, it is misleading (mistaken, a categorical error) to say that affordances are *of* things in an environment *for* a given organism. Rather, we might instead say that affordances (1) are *for* a respective live creature (extended across an organism/environment divide, however one might make that cut for analytical purposes) and (2) are *of* different pieces or aspects of situations as concrete arrays of circumstances in which the live creature finds itself. Affordances thus are *of* organism/environment entities (in general) *for* organism/environment entities (of a certain type).

This "externalist" way of talking may initially sound odd, but one of its virtues is that it sidesteps various epistemological and metaphysical quagmires by avoiding now standard presumptions of hard-and-fast divisions between body and world or body and mind or mind and world. The latter distinctions are of course meaningful and even useful, sometimes, but they are not obviously black-and-white divisions on the order of Cartesianesque substance dualities and trialities. Whatever the problems may be for ecological psychology, bridging such unbridgeable metaphysical chasms is not one of them.

There are, of course, compelling arguments against cognitive externalism (e.g., Adams and Aizawa 2001; 2008), but the position here is that (1) such arguments can be deflected (Everett 2013; Burke and Everett 2013) and (2) the larger battle will not be completely won or lost on such grounds anyway. The internalism/externalism issue rather highlights *a competition between paradigms* in cognitive science. We thus return to the fundamental assumption that the regularities that characterize habits (as organism/environment attunements) are subject to mathematical modeling. The viability of ecological psychology (and that of externalist positions in cognitive science more generally) rests on the explanatory power and empirical testability of such models. It will be successes and failures in this regard that will decide the internalism/externalism debate.

A crucial issue for ecological psychology in this regard concerns how to characterize different kinds of perceivable objects not in terms of property bundles but as systems of affordances. It has already been suggested that we begin at a functionally basic level with collections of primitive (lower-order) invariant-extraction abilities (each involving flows of some respective type of sensory excitation) and that, for each such ability, we associate variables that range over the respective set of possibly extractable invariant-types (specifically, types of invariants in some respective type of flow of sensory excitation). Furthermore, these lower-order stimulus variables may serve as the basis for a kind of "syntax" of sensory stimulation. We should be able to construct *models* for any such syntax by way of specifying dependencies among the respective stimulus variables. Any such model determines ranges of possible values (i.e., sensible results) for certain stimulus variables given values for other stimulus variables related to the former in ways characteristic of the model, i.e., in accordance with the sensory dependencies (represented by *sentences* in the given sensory syntax) that are "true" in the model. This in effect provides a way to specify affordances insofar as such models determine spaces of sensory possibilities in accordance with law-like dependencies (systemic attunements) involving respective stimulus variables.

One more move is needed, then, given that it is not likely that a kind of perceivable object can be fully characterized by any one such model. Borrowing an idea from the semantic view of scientific theories (Suppes 1960; 1962; 1967; Suppe 1977; 1989; Hughes 1996; van Fraassen 1980; 2000), we may characterize perceptual kinds (that is, kinds of perceivable objects) as *collections of* such models.

There are, of course, many ways to specify such sets of models, from making random lists to citing some inexplicable family resemblance. One nicely tractable way to do it would be to specify one or more invariance relations (regularities, laws) among the basic stimulus variables that must hold (be "true") in a given model in order for that model to be in the set. In this case the perceiver could be said to be attuned or habituated to (by being such that one's activities are constrained by) the respective defining invariance relations for that set of models.

In this view, such a model may allow a range of activities (constrained by respective invariance relations), all of which may be associated with affordances of a perceptual object of that kind. We can in this way capture the idea that a perceivable object is essentially a structured system of affordances. We thus will have captured the idea that affordances are specified by (though they are not identical to) attunements as invariance relations among lower-order stimulus variables.

An example or two may be helpful here.

Optical Texture Density

Consider cases of uniformly flat and hard horizontal surfaces (approximated by sidewalks, dance floors, tennis courts, grassy meadows, grain sorghum fields in the Texas Panhandle, etc.). An instance of this kind of object affords (among other things) a range of locomotive activities—walking, running, and so forth. Such objects tend to be limited in their spatial scope in different ways—sidewalks are long and narrow, tennis courts are bounded on all sides by more or less impassable vertical surfaces, grassy meadows disappear into underbrush and trees, grain sorghum fields in Texas seem to go on forever, etc. That one may walk on such a surface, e.g., a flat horizontal sidewalk, is something that is directly perceived. One will visually perceive at least minimal surface-walkability (the affordance of walking) in certain directions and not in others as a result of registering a constancy of *optical* texture density in those directions, i.e., an invariant ratio of the number of texture elements of the surface per unit area of the *terrain* in those directions (Gibson 1950, chap. 5–7; Gibson 1979, 162–163, Figure 9.5). This constancy will be detectable to the extent that, in the course of many actual past walkings, one will have become attuned (habituated, accustomed) to such constancies as indicators of uniformly flat horizontal walkable surfaces, allowing one *now* to visually *perceive* such affordances of the given object (the sidewalk surface) just by detecting an invariant involving optical texture density.

The proposal here is that, by detecting an invariant optical texture density, one will have instantiated and thus "activated" (and thus made salient for perceptual-qua-interpretive purposes) a certain set of models characterizing the object-type "walkable surface." This will be a set of models for a language of optical stimulation, namely, models in which that particular optical-texture-density invariance relation holds.

What invariance relation is that exactly? These models will be models for "grammars of sensory stimulation" based on or built upon certain lower-order invariant-extraction abilities determining respective stimulus variables. There are a number of basic stimulus variables in this case, each being associated with one or more respective *optical* invariant-extraction abilities. The value of a given variable in any given instance (if not "assigned" by way of lower-order "inferences" constrained by relevant invariance relations) may be the "sensible result" of actually exercising a respective ability (i.e., creating some kind of flow of excitation within which constancies may be detected). For instance:

TERRAIN SURFACE AREA

The surface area, S, of a given bit of terrain is what one would measure on the spot with a meterstick, for example, or with surveying instruments. The area of a rectangular hull for your own footprint, say, can be estimated by multiplying the results of two measurements, one of maximum width and one of maximum length. We do not want to get sidetracked by minutiae, but to measure, for instance, the *length* of the footprint, one might do the following:

(1) Locate the most extreme heel point, H, and position the zero mark on the meterstick at that spot.

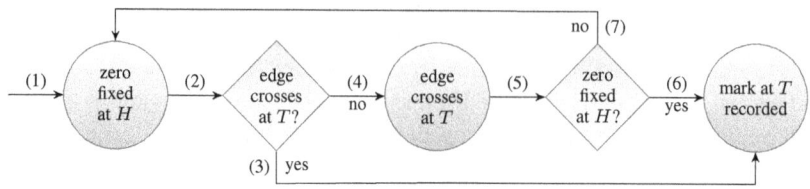

FIGURE 1: Measuring the length of a footprint. Arrows represent actions, circles represent achievements, and diamonds represent choice points.

(2) Check whether the meterstick edge intersects with the toe-end curve of the footprint at the furthest point, T, away from the heel point. If so,
(3) Read and record the numerical counterpart of the meterstick mark at T and stop. If not,
(4) Pivot the meterstick around the point H so that its edge intersects the toe-end curve of the footprint at T.
(5) Check whether the zero mark is positioned at H. If so,
(6) Read and record the numerical counterpart of the meterstick mark at T and stop. If not,
(7) Pivot the meterstick around the point T so that its edge intersects the heel-end curve of the footprint at H while adjusting the position of the meterstick along the line determined by H and T so that the zero mark is again at H; then do procedure (2).

This process may be depicted as in Figure 1. The circular nodes denote achievements resulting from various procedures of looking, manipulating the meterstick, etc. The arrows denote the various procedures, executions of which are not completed until they produce the required (circled) results. The diamonds are choice points based on visually comparing meterstick marks and points on the edge of the footprint.

The recording of the numerical counterpart of the meterstick mark at the toe point T is the key outcome of this process as a whole. Producing this outcome is a registration of invariants in several senses. Repetitions of the process as a whole would yield (very close to) the same result. It is important to notice, though, that a single execution of the process essentially incorporates such repetition. Namely, the process (as depicted) does not stop until merely looking (without further positioning of the meterstick) reveals that the zero mark is fixed at H *and* the marked edge crosses through T. Either choice point in this case may involve not so much a simple yes/no judgment as it does a tentative-doubt ("maybe not?") versus final-removal-of-doubt ("definitely so") assessment. A final removal of doubt as to the length of the footprint depends on stable removals of doubt as to meterstick alignments at H and T, respectively. If one can repeatedly get from one choice point to the next by way of negligible or no readjustments at H and T, then a kind of constancy qua stability of the results of these subroutines will have been achieved, thus warranting the recording of the mark at T.

This whole process of measuring a small length with a meterstick can in some cases be regarded as a so-called black box, that is, as a type of primitive (internally opaque) action that produces the measurement. Otherwise, a single execution of this process is constituted by executions of subprocesses (the arrows) involving productions of various temporal and spatial constancies in their own right—locating the heel-point H, fixing the zero-point pivot at the heel, locating the toe-point T, aligning the edge of the meterstick with the segment $\overline{HT}$, identifying the meterstick mark aligned with T. Each of these sub-processes involves *looking*—over time and from slightly varying positions directly above the heel point and toe point, respectively—and manually (*re*)adjusting the meterstick until positions are fixed and both alignments are achieved. The visual registration of each of these constituent results in itself is the registration of an invariant, namely, an optical constancy (of relative place and alignment) over time in a dynamic setting.

This kind of process is of course just one illustration of any number of processes possibly associated with gauging spatial distances. The point is that such invariant-extraction processes are resolvable into invariant-extraction subprocesses, themselves likewise resolvable, etc., and that such processes (or, rather, engrained abilities to execute such processes) ground our sense of terrain surface area.

Terrain surface area may of course be gauged in reliable but less precise ways. For instance, the time and/or energy expenditure required to traverse a given horizontal expanse is a direct sensible indicator of the size of that expanse in the direction of traversal. Short hikes usually require less time and energy than long hikes. Generating such sensible results will be a matter of detecting instances of a general invariance relation between energy levels (say) and distances.

A natural unit of horizontal terrain distance would be one's walking step length geared just-in-time to current surrounding conditions (versus, for example, the length of some unique platinum rod kept under conditions of constant temperature, pressure, humidity, etc.).

OPTICAL SURFACE AREA

For any given terrain surface with area, S, there is a corresponding *optical surface area*, A—the area of the solid angle of the given terrain surface projected onto a unit sphere centered at an observation point. In particular, terrain surfaces of uniform area that are farther away will have smaller *optical* surface areas than those that are closer to the observation point (Figures 2–3).

Let S be the area of a given terrain surface that is, say, n step lengths away from one's current location. This terrain surface will have a respective optical

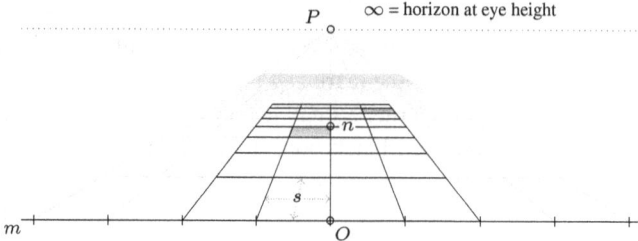

FIGURE 2: Single-point perspectival rendering of a flat horizontal tiled surface—not unacceptable for nearby objects but incorrect for lack of depicting the *curvature* of available optical information (so that the highlighted tiles appear to be headed toward a point below the perspective point P).

surface area A. For instance, if S is the terrain surface area of a round penny lying several paces away on a flat sidewalk, A will be the optical surface area of an ellipse. A second identical coin lying farther away will have a smaller optical surface area with smaller major and minor axes. Figure 2 is a single-point perspectival drawing of not pennies but what might be a number of identical square tiles on a flat floor, the optically larger shaded tile being closer than the optically smaller shaded tile.

Let s, the length of a single step, be the terrain length and width of each of the tiles in Figure 2. Let h be the vertical height of the observation point, P, from the terrain surface. The horizon, infinitely many steps away on the terrain, is at eye height optically. The observation point thus coincides optically with the perspective point on the horizon.

Let $S_{n,m}$ be the terrain surface area of the tile whose farthest corner is n steps ahead and m steps to the left. For instance, the closer shaded tile in Figure 2 has terrain surface area $S_{4,1} = s^2$ while the other shaded tile has terrain surface area $S_{7,-2} = s^2$.

Let $A_{n,m}$ be the respective optical surface area corresponding to terrain surface area $S_{n,m}$. Figure 2 does not accurately represent optical surface area, whereas Figure 3 is more successful in this regard, providing two perspectives on a projection of $S_{4,1}$ onto an optical sphere. In Figure 2 it is as if the observer is several steps away from the beginning of the tiled surface at point O. Figure 3 positions the observer's toes at point 0 and depicts the kind of momentary optical information about the tiled expanse that is available at point P—that is, as radiating from all directions toward the point P. The (hemi)sphere onto which the tiles are projected in this case has radius h to make the optical surface areas large enough to be visible to the reader. In these particular figures, if the step length s is something like 24 inches, then h is about 60 inches. A unit sphere centered at P with one inch as the unit radius would rather intersect the bridge of a human observer's nose. But the size of this projection sphere does not matter since spherical

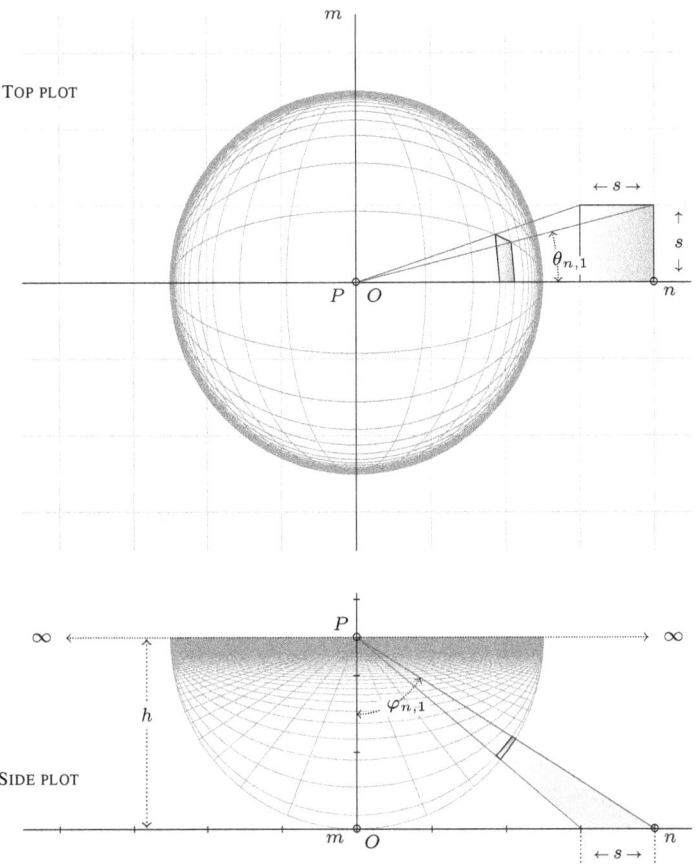

FIGURE 3: Top and side plots of a momentary OPTICAL SURFACE AREA A_n of a terrain square S_n whose far edge is n step lengths away, as visually accessed from a single location P that is at a vertical height h from the ground. Projected onto a sphere of radius h (eye height) centered at P. The plot from the top is like looking down into a bowl with the projected optical surface area being on the transparent surface of the bowl.

solid angles are measured in steradians which, like angle measurements in degrees or radians, are independent of the chosen unit of length or the radius of the sphere (a 45°-angled piece of pie from a small pie is smaller than one from a large pie, but a 45° angle is just a 45° angle). Figure 3 as drawn makes it possible to more easily compare the relative sizes of optical surface areas of different tiles.

It is obvious from these figures—from the spherical "inverse gnomonic" projections of the terrain grid of tile boundaries—that optical surface area varies regularly as m and n vary, decreasing as either of the latter two variables increase. It is

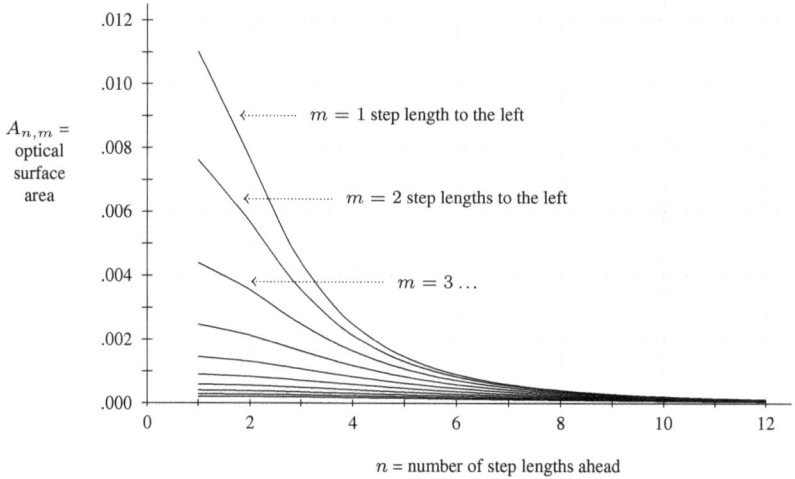

FIGURE 4: Graph of OPTICAL SURFACE AREAS $A_{n,m}$ (in steradians) on a unit sphere centered at P, versus distances to respective terrain squares, each with its far corner lying n steps ahead and m steps to the left and all having uniform terrain size $S_{n,m} = s^2$.

not exactly trivial to describe the nature of this regularity mathematically. Calculating the simple optical surface areas $A_{n,m}$ of projected rectangles $S_{n,m}$ utilizes a somewhat complicated trigonometric function with independent rectilinear variables m and n (or, alternatively, polar coordinates with colatitude $\pi - \varphi_{n,m}$ (polar angle) and longitude $\theta_{n,m}$ (azimuth)).

The formula for this function involves only elementary trigonometry, though it is messy (Forney 1991, 14–16). There is no need to write it out here, but see appendix A for details. Graphs of values for $A_{n,m}$ for different values of n and m have been depicted in Figure 4. These graphs roughly indicate the nature of the inverse relationship between optical surface area and terrain distance.

It should be emphasized that Figures 3 and 4 depict a momentary *snapshot* of optical information that is available at observation point P. The visual system of any known type of live creature is *not* like a camera taking such a snapshot as an array of data points from which optical surface areas may be internally computed using the kind of mathematical function used to produce the graphs in Figure 4. On the contrary, that mathematical function is just a model—a description—of a regularity to which the observer is supposedly attuned, modeling or describing the attunement but not thereby ascribing respective calculation capabilities to the observer (just as Newtonian physics does not claim that Mars *computes* its way around the sun, etc.). It is more plausible (more in line with the kind of time and energy resources available to the observer) to think that the regularity is detected by the observer's perceptual systems being sensitive to relational constancies across multiple samplings of such complex information.

For one thing, we have two eyes; and thus we have not one but (at least) two observation points P. We must allow that *each* eye alone is capable of accessing the kind of information depicted in Figures 3 and 4. This binocular infrastructure makes possible a kind of triangulation capability, triggered and utilized in the presence of constancies across samples of information from the two eyes respectively. Such constancies may be modeled by the kind of mathematical formula used to produce Figure 4, not that the observer calculates anything in terms of such a formula but that the formula describes (models) a regularity across different samplings of information that may be registered (detected) as a relational *constancy* in a controlled but varying flow of information from two distinct sources. What is *sensed*, namely, is a higher-order *invariance* that may, upon reflection, be modeled theoretically by the kind of mathematical formula used to produce Figures 3 and 4 but which need not be represented symbolically by the observer's perceptual apparatus. Such a model—as a bit of ecological physics, as it were—is designed simply to argue for the existence of such a regularity. What a given perceptual apparatus needs to be able to detect is whatever stays the same in a changing flow of information. Typically, what stays the same will not be the basic data but rather higher-order relationships among parametrized variations of that data. Such relationships are what is *sensed*—in the most basic sense of the term "sensed." (This is an essential pillar of James's radical empiricism.)

In addition to a binocular visual apparatus, even a single eye is not statically pinned to one observation point P. It should be clear—from the existence of extremely fast involuntary "minor saccadic" movements as well as slower more or less voluntary movements of the eyes, head, and body (even while standing in one place, e.g., with toes fixed at point 0)—that a single eye will access and ingest optical information not just from a single fixed point but from a more or less continuous path of points P. This is the case all the more if the organism is traversing the terrain surface. This suggests a kind of extensive non-stop sampling capability, triggered and utilized in the presence of constancies across samples of information from a single eye in continual motion. Such constancies, again, may be modeled by the kind of mathematical formula used to produce Figures 3 and 4. And again, it is not that the eye or brain or any other neural system calculates anything in terms of such a formula but that the formula models a regularity across different samplings of information that may be detected as a relational constancy in a controlled but varying flow of information from a single moving source. What is sensed even by a single moving eye is the same high-order *invariance* referenced in Figure 4.

The claim that such an invariance relation exists is supported by the fact that it may be modeled by some such formula. It is, again, a general relation among optical and terrain distances characteristic of flat horizontal surfaces as plotted from a position that is a couple or so "step lengths" above the surface—a regularity as real as the regularity of the vertical pull of gravity across such an expanse.

In systemic conjunction with any number of such relations among these and other optical and physical variables, this trigonometric relation, in the present view, is engrained as a constraint on the observer's activity (such as walking or running, but also including the activity of employing one's eyes in specific ways to ingest information). Evolution of the human species will have fitted the human visual perceptual system to pick up and utilize the information that such relations represent. The growth and development of the individual human being with normal eyesight will more finely attune the individual's visual perceptual system as a result of the ongoing experience of traversing and looking at such surfaces, from an early crawling stage to the present, depending on unique characteristics of the individual's changing anatomy and terrestrial locale. The observer will detect instantiations of this particular relation primarily because the observer's visual perceptual system will already be attuned to that and other relations.

In that case, if one is attuned to such relations, the respective information regarding its current instantiation can be said just to be there in the ambient optical field. Otherwise, without an appropriate attunement, the information is essentially unavailable. Infrared or ultraviolet or x-ray information is ubiquitous, but humans cannot access it because we seem not to have any of the "wiring" (etc.) that could embody the requisite attunements.

Ecological-physical models of such attunements are (typically) externalist in character. Such models are in principle as experimentally testable as any hypothetical model worth its scientific salt. So far as the internalism/externalism debate goes, externalism should thus be as much in the game as internalism is. The contest here should be regarded as a contest between scientific paradigms rather than as an armchair debate.

There is still one point worth making here before going on. Namely, the internalism/externalism debate cannot be settled either way by claiming that internalism is computation-friendly whereas externalism is not. Internalism, at least on historical grounds, is more or less the default position that was taken for granted in classical good old-fashioned AI and robotics research in the 1970s and 1980s. The idea there was to liken the brain (where the mind is) to a computer. Fodor's modularity thesis made this quite explicit (Fodor 1975; 1983). Connectionism offered a different kind of computation to supplement if not replace the standard symbolic-representational conception of computation, but it did not question internalism as such.

It would be a mistake, though, to think that giving up internalism is tantamount to giving up the computer metaphor. Externalism is computation-friendly as well, but in an interestingly different way. The example we are currently developing nicely illustrates at least one way to think about computational modeling from an externalist perspective.

Namely, if a perceiver is comparable to a computer, then we might liken the perceiver's brain not to an entire computer but to some identifiable feature or part of a motherboard. It may best be regarded as a processing unit, or perhaps only as a data storage device; or perhaps it is better regarded as a chipset or a chipset-plus-bus-system whose task it is to coordinate the transfer of data among various processing, storage, and peripheral components on the motherboard (Wikipedia 2012a). Otherwise, the perceiver's somatic constitution along with key parts of the accessible world outside of the perceiver's somatic boundaries might also be likened to other parts of the computer, including different kinds of processing and storage units built into the motherboard itself.

For example, it may be more fruitful to regard pencil-and-paper processes (making lists, calculating sums, etc.) as occurring in an extended "CPU" rather than as "peripheral" sequences of events. Similarly, it may be more fruitful to regard an ambient optical field as a storage device whose data are directly accessible for processing purposes. The latter need not be a bank of binary digital devices, meaning that (1) elementary visual data need not be binary, and (2) bottom-level storage elements may not be best regarded as *things* at fixed spatial locations (capable of being in various distinct states, etc.). Rather, what matters is that specific types of interactions with the ambient optical field will result in the perceiver's detecting (registering) certain stable (constant, invariant) states distinguished by their relative *stability* (constancy, invariance), however many such stable states may be possible per type of interaction. That is, think of the ambient optical field itself as a non-binary read-write information storage device that reliably stores data that is dynamically over-written (1) by virtue of independent changes in the external world (planetary rotation, external environmental activity, swats out of the blue, etc.) or (2) as the results of specific types of interactions (on the perceiver's part) designed to detect *and* process information that is present there. (A processing unit and a storage device may of course be very tightly coupled.)

All of this is speculative, but it is not inconsistent. The point here is that, from an ecological perspective, what is inside and outside of a typical desktop computer or what is or is not on a given motherboard need not correspond closely if at all to what is inside and outside of an animal's skin or skull.

This general line of thought would also account, by the way, for Gibson's key insight about perception being *direct*. "Representation" is an essential part of characterizing human intelligence, such as it is; but perception—*mere* perception by itself—would not require the *representation* of information that could just as well be directly accessed on the motherboard whether it be inside or outside the skull. Not everything in the world is on the motherboard, but the motherboard itself may extend outside of the skull so that the processes that constitute perception are expected to be in the world outside of the skull as much as they are in the world inside of the skull.

Optical Texture

A given visual solid angle of the optic array typically will enclose some amount, T, of optical texture. Gibson contended that "the pickup of the *amount of texture* in a visual solid angle of the optic array is not a matter of counting units, that is, of measuring with an arbitrary unit" (1979, 162). But an invariance relation characterizing a set of models for a "flat walkable surface" would reflect a constancy of terrain texture T relative to terrain surface area S—an invariant "rule of *equal amounts of texture for equal amounts of terrain*." Namely, $T = \delta S$ for some *constant* δ (terrain texture density).

Constancy of terrain texture density δ entails constancy of *optical* texture density $\delta_{1,1}$ of step-sized squares at one's feet as one traverses that terrain. The amount of texture $T_{1,1}$ in a step-sized square at one's feet would be a constant $\delta_{1,1} A_{1,1} = \delta S_{1,1} = \delta s^2$, since the optical surface area $A_{1,1}$ remains constant as one traverses an extended flat terrain. If one were to stop walking and visually pan upward toward the horizon, the optical texture density would increase in a regular way, being inversely proportional to decreasing optical surface areas of successively more distant step-sized terrain surfaces. This invariant can be modeled by the equation $\delta s^2 = \delta_{n,m} A_{n,m}$.

In short, if the visible surface is a uniformly textured flat horizontal plane, then there are equal amounts of texture for equal amounts of terrain, in which case optical texture density varies inversely with optical surface area in a simple linear way. In light of one's attunement to this invariance relation, detecting that $\delta_{n,m}$ and $A_{n,m}$ are inversely proportional as one visually scans the terrain supports the *abductive* inference that the terrain within one's visual purview is a uniformly textured flat horizontal plane and thus (if solid) is a walkable surface. Thus the *affordance* of walkability over yonder is directly perceivable (abducible) at a distance from over yonder (without actually having to be walking over yonder).

It is understood, of course, that such perceptions (qua abductions) may not be veridical (Gibson 1979, 142–143). Various optical illusions may be results of engrained attunements failing to be veridical in instances where all indications are that they *are* veridical—in statistically rare cases, that is, where certain invariants of invariants are detected but where the affordances that such invariants usually specify are not actually afforded. The claim that perception is direct does not entail that it is always veridical, though the fact that perception is nonetheless so often veridical and thus successful points to the depth and degree of regularity in the world that makes such attunements possible. This analysis, including the fact that perception is so often veridical but sometimes fails, agrees with Peirce's characterization of perception as a kind of abduction (1903f, EP2:229).

Many if not all models in the set of models associated with the object-type "walkable surface" will be models in which some such invariant (constant, lawlike) relation holds between similar kinds of stimulus variables. The value of $\delta_{n,m}$

will depend on the given surface, the nature of the optical texture, and so forth; but the key point is that, while specific numerical values for these variables may not be determined by the perceiver (that is just a feature of the mathematical model), what is directly detected is the inverse proportional (linear) variation of $A_{n,m}$ and $\delta_{n,m}$. One will thus be *aware of* a walkable surface because one *perceives* its surface-walkability. One may perceive this by *detecting* an instantiation of an invariant linear inverse relation between stimulus variables $A_{n,m}$ and $\delta_{n,m}$ to which one has become attuned as a sign of horizontal walkable surfaces.

Note how the dual reading of the pragmatic maxim is exemplified in this simple case of awareness of a walkable surface. Figure 4 depicts optical surface area $A_{n,m}$ for fixed m as a strictly decreasing function of step distance n. Let $m = 1$ (as if one were to visually scan the terrain essentially straight ahead in front of one's fixed position). Appendix A shows how $A_{n,1}$ is a function of n, namely, $A_{n,1} = \Omega_{n-1,n,0,1}$. Abbreviate the latter by $\mathcal{F}(n)$. Since $\mathcal{F}$ is strictly decreasing for $n \geq 1$, there is an inverse function $\mathcal{F}^{-1}$ that depicts step distance n as a function of optical surface area, namely, $n = \mathcal{F}^{-1}(A_{n,1})$. So, consider the stimulus variable n. One might traverse the distance and count steps as one goes. Or one may have some grasp of its relations to other stimulus variables that would sanction *assignments* of values to n without having to step off the distance. Values for n that are produced by walking the distance are operational sensible results. Values for n that may be assigned simply because of its systemic relationship to $A_{n,1}$, for instance, are inferential sensible results.

Looming Objects

Without going into details, another quick and dirty illustration of affordances and invariance relations comes from David Lee's analysis of the *optic flow field* associated with simple rectilinear motion of the head relative to the environment—e.g., as one walks, runs, drives, or flies in a straight line over a flat surface (Lee 1980). Lee's paper is a classic in the ecological-psychology literature, illustrating how one could be aware of various objects that are "looming straight ahead" by detecting various affordances (collisions, crashes, etc.) that are specified by simple invariance relations holding among a small number of stimulus variables whose values are directly detectable in the optic flow field itself. One is able to directly gauge distances, sizes, and orientations of surfaces and objects in the environment simply by being attuned to such higher-order invariants, thus affording control of various kinds of locomotor activity (think of a bird preparing to land, a horse preparing to leap a fence, or a long jumper approaching the take-off board—examples used by Lee to illustrate his analysis). Again, the key invariance relations here reflect regularities characteristic of certain kinds of objects—objects present *and looming* in or near one's path of motion. A mathematical development of this range of examples would first call for identifying the key stimulus variables that determine a relevant "grammar of optical stimulation" associated with moving in a straight line through a level environment. Various invariance relations among these variables would then be taken to determine the sets of models definable on such grammars that characterize looming objects of various kinds in such settings.

Fast and Frugal Heuristics

A third kind of example is found in discussions of "fast and frugal heuristics" in the literature on bounded rationality (Gigerenzer and Selten 2001; Gigerenzer 2004). In particular, consider the case of running across a baseball or cricket field in order to catch a fly ball. This is similar in many respects to the kind of scenario analyzed by Lee (above); but in the case of catching a fly ball, there is a moving object high in the air—the fly ball—that will land somewhere in front of or behind one's position such that one wants to approach that position in a timely fashion so as to catch the ball (as if seeking to collide with the moving object).

> Experimental studies have shown that players actually use several heuristics. One of these is the *gaze heuristic*. When a fly ball approaches, the player fixates the ball and starts running. The heuristic is to adjust the running speed so that the angle of gaze remains constant (or within a certain range; see McLeod and Dienes 1996). The angle of gaze is the angle between the eye and the ball, relative to the ground. [A player who] uses this heuristic does not need to measure wind, air resistance, spin, or the other causal variables. It can get away with ignoring every piece of causal information. All the relevant information is contained in one variable: the angle of gaze. Note that a player ... using the gaze heuristic is not able to compute the point at which the ball will land. But the player will be there [when and] where the ball lands. (Gigerenzer 2004, 63)

Obviously, catching a fly ball is in large part a perceptual task. As opposed to birds, airplanes, clouds, or even fly balls whose projected path of motion extends too far in some direction from one's present position, being aware of a catchable fly ball requires the perception of certain affordances—like catchability or what we might call interceptibility. These affordances will be present in a scenario that is constrained by the following rule: fixate the ball, begin running, and adjust running speed so that the angle of gaze remains constant. This "heuristic" specifies an invariance relation that one does not simply detect but which one will have to *produce* if possible. Nevertheless, the claim is that careful analysis of this kind of scenario, based on an initial determination of relevant stimulus variables to generate an appropriate grammar of sensory stimulation, would treat the object-type "catchable fly ball" as a set of models for this grammar all of which are such that the stated heuristic would hold.

Most of the details of the preceding examples are missing; and the given analyses such as they are, if they are not mistaken altogether, are simplistic. But such examples help to clarify what is being proposed here as a general method of analysis that is in line with the pragmatic maxim. Values for various variables must be *operationally producible* (extractable, detectable), though they should also be *inferentially assignable* given that respective variables stand in various higher-order relations with other variables.

We have argued in the previous chapter that science cannot sustain a passively-detached-spectator conception of observation. In the present chapter we have argued that we cannot even allow a passively-detached-spectator conception of *perception* (as if perception were mere sensory "input," for instance).

This in itself should help to clarify what *pragmatism* is. Namely, on one hand, the discussion above shows that we can apply the pragmatist maxim to the "hard words" in Gibson's ecological theory of perception (see page 90 above). We certainly should be able to do that after all, no matter what the subject matter, if pragmatism is worth its salt.

On the other hand, note that where Peirce talks about clarification of concepts and thus definitions of "hard words" in operationalist terms, Gibson is intent on specifying the operational character of affordances themselves as perceptual kinds, namely, with specifications of affordances in terms of activities of invariant detection (1967, 140). This shows that the pragmatist formula can be pushed all the way down to neuronal activities if necessary to account for a wide range of fundamental cognitive functionality (page 113), though many *operations* and respective ranges of detectable (producible, extractable) "invariants" that constitute contents of our perceptions are appropriately specified only at terrestrial scales, whatever the micro-physiological infrastructure may be. The point we want to make, in any case, has been made, namely, that actions and tangible results lie at the basis of the form of enactivism exemplified by ecological psychology.

Much of the force of the pragmatic maxim lies in the fact that animal experience (including perception) is not just *rooted in* action but is *constituted by* it. This is a mere elaboration of the kinds of concerns Peirce appealed to in motivating the pragmatic maxim to begin with (see chapter 1 above). It should be no surprise, then, that actions and their sensible results are going to be the kinds of considerations on which one ultimately depends to clarify one's thinking.

In the next chapter, we will look at a particular piece of history that nicely illustrates the difference between sensationist empiricism and operationalist pragmatism. The example is taken from the prehistory of sociology in the United States at the end of the nineteenth century and at the start of the twentieth. A wedge between empiricism and pragmatism is provided by considering the role of participant observation in the social and behavioral sciences. Essentially, a passively-detached-spectator conception of observation cannot accommodate the interactive nature of observation in this kind of example whereas operationalist pragmatism easily can.

EIGHT
Addams and the Settlement Movement

Implicit in much of the preceding discussion is a distinction between several kinds of action. In one sense, we act in order to perceive, and in another sense, we perceive in order to act. In the one case, we act in order to be *informed* about the world around us. In the other case, given such information, we are in a position to *reform* the world around us. In yet another sense, for that matter, the thinking and research that goes into exploring possible avenues of reform based on available information by itself encompasses a range of distinct kinds of activity. The first two kinds of activity are what we want to highlight in the present chapter. They are key to distinguishing empiricism and pragmatism.

On one hand, to be capable of being informed about the world around us, we should be able (in the interest of greater clarity, etc.) to "operationalize" our concepts and terminology in terms of low-order routine abilities that reflect our embeddedness in the world (this is operationalist pragmatism). In science, this includes the kinds of abilities exercised in the laboratory or otherwise in settings of controlled experimentation and observation. Many ordinary everyday concepts should in this way be explicable in terms of the affordances of the objects that fall under those very concepts. The manner in which we act in order to determine the affordances of a given environment is the manner in which we act in order to perceive.

On the other hand, the activities of daily living cannot be limited to the exercising of such automatic routines. At some level, particularly in unusual circumstances, we attend to evolving conditions in the world that may call for deliberate modification. Our daily lives are typically a succession of decisions and choices that are not merely the results of automatic routines (though the machinations of habit and instinct are perhaps more ubiquitous than we might be inclined to notice). In the sense of inferentialist pragmatism, what we *mean* by certain beliefs couched in certain conceptual terms is determined by the instrumentality of those beliefs in promoting such deliberate modifications—determined by how such beliefs *work* systematically (inferentially) to help implement such changes. Ample doses of perceptual content will contribute information essential to acting rationally and effectively in this way—this being the sense in which we perceive in order to act.

This distinction between acting as a way of becoming better informed about current circumstances and acting as a way of purposefully modifying those circumstances is well illustrated in the work of Jane Addams and others involved in the "settlement movement" at the end of the nineteenth century and early in the twentieth century.

In 1906, Simkhovitch proposed an analysis of settlement house methods as part of an explanation of what the settlement movement was and how it worked. Because of her emphasis on interpretation and action, and because of the very nature of the settlement movement as a concrete social reform effort with vitally important consequences for everyone directly or indirectly involved, it might be thought that her analysis would be pragmatist in character. But what is a "pragmatist" analysis supposed to look like? I argue in this chapter that her analysis is decidedly empiricist, not pragmatist, and offer an alternative pragmatist sketch of settlement house methodology. The point of this exercise is to show by way of an example what pragmatism is, that is, in the sense(s) originally proposed by Peirce and James.

An operationalist reading of the pragmatic maxim emphasizes the possibility of observational *evidence* as a necessary component of the constitution of our concepts of things in the world. But it is not enough to focus just on evidence. Evidence is what it is depending not only on its inferential role as such but also essentially on *how* it is acquired. In particular, as indicated in previous chapters, observation is active—indeed, it is *inter*active (participatory, etc.). The following illustration makes this point in terms pertaining specifically to the social sciences. What is peculiar about this example is that various attempts so far to explain it have failed to convey its value as an illustration of operationalist pragmatism, given that all of the interactional, operationalist trappings of operationalist pragmatism are so obviously present.

As we have seen in chapter 6, any number of examples from anthropology or other social sciences could be used to illustrate operationalist pragmatism. Of special interest here is the body of methods employed in and by the settlement movement in the United States. It will take a few paragraphs first to describe the settlement movement as a kind of reform movement that directly influenced the emergence of sociology as a stand-alone scientific discipline (Deegan 1990; Hull-House 1895). We will then look at one particular attempt (Simkhovitch 1906) to analyze its methods of operation as an agency for social reform. Once again, while the latter analysis may appeal to some proponents of pragmatism given that the settlement movement was dealing with highly "consequential" matters of vital importance for all concerned, I want to argue that that analysis is not pragmatist at all. At bottom, it is merely the product of a kind of sensationist empiricism and to that extent falls short. The settlement movement can after all be understood as quintessentially pragmatist in its methods, but a different analysis is needed to justify that claim. Simkhovitch's mistaken analysis thus will allow us to highlight the difference between operationalist pragmatism and sensationist empiricism.

Specifically, consider again the nature and role of *participant observation* in the social sciences and in cultural anthropology in particular. Contemporary cultural anthropology has successively honed participant observation as a key research methodology. The method grew out of the ethnographic fieldwork of social anthropologists, including Boas (1897; 1911) and his students in the United States, and Malinowski (1922; 1929; 1935) and his students in Britain. Ethnographic fieldwork and participant observation also played an important role in the 1920s and 1930s in early studies of city environments by the Chicago School (or Ecological School) of urban sociology. Boas was committed to the notion that, as a method of collecting data, an anthropologist should reside for an extended period of time among the people being researched, conducting research in the native language and in collaboration with native researchers. Generally speaking, the aim of the participant observation method is to acquire familiarity with a given group of people by participating for an extended time in their normal life activities in their home environment.

Some twenty or so years prior to the beginnings of academic recognition and development of the method of participant observation, similar methods were already being utilized throughout the so-called Progressive Era (roughly 1890 to 1920) in the settlement (house) movement, first in the 1880s in England (particularly Toynbee Hall in London's East End slums) and from the late 1880s to 1920 or so in the United States. The latter included Chicago's Hull House, founded in 1889 by Jane Addams and Ellen Gates Starr, and the Henry Street Settlement in New York, founded in 1893 by Lillian Wald. These and other settlement houses (for example, Lenox Hill Neighborhood House, founded in 1894, and University Settlement House, the oldest in the United States) were important sites for Progressive Era reform.

Progressivism was a social reform movement championed by mostly middle- and upper-class individuals advocating a wide range of economic, political, social, and moral reforms in response to major social and cultural changes introduced by industrialization. In particular, the settlement movement in the United States was typically aimed at serving immigrant communities in larger urban centers like Chicago and New York. Settlement houses were a kind of nonprofit agency that addressed the needs of immigrants or urban poor. "The name 'settlement house' came from the idea that reformers, often well-educated and wealthy individuals, 'settled', or resided, in the area they served, in the house or agency building itself" (Tuennerman-Kaplan 2007). This notion of residing with a community for an extended period of time (in this case, as an integral part of serving that community) is, as we have seen, a key feature of the participant observation method in cultural anthropology.

Undeniably the settlement movement was largely supported and promoted not as scientific research but as a kind of charitable activity. Settlement houses were centers for neighborhood social services and reform activities aimed at bridging gaps between social classes and at solving social problems endemic to tenement living.

> The settlement movement was responding to an array of urban social problems stemming from massive immigration and overcrowding, unrestrained capitalism, and the severe economic depression of 1893. Social settlement residents, who were primarily wealthy, white, well-educated women, strove to fulfill a "neighborhood ideal." They believed that their living in the heart of impoverished immigrant communities would help to solve many of the problems that plagued modern industrial cities, such as disease, alcoholism, prostitution, overcrowding, and harsh working conditions. Many settlement workers were guided by a religious call to service and a quest to fulfill their professional ambitions in an era of restricted choices for women. Settlement workers were optimistic that a blend of residence, research, and reform would offset the major social ills of the modern age. (Abrams 2003)

As agencies for social reform, settlement houses focused less on giving aid to individuals and more on identifying and eliminating shared problems within their neighborhoods and beyond. Charitable motivations aside (but probably never being able to shake a reputation as do-gooder outsiders), practitioners of the settlement movement were continually critiquing their own practices, speculating about what they should be doing, and deliberating about how better to do it.

In particular, Jane Addams (1893a; 1893b; 1899), from her earliest days at Hull House, was intent on clarifying what the settlement movement was—to dispel persistent misconceptions but also perhaps to explain something that even she did not fully comprehend and yet probably knew as well or better than anyone could know. Here are some representative quotes conveying the general tenor of Addams's thinking about settlement house activities:

> The Settlement, then, is an experimental effort to aid in the solution of the social and industrial problems which are engendered by the modern conditions of life in the city. It insists that these problems are not confined to any one part of the city.... From its very nature it can stand for no political or social *propaganda*.... The one thing to be dreaded in the Settlement is that it lose its flexibility, its power of quick adaptation, its readiness to change its methods as its environment may demand. It must be open to conviction and must have a deep and abiding sense of tolerance. It must be hospitable and ready for experiment. It should demand from its residents a scientific patience in the accumulation of facts and the steady holding of their sympathies as one of the best instruments for that accumulation.... Its residents must be emptied of all conceit of opinion and all self-assertion, and ready to arouse and interpret the public opinion of their neighborhood. (Elshtain 2002, 25–26)

Here we see an emphasis on the *experimental* nature of settlement house activities, requiring a flexible and tolerant open-mindedness free of any particular agenda other than a readiness "to arouse and interpret the public opinion of their neighborhood." This is markedly similar to Peirce's characterization of pragmatism not as a doctrine but as a methodological stance—not that that shows anything other than an alignment of attitudes. In the following passage, Addams downplays philanthropy in favor simply of good citizenship:

> I am always sorry to have Hull House regarded as philanthropy, although it doubtless has strong philanthropic tendencies, and has several distinct charitable departments which are conscientiously carried out. It is unfair, however, to apply the word philanthropic to the activities of the House as a whole. ... Working people live in the same streets with those in need of charity, but they themselves, so long as they have health and good wages, require and want none of it. As one of their number has said, they require only that their aspirations be recognized and stimulated, and the means of attaining them put at their disposal. Hull House makes a constant effort to secure these means for its neighbors, but to call that effort philanthropy is to use the word unfairly and to underestimate the duties of good citizenship. (Elshtain 2002, 45)

Such remarks emphasize the degree to which settlement residents functioned as citizens of their neighborhood. A settlement house, in her view, had a peculiar status that to some extent set it apart in the neighborhood as a special problem-solving agency, and yet the best methods available to it for gathering the information that it needed in order to exercise this function were more or less just the methods of ordinary good citizenship. Social mores against cheaters and freeloaders allegedly run deep, not that we will not instinctively jump at any opportunity to benefit from given circumstances whether it be at the expense of others or not, but that we tend to lose social stature when inequities in our own favor are discovered and publicized (Dunbar 1997, 44–45). It is as if openly accepting charity would put one in the role of being a freeloader who has been caught. Perhaps then as a potential threat to our own social stature, we tend to shy away from overt charity the way we avoid taking on unnecessary debt. At the same time, when our own community is facing dire circumstances, we are able if not willing to face the difficulties and promote improvements on an equal footing with other members of our own impacted community so long as those other members also carry their own weight (etc.). Addams was emphasizing that settlement workers should present themselves in just that way if they intend to be at all effective in their work.

> We sometimes say that our charity is too scientific, but we should doubtless be much more correct in our estimate if we said that it is not scientific enough. ... Collecting data in sociology may mean sorrow and perplexity and a pull upon one's sympathies, just as truly as collecting data in regard to the flora of the equatorial regions means heat and scratches and the test of one's endurance. Human motives have been so long a matter of dogmatism that to act upon the assumption that they are the result of growth, and to study their status with an open mind and a scientific conscience, seems well-nigh impossible to us. ... A man who would hesitate to pronounce an opinion [about what he regards to be a scientific matter] will, without a moment's hesita-

tion, dogmatize about the delicate problems of human conduct.... We are singularly slow to apply the evolutionary principle to human affairs in general, although it is fast being applied to the education of children. We are at last learning to follow the development of the child; to expect certain traits under certain conditions; to adapt methods and matter to his growing mind.... But in our charitable efforts, we think much more of what a man ought to be than of what he is or of what he may become; and we ruthlessly force our conventions and standards upon him, with a sternness which we would consider stupid, indeed, did an educator use it in forcing his mature intellectual convictions upon an undeveloped mind.... There is no doubt that our development of charity methods has reached [this] pseudo-scientific and stilted stage. We have learned to condemn unthinking, ill-regulated kind-heartedness, and we take great pride in mere repression, much as the stern parent tells the visitor below how admirably he is rearing the child who is hysterically crying upstairs, and laying the foundation for future nervous disorders. The pseudo-scientific spirit, or rather the undeveloped stage of our philanthropy, is perhaps most clearly revealed in this tendency to lay stress on negative action.... For most of the years during a decade of residence in a settlement, my mind was sore and depressed over the difficulties of the charitable relationship.... Recently, however, there has come to my mind the suggestion of a principle, that while the painful condition of administering charity is the inevitable discomfort of a transition into a more democratic relation, the perplexing experiences of the actual administration have a genuine value of their own.... The social reformers who avoid the charitable relationship with any of their fellow men take a certain outside attitude toward this movement. They may analyze it and formulate it; they may be most valuable and necessary, but they are not essentially within it. The mass of men seldom move together without an emotional incentive, and the doctrinaire, in his effort to keep his mind free from the emotional quality, inevitably stands aside. He avoids the perplexity, and at the same time loses the vitality. (Elshtain 2002, 72–74)

One can see in all of these passages a certain amount of ambivalence as to whether the settlement movement was science or charity, sociology or social work. Addams managed to blend the one into the other by way of some sophisticated insights into the "perplexing" nature of *participant observation*. In the first of the three passages above, note the call for "scientific patience in the accumulation of facts and the steady holding of [one's] sympathies as one of the best instruments for that accumulation." This is hardly what one would hear in a chemistry laboratory, not because settlement house activities do not have scientific import but because of the fact that we are now talking about human relations and social interactions—interactions that may "pull upon one's sympathies." (In a chemistry lab one would want to have rather a steady hand and a penchant for cleanliness and accurate measurement.) Throughout the whole of the third passage Addams makes clear the tension between maintaining impartial objectivity versus *going native*, as it were, in the face of the "sorrow and perplexity" that participant observation often involves. Going native is not the answer; and yet giving oneself over to the "emotional incentive" of the "charitable relationship" is just what makes possible a viable and valid accumulation of facts in the course of being "emptied of all conceit of opinion and all self-assertion, ... ready to arouse and interpret the public opinion of [one's] neighborhood," as she puts it.

But why be "ready to arouse and interpret ... public opinion"? One of our main concerns here is operationalist pragmatism. Participant observation as practiced in the settlement movement was a perplexing, emotionally charged affair that nevertheless need not for those reasons compromise the possibility of impartial, objective accumulation of facts. The notion of being ready to "interpret the public opinion of [one's] neighborhood," meanwhile, moves us toward inferentialist readings of the pragmatic maxim. Looking more widely beyond the operations of observation as such, the notion of *interpretation* introduces a different array of concerns—the kind of concerns, as a matter of fact, that many self-professed pragmatists might prefer to dwell on. The function of a settlement house in a given neighborhood was not just to accumulate facts but also to help institute some manner of "reform," to craft solutions, when those facts yielded evidence of present or impending problems for the neighborhood. Indeed the whole idea of social reform suggests activities that are more like engineering than pure science. Unlike the activities of a contemporary engineering agency like NASA, for example, that both exploits and advances the progress of science, the activities of the settlement movement in its day probably gave more to social science than it got from it, particularly since it predated the very existence of sociology as a viable stand-alone science. These contributions to science included not just valuable insights concerning participant observation. Hull House residents in particular were early pioneers in the use of quantitative statistical methods in sociology, perfecting a method of mapping demographic information about urban populations according to their geographic distribution (Hull-House 1895; Deegan 1990). In this regard they were social engineers advancing the goals of pure science.

The settlement movement thus successfully combined science and service. Conflicting priorities between these two concerns alone would have generated a bit of critical self-examination as to the proper role of a settlement house in a respective neighborhood. As evidence of an attempt to bring some sort of common organizational clarity to bear, one finds references to the "three Rs" of the settlement movement: "residence, research, and reform" (Trattner 1998; Tuennerman-Kaplan 2007; Abrams 2003; Answers.com 2006). This characterization (whatever its origin) seems to have hit the mark as an organizational ideal, succinctly summarizing in broad strokes some defining features of settlement house practices.

The notion of *residence* is essentially the idea behind the method of participant observation, requiring that settlement workers live (dwell, participate, interact) in the neighborhoods they served.

The notion of *reform* points to the settlement's mission to recognize problems in its neighborhood and to implement solutions to those problems with the aim of improving living and working conditions in the neighborhood. Such solutions might occur in the form of legislation if not in the form of direct services such as child care, libraries, cultural programs, nursing services, after-school clubs, or job training (to name just a few examples).

The notion of *research* involves a critical concern for developing ways to identify and understand problems and to devise possible solutions so as to facilitate implementation of neighborhood activities designed to eliminate those problems. Implicit in the very notion of accumulating hard *facts*, the notion of *interpretation* becomes centrally important in the face of a persistent need for flexible and innovative problem solving. Creative design of new and effective solutions calls for insightful interpretation of problematic situations and of what the respective consequences may be of various ways of readjusting neighborhood activities to deal with those circumstances. Addams identified the settlement's function in this setting *primarily* in terms of reciprocal interpretation—"clarifying and making accessible American institutions to immigrants" as well as "explaining immigrant customs and experiences to non-immigrant Americans" (Fischer 2009). "The Settlement is valuable as an information and interpretation bureau. ... The attempt to interpret opposing forces to each other will long remain a function of the settlement, unsatisfactory and difficult as the role often becomes" (Addams 1910, 99, 134). "Her aim throughout was to encourage sympathetic understanding among disparate groups and thereby foster growth toward social democracy" (Fischer 2009, 1).

Fischer discusses this theme of interpretation at some length, initially by way of examining Addams's attempt (1908) to explain the actions she and others undertook in response to the Chicago police chief's shooting of a Russian-Jewish immigrant, Lazarus Averbuch, an alleged assassin and anarchist, at a time and place (Chicago in 1908) when anarchists and anarchism were perceived by many to be as much of a clear and present danger to the country's security as "terrorists and terrorism" are so perceived today in the United States and elsewhere. We need not repeat Fischer's discussion except to pick out some choice claims and observations that nicely summarize Addams's conception of the settlement's interpretive function as a professional duty.

Fischer emphasizes early in her paper that Hull House as Addams saw it was first and foremost a neighborhood residence where "neighborliness" entails *duties of citizenship*, requires *sympathy* as the primary mode of social interaction, and promotes *fellowship* as the means for sustaining social relationships (2009, 2). *Interpretation* on many levels—of neighbors to one another, of the neighborhood to the larger community and vice versa—was a primary feature of settlement residents' work (2009, 4). Competence and authority to fulfill such a role could only be "obtained from a standpoint of immersion in a group, so that sociological data is sympathetically cast within the context of the group's aspirations, dreams, and modes of thought and feeling" (2009, 10).

In performing this interpretive function, settlement house activities were notably different from charitable social work:

> Charitable social workers and settlement workers appreciated each other's work. ... There were tensions, however. "Diagnosis" and "treatment," as sought by charity workers, did not exist in settlement workers' vocabulary. Settlement workers made literal neighborhood residence the central tenet of their lives and work, and the basis of their authority to interpret. By having no initial agenda, and simply responding as neighbors, settlement workers claimed they came to know their particular neighbors' personalities and concerns with nuance and specificity. ... [S]ettlement workers' authority to interpret was grounded [both in a knowledge of] sociological data and knowledge that is "gossipy, intimate, and interested," that is, the kinds of knowledge obtained through long dwelling and sympathetic exchange. (Fischer 2009, 6–7)

On the surface, in some instances, settlement residents' work might be difficult to distinguish from charitable work; but the residents regarded what they did simply as "neighborhood citizenship," attempting to show by example that all citizens of a neighborhood "were responsible for improving their neighborhoods on their own initiative" (Fischer 2009, 9).

A settlement house was thus in a position to "use its advantage of residence as a local force for civic reconstruction," as Addams herself put it (Fischer 2009, 9). At the same time, Addams found that her own perceptions and understanding were changing as a result of being swept up in the "cares and joys, desires and frustrations, needs and generosities" of the people in the neighborhood in which she lived. The reconstruction thus was mutual: "From such neighborly fellowship, personalities were transformed, and joint activity was a natural outgrowth" (Fischer 2009, 8).

For the record, to put it somewhat abstractly, Fischer's discussion clearly links the validity and effectiveness of interpretation to properly executed participant observation, so to speak, so that an interpreter of neighborhood activities, to be competent as such, would have to be interactively embedded in the neighborhood. Note, in this regard, that an analogy between charity workers and physicians is not appropriate for settlement workers since the latter are not like doctors observing live patients from a distance.

This is all interesting for its own sake; but what is even more interesting for present purposes is Fischer's subsequent discussion of other attempts besides those of Addams to analyze and explain settlement movement methods. One of these in particular was an attempt by Mary Kingsbury Simkhovitch (1906) to explain settlement work in terms of three *stages*. This three-stage analysis is in fact the target we have been aiming at in the present discussion of the settlement movement insofar as it nicely exhibits a mistaken *empiricist* analysis of a kind of life and experience that is better understood in *pragmatist* terms. Looking at its details helps to more clearly highlight just what the difference is.

For Simkhovitch, like Addams, settlement work was primarily "a method of living, through which fine-grained knowledge of the neighborhood gave authority to interpretation" (Fischer 2009, 11). Her three stages of settlement organization were labeled and described as follows (Simkhovitch 1906, 568):

- *Social impressionism*: "The first stage ... is the pouring in of the vivid life about one upon the sensitive and waiting personality. Group impressions then come into existence. A group must get a more varied, a more complex and a truer picture of life than any one individual can hope to obtain."
- *Interpretation*: In the second stage, "the settlement group has to impart what it knows—not the intimate confidences which belong to one person alone—but it has to tell what it finds of virtue and beauty, of hampered life, of tragic economic conditions. It may tell this in a thousand different ways."
- *Action*: "To act on the basis of the knowledge gained is the purpose of the settlement. Without such action the life of the settlement is sterile; it is only an interesting and highly educational life for the residents. ... There are countless methods by which [positive action] can be brought about. It is not in the least essential that the settlement itself shall do the work. Its responsibility is only to see that it gets done. [That] will depend on the environment in the given case."

We have here a description of the settlement house residents as a coherent group, functioning like a single participant observer and agent of change. This three-stage description of their method, though, is oddly familiar: the soaking in of impressions by the waiting observer is followed by appropriate actions of the observer upon the environment as mediated by reflection upon and interpretation of those impressions.

> What a settlement should seek to undertake depends then upon a whole series of other social phenomena. But the underlying method remains the same and we hold the key to the genuineness of the settlement by the test of this method. If it be the simplest group in the tiniest house, or if it be a large group occupying a whole block of imposing buildings with hundreds of activities, *it is in both cases a settlement if whatever action takes place is based on the knowledge gained by the group through its own impressions of the surrounding life.* (Simkhovitch 1906, 568–569)

It is clear from this summary statement and from her descriptions of each of the three stages that Simkhovitch has given us nothing other than a kind of "impressionist" empiricism (applied to a group of settlement residents working together as a single collective agent). Everything else she says, other than this three-stage analysis, points to the importance of, for example, being "in vital touch" with neighborhood life, or of the identification of settlement life with the life of the neighborhood—an interactive immersion, that is, in the life of the neighborhood. Everything Addams or Simkhovitch or other proponents of the settlement movement have said suggests pragmatism at work in the trenches. Simkhovitch's three-stage analysis of this scenario, on the other hand, depicts the settlement as a passively detached spectator—a loving, caring, sympathetic, neighborly, committed, honest, objective, passively detached spectator, acting in the world only in a way that sensationist empiricism would characterize such involvement. (Apparently sensationist empiricism weighs heavily on our imaginations even when the evidence runs so forcibly against it.)

But what exactly is the problem here? If Simkhovitch's sensationist empiricism is not acceptable, what is the pragmatist alternative? The first big hint that Simkhovitch's analysis is on the wrong track is the fact that she has made the same kind of mistake that Carnap and James made by focusing at bottom merely on "impressions" (that is, "evidence") without properly accommodating the different kinds of interactive means by which such impressions may be acquired. *Action* comes into Simkhovitch's picture only at a third stage whereas we have seen throughout our account of settlement house activities that the first stage requires an *interactive* immersion in neighborhood life that enables a kind of *participatory* observation. She says as much, and yet it falls through the holes of her analytical net. Action—interaction, participation—should also be there in the first stage. Impressions are the results of the operations of participation in the life activities of the neighborhood. Third-stage activities are something else altogether, namely, the kind of adjustments and readjustments of the life activities of the neighborhood ("reforms" based on settled agenda) that inferentialist pragmatism deals with. That, in any case, is what a dual reading of the pragmatic maxim would have us believe.

So what might a pragmatist analysis of settlement organization look like? It would be better perhaps to frame such an analysis in terms of the three Rs of the settlement movement. Something like the following is what Simkhovitch should have said, putting aside the notion of "stages" and working instead in terms of three coexisting aspects or features of settlement organization:

- *Residence*: The foundation of settlement work is active immersion in the life of the neighborhood. Where well-intentioned charity workers come to a neighborhood with ready-made solutions to preestablished problems (often a useful and important thing to do, for example, in the aftermath of large-scale natural disasters), settlement workers become integral parts (active "long-dwelling" citizens) of the neighborhood—engaging in the life of the neighborhood more or less on its own terms as a way, first, of establishing baselines for what is factually "normal." This is a matter of embracing and participating in the ethos and pathos of the neighborhood just to be able to observe what in fact neighborhood life is like. This first function of "residence" is to foster opportunities to observe neighborhood life honestly and objectively, free of preconceptions. A second function of residence in the neighborhood is to utilize these opportunities of observation, given an always-developing sense of what is normal and not normal, to discern and highlight the neighborhood's shared *problems* on its (the neighborhood's) own terms—to see (feel, know) these problems in the way that citizens of the neighborhood see (feel, know) them. One can be in a position to do this by being an engaged and responsible citizen of the neighborhood.

- *Research*: With a sense of what the neighborhood's problems are, as felt and owned by the neighborhood itself, efforts can be made to discover efficient and effective ways to solve them. Almost any citizen will bring unique perspectives and resources to bear in such efforts. The settlement movement is premised on the assumption that settlement residents come to neighborhoods with particularly useful perspectives and potentially powerful resources that would otherwise not be available within a poor urban neighborhood by itself in the absence of the settlement residents. Nevertheless, settlement workers do not come to a neighborhood with ready-made solutions but rather, presumably, with enhanced capacities to assist a neighborhood in acknowledging, understanding, and solving its own problems—not to dole out solutions, but to enhance the neighborhood's capacities to conceive, test, and implement its own solutions. As noted earlier, a capacity for insightful *interpretation* is crucial in the face of a persistent need for flexible and innovative *problem solving*. Creative intelligence in the design of efficient and effective solutions to clear and present neighborhood problems requires interpretation of problematic situations and of possible consequences of readjusting neighborhood activities in various ways to deal with such situations. A settlement house may enhance potentials for fostering such intelligence—as a repository of information about reusable techniques and solutions to recurrent problems, as a facilitator of discourse aimed at fathoming given problems, as a source of expertise relevant to given problems, as an organizer of local expertise, as a facilitator of communication between the neighborhood and larger communities, as muscle to implement viable solutions formulated by the neighborhood at large, and so forth.

- *Reform*: The life of a neighborhood, like life in general, is dynamic. Besides recognizing problems emerging in an ongoing flow of activities and designing solutions to those problems, the settlement's mission is to aid in the implementation of such solutions with the aim of improving living and working conditions in the neighborhood. Such solutions might be in the form of legislation if not in the form of more direct services like child care, cultural programs, nursing services, job training, and the like. Where Simkhovitch speaks simply of action at this stage, the emphasis should rather be on reform as adjustment and *readjustment* of the dynamics of neighborhood life. This is indeed a kind of action, but in the sense of implementing overall programs for change in the way lives are lived, as a way of solving recognized problems inherent in current ways that lives are lived. This is action of a sort that is distinguishable from actions inherent in one's participation in "normal" neighborhood life.

On this account, *residence* is a kind of embedded interaction aimed primarily at being informed about the facts of normal neighborhood life. *Reform* is a kind of action aimed at changing those facts. As briefly acknowledged at the beginning of the chapter, *research* is itself a kind of intermediate reflective, deliberative (inter)activity aimed at interpreting the facts and surveying alternative avenues of reform. On this view, the ambiguity of the words 'action' and 'interaction' can be rather problematic when one fails to notice it.

A simple example might help at this point.

(1) Suppose that, after residing in a given immigrant community for a while, settlement residents detect that a notable proportion of the neighborhood children to varying degrees are becoming unduly lethargic by comparison with children elsewhere of comparable ages. That is a *problem*—one whose emergence might be too subtle to notice except as a consequence of living in the neighborhood for a long enough time to see it in the course of one's interactions with the children.

(2) Openly or discreetly, settlement residents would proceed to look for possible explanations (reasons, causes). Is the lethargy evidence of psychological or physical abuse? Substance abuse? Dietary deficiencies? Environmental toxins? An infectious disease? One particular role of the settlement house as a whole is that of wielding a broader sense of what the alternatives may be or at least of how to discover what they are. The residents may seek out medical and other expert advice. They may look for unique common factors among the children and their living conditions. They may look more broadly at other neighborhoods to see if it is not just a local problem. They will deliberate, explore, observe, and experiment in order to zero in on the cause or causes so that they can also explore possible solutions. These kinds of activities constitute *research*. Suppose then that the root cause is found to be malnutrition, even among the more well-to-do families, due to certain dietary customs that do not easily survive transplantation to this country and clime from other parts of the planet.

(3) The real solution to the problem would be to alter dietary practices of the community. In the short run, as a temporary measure, one might pursue direct nutritional intervention (financing school lunches, distributing food supplements, etc.). Ultimately, though, with the long term in view, the settlement house might also establish classes in nutrition for parents as a way of adjusting established dietary habits. This is an effort at *reform*, an effort to change what is normal, not merely a treatment of symptoms.

The difference between a pragmatist analysis of settlement organization and an empiricist analysis thus hinges on how we think about action. There are two kinds, two orders, of action in the pragmatist picture. The difference between the interactions required by "residence" and the adjustments that constitute "reform" are not unlike the distinction between the mechanics of operating an automobile (steering, accelerating, braking, beeping the horn, etc.) versus actually driving an automobile in the midst of changing road conditions (dealing with curves in the road, intersections, other traffic, etc.). One must be able to do the former to do the latter properly (thus the necessity of interactive "residence" in the driver's seat in a car on a road); but one could be capable of the former without a clue or any experience concerning the latter. These are two different kinds of action that should not be confused one for the other. Likewise, one may know how to move all of the pieces on a chessboard but still not be able to play chess. Peirce drew a similar distinction between playing musical notes versus playing melodies (1878a, EP1:128). Or consider Dewey's example where "the ultimate meaning of the noise made by a traffic officer is the real consequent system of social behavior, in which individuals are subjected by means of noise to social coordination; its proximate meaning is a coordination of the movements of persons and vehicles in the neighborhood and directly affected" (Dewey 1925, LW1:150). The proximate interactions of residence and the ultimate changes brought about by reform are quite different in an analogous way. Inferentialist pragmatism tends to focus on the activities and results of "reform." Operationalist pragmatism highlights the activities and results of "residence."

The point is that a sensationist brand of empiricism would seem to recognize actions of reform as the one and only form of action as such. A Peircean brand of pragmatism, on the other hand, would have to acknowledge multiple kinds of action with distinguishable functional roles. In particular, perception itself is active, and not just in the way that actions of "reform" feed back into *what* one perceives.

It should be clear, given this result, that one cannot simply tack discussions of "real-life" practical applications and their consequences onto presentations of existing philosophical positions (for example, Carnap's sensationist empiricism) as if that is all there is to embracing pragmatism. It may indeed be expedient, prudent, or otherwise useful if not financially lucrative for anyone in any profession to address real-world vital concerns in science, engineering, politics, religion, law, medicine, economics, or wherever. In particular, this is true of academic philosophy as a profession. We cannot say that one cannot pursue the business of academic philosophy as usual and then simply append or superimpose concerns for real-world applications onto one's work because it is professionally expedient to do so. The point, rather, is that this strategy by itself will in many cases have nothing to do with pragmatism. To be a pragmatist (as opposed to being merely professionally prudent), it will be necessary in many cases to start over from scratch to reformulate basic concepts and assumptions along pragmatist methodological lines, specifically in accordance with operationalist and inferentialist versions of the pragmatic maxim.

NINE

Truth, Justice, and the American Pragmatist Way

Pragmatism is a methodological stance concerning how best to define one's terms, or, as Peirce put it, how best to clarify one's ideas. It has been argued in previous chapters that, by pragmatist lights, there are two kinds of clarity—third and fourth grades of clearness—above and beyond the first and second Cartesian standards of "clarity and distinctness" characteristic of axiomatic mathematics. That is, (third) to ground ideas concretely, they must be operationalized; and (fourth) to be made reasonable, they must be inferentialized (if it may be put that way). James's *inferentialism* has been the dominant identifying feature of pragmatism for the past century or so. Peirce's *operationalism*, on the other hand, has been largely ignored. Both are essential.

To better understand this double-aspect conception of pragmatism, examples are especially helpful. We will want to recall a number of examples that have already been discussed or at least mentioned. As already noted, one of the more remarkable examples is Peirce's definition of the word 'reality' with a corollary definition of the word 'truth' (Peirce 1877; 1878a). It will be shown below that this definition also supplies for free another corollary definition, namely, an operational definition of the word 'knowledge'. Moreover, the same *type* of definition (involving a long-run perfectionist ideal of some sort) can be given for the words 'democracy' and 'justice'.

Lithium, Diamonds, etc.

Applications of the pragmatic maxim that have been discussed so far include James's example of *going around the squirrel* (in the opening pages of James 1907c; see page 13 above). This example is particularly instructive as an everyday illustration of the need to get clear about what words might mean in order to resolve conceptual disputes. The important point here is that the notion of *going around something* is easily operationalized in two distinct ways which, if not understood, could lead to interminable debate. James essentially ended the debate not by casting a deciding vote but by disposing of the debate altogether, having revealed the misunderstanding and thus miscommunication that was involved. The aim of pragmatism, of course, is not to dispose of debates as such but rather to clarify the ideas employed in a debate so that some kind of resolution is more likely to be achieved. In that particular case, the debate was confused from start to finish.

But that perhaps is as much as one can find in James's writings in support of an operationalist interpretation of the pragmatic maxim in spite of his emphasizing the importance of empirically grounding one's concepts. He does provide many examples of pragmatism at work, though what is uniquely pragmatist in these examples as rendered by James is inferentialist in nature. It would be fairly straightforward to amend some of them (as with the 'going around' example) to accommodate Peirce's operationalism, but that is not the point. Peirce's and James's respective discussions of transubstantiation of the sacrament (chapter 4, pages 45ff. above) showed in fact how Peirce's treatment could just as well be amended to accommodate James's inferentialism. The point rather is to better understand what operationalism is in the first place.

Peirce provided several examples. After presenting the first formulation of the pragmatic maxim (1878a), Peirce looked in turn at the three words 'hard', 'weight', and 'force' (see page 22 above for a brief overview). Also, in 1897, he illustrated in great detail *each* of the three grades of clarity as applied to the term 'relation'.

Later, in 1905b, Peirce criticized the anti-realist flavor of his own earlier accounts of 'hard' and 'force', harking back to earlier discussions of realism versus nominalism (1872) that were glossed over in the 1877–78 *Popular Science* articles (see also Peirce 1905d; 1911). The later assessment is probably correct, but as interesting as that issue may be, we need not pursue it here.

In his later discussion of the meaning of the word 'hard' in 1905b (EP2:356), in order to make his point about the reality of *possibilities*, he also defined the word 'diamond' in a way that might stand with the *lithium* example (1903g, EP2:286; page 30 above) as paradigmatic of what an operational definition is, assuming one reads these definitions with an eye on distinguishing expected results of executing actions characteristic of identifying such materials:

> Being a diamond, it was a mass of pure carbon, in the form of a more or less transparent crystal (brittle, and of facile octahedral cleavage, unless it was of an unheard-of variety), which, if not trimmed after one of the fashions in which diamonds may be trimmed, took the shape of an octahedron, apparently regular (I need not go into minutiæ), with grooved edges, and probably with some curved faces. Without being subjected to any considerable pressure, it could be found to be insoluble, very highly refractive, showing under radium rays (and perhaps under "dark light" and X-rays) a peculiar bluish phosphorescence, having as high a specific gravity as realgar or orpiment, and giving off during its combustion less heat than any other form of carbon would have done. From some of these properties hardness is believed to be inseparable. For like it they bespeak the high polymerization of the molecule. (Peirce 1905b, EP2:356)

To be more explicit, one would have to describe the respective actions required to produce each of these sensible results (where it is not already obvious), but that would be easy enough for someone who actually knows what those actions are. That is, this definition will literally be more meaningful to anyone who knows their way around physics and chemistry laboratories (not in general, but because these are the relevant operations in this particular instance).

The aim of chapter 8 above was to use the settlement movement to illustrate the difference between operationalism and empiricism. Operationalism as illustrated in real-world sociological "laboratories" was exemplified by the activities of *residence* while processes of *reform* exemplify experimental efforts informed by the operational grounding supplied by *residing* in the given neighborhood. Reform efforts were of course also informed by *research* efforts, the latter illustrating the equally important role of inference (broadly conceived) in engaging and exploiting a broad range of expertise including but not limited to that of neighborhood residents.

In chapter 7, exploring Gibson's ecological psychology, the aim was to show how far an operationalist perspective can reach. Contrary to Peirce's focus only on *intellectual concepts*, we can in much the same way characterize perceptual kinds (e.g., a flat surface that would accommodate our walking or running) in terms of the activities characteristic of various perceptual systems. Intellectual concepts may or may not correspond to respective perceptual kinds, but the point is that the logic of perception and the logic of science are one and the same logic even if some of the technical terminology one uses in these two cases may differ.

Reality and Truth

After defining the words 'hard', 'weight', and 'force' in the 1878 article, Peirce presented operational definitions of the words 'reality' and 'truth' to further illustrate how to use the pragmatist method. A preliminary discussion of Peirce's definitions of the latter words can be found above in chapter 3 (pages 31ff.), so we need not present those details again here. But we do want to outline a kind of template that these examples provide and that may be taken advantage of to define other equally difficult words. In particular, we want to look at three other intellectual concepts that also signify *ideals* of some sort. Respective operational definitions will in a similar way appeal to a *perfect* scientific employment of otherwise common practices.

How did Peirce proceed?

First, he would give a rough-and-ready definition of the target word that was at least clear$_1$ if not clear$_2$. While not clear$_3$, yet, this would put matters in some kind of perspective that might be operationalized. Three more steps would then be required to achieve clarity$_3$. Specifically:

1. specify appropriate types of *operations*,

134 / What Pragmatism Was

2. characterize respective types of *tangible effects* of executing those operations, and then
3. define the target word in just those terms, in some way indicating which procedures to execute in expectation of achieving which tangible results.

In the case of 'reality', Peirce's rough-and-ready characterization is that it denotes that which is independent of whatever anybody may think it to be. Obviously that is not clear$_3$. So here are the three steps in a clear$_3$ definition:

1. Peirce's operational definitions of 'reality' and 'truth' are couched in terms of *inquiry* as a type of *operation*,
2. with settled *beliefs* resulting from inquiry being the designated *tangible effects*. But these cannot be just any beliefs. We want to consider only results of the type of inquiry—*scientific inquiry*—which already has built into its methodology an explicit critical concern for distinguishing true versus false beliefs.
3. Thus, what we should *mean* by the phrase 'the truth' is the opinion that would be ultimately agreed to ("by all who investigate") as the result of the *perfect* employment of *scientific* methods of inquiry. By 'reality', then, we should mean simply that which is represented in such a belief.

Again, see pages 31ff. above for an extended discussion of this way of rendering Peirce's definition of these words. The question now is whether we might use the same kind of procedure to define other hard words.

Knowledge

Establishing the meaning of the word 'truth' clearly$_3$ will impact the meanings of other words. Note that 'reality' and 'truth' were defined not circularly in terms of each other but *jointly* in terms of a common set of characteristic operations and sensible effects. In fact, with very little further effort, we also have a plausible operational definition of the word 'knowledge'.

Namely, Peirce refers to "the opinion which is fated to be ultimately agreed to by all who [scientifically] investigate" as a "belief in the real" and thus as a *true belief*. In Peirce's sense of these terms, a true belief is a belief that may be or would be or will have been *perfectly justified*. We thus get an immediate semantic freebie: *true belief* as *perfectly justifiable* (PJTB) in the present sense is what we should mean by the word 'knowledge'. The operational definition of 'reality' (in terms of *inquiry* as a kind of operation that "settles opinion" or "fixes belief") thus yields operational definitions of the words 'truth' and 'knowledge' (not just two but *three* birds with one stone).

But this is perhaps too quick. We do not want to say that the words 'truth' and 'knowledge' are identical in meaning. One difference of meaning between the latter two words would concern the "modality" of the reference to justification in the respective definitions. For instance, one's saying (correctly or not) that it is *true* that *p* will make sense whether or not any effort has been made to justify that claim. No actual inquiry is required for the definition to apply in that case, though the speaker will have thereby taken the position that perfect scientific inquiry would confirm that *p*. On the other hand, one's saying that one *knows* that *p* suggests that some such inquiry has already been pursued, deferring to experts as needed (perhaps entirely), and that one is now committed to the further claim that any further (e.g., perfect) scientific inquiry would confirm that *p*. A truth claim does not *presuppose* that some justificatory effort has actually taken place at the time of the utterance, whereas a knowledge claim does. In the latter case, a challenger may legitimately ask for supporting evidence, while in the former case one may simply have made a blind bet.

It should be noted that Peirce proposes essentially this definition of the word 'knowledge', or as he put it, 'perfect knowledge' (Peirce 1893, CP4:61–64). We should resist the temptation to call this *the* pragmatist definition of 'knowledge'. It is simply *a* pragmatist definition. There may be any number of other ways to define the word operationally.

Nevertheless, this particular definition of 'knowledge' easily sidesteps Gettier-style counterexamples which typically pick away at the justification element of a standard JTB conception of knowledge. Any such alleged counterexample points to something that will otherwise have been dealt with successfully, one way or another, in a perfect inquiry. The self-critical nature of scientific inquiry requires that the possibilities on which such present or future counterexamples turn will have been among the possible disconfirming scenarios that will already have been investigated in a perfect scientific inquiry.

Granted, in actual practice we rarely achieve such perfection. Perfection is a long-run *ideal*. Nevertheless, while these definitions do not provide *decision procedures* for distinguishing true and false beliefs or for determining which beliefs are or are not knowledge, they do provide a meaningful *standard*: Actual practice measures up to such a standard to the extent that actual results of actual inquiry comport with (i.e., would not be undone by) what would be perfect results of perfect inquiry. We have not compromised common usage of the words 'truth', 'know', etc. One may meaningfully claim that the sentence 'grass is green' is *true* or that one *knows* that grass is green insofar as such a claim only commits one to a wager that further inquiry will not disprove it.

Of course, Gettier-type counterexamples are not the only threat here. For instance, does the "lottery paradox" pose a problem? The lottery paradox (Kyburg 1961) was designed to show that three principles governing the "rational acceptance" of a proposition are jointly inconsistent. Namely,

(1) it is rational to accept a proposition that is very likely true,
(2) it is not rational to accept a proposition that is known to be inconsistent, and

(3) if it is rational to accept a proposition p and it is rational to accept another proposition q, then it is rational to accept $p \wedge q$.

These jointly entail an inconsistency, namely, that none of the tickets in a lottery will win (since each will not) and yet that exactly (and thus at least) one of the tickets *will* win.

Given the inconsistency, Kyburg rejected principle (3); *but* principle (1) is in any case unacceptable as stated. The PJTB alternative would be that

(1′) it is rational to accept a proposition that is very highly if not perfectly justified by scientific means.

Thus, before the drawing, one *could not* rationally believe that lottery ticket A will not win (or one might sooner dispose of it), but one *could* rationally believe that it *probably* will not win (but would keep it until the drawing). After the drawing, after one hears that another ticket has won, one may rationally believe (say it is true, say that one knows) that ticket A did not win (and at that point could easily dispose of it), thus committing oneself to the wager that one's warrant for that claim cannot subsequently be shown to be in error. There is no inconsistency here. The lottery paradox thus poses no problem for PJTB.

How about the "preface paradox"? The preface paradox (Makinson 1965) is similar to the lottery paradox and is handled similarly. Namely:

- Suppose that in writing a book, one will have rationally asserted (by virtue of rationally believing) a large number of propositions: that p_1, that p_2, ..., that p_N, each taken singularly.
- If we accept Kyburg's "aggregation" principle (3) above, then it is rational to believe that $p_1 \wedge \ldots \wedge p_N$ (of which the book as a whole is an assertion).
- Yet, as such things always seem to go, one might rationally believe (and acknowledge in the preface) that among such a large number of propositions in such a book, mistakes will have been made and thus that $\neg(p_1 \wedge \ldots \wedge p_N)$.

This apparent inconsistency rests on the assumption that to believe that *it is highly likely* that there are errors in the book is tantamount to believing that *it is the case* that there are such errors. The problem, again, is due essentially to Kyburg's principle (1). The typical situation by PJTB lights is, rather, that

- The book is a rational assertion that $p_1 \wedge \ldots \wedge p_N$. One is thereby committed to the wager that mistakes will not be found.
- On the other hand, in the preface, one acknowledges one's fallibility, admitting that what is rationally asserted but imperfectly justified in the book may not hold up in the course of *perfect* inquiry. This denies neither the assertion nor the commitment; but (as a plea for civility?) it acknowledges the risk of the wager.

Again, there is no problem here for PJTB.

Another possible range of issues may arise depending on how and what one thinks about Peirce's notion of an "ideal limit of inquiry." In short, we would want to say that Peirce's conception of "the opinion which is fated to be ultimately agreed to by all who investigate" need not be interpreted as an opinion finally formed at the end of all inquiry, at the end of time, etc. Careful repetition and successive refinement of scientific experimentation is in fact time-consuming (and resource-limited). But in characterizing what is meant by *ideal* long-run results of such inquiry, we may minimize if not ignore the temporal aspect of actual inquiries. (See the discussion of Achilles and the tortoise above, page 25.)

For example: the *reality* of the decimal expansions of the numbers π, e, $\sqrt{2}$, etc., is not disputed, though they would require an eternity to write out when calculated by hand or computer. Any such expansion, in full, is non-temporal and thus takes no time at all when characterized as the *limit of a sequence* of respective partial sums (no writing out of digits required).

Confirming convincingly if not conclusively that a given die is unfair may take time but does not require tossing the die until the end of time. The *real* nature of the die *is* what it is and thus determines the mean distribution of *all possible samples* of N throws of that particular die. The fair/unfair question can be convincingly answered with just one such sample if N is large enough. The "long run" refers not to the end of time but to the infinite totality of these possible samples considered all at once, simultaneously.

A buyer randomly samples a load of coffee beans just *once* in a reasonably short amount of time to assess the current overall quality of the cargo. Given that the coffee beans are subject to spoilage, the *real* quality is assumed to be indicated by the mean result from all possible random samples of the same size *at that time* (any one of which will be a good enough estimate if the sample size is sufficiently large). Again, the "long run" refers not to the end of time but to the whole of these possible samples considered all at once, simultaneously.

Election polls are highly time-dependent (such that considerations of voter preferences at the end of all time are irrelevant if not meaningless). Such polling gets at a quickly changeable reality such that *perfect* polling should be regarded as instantaneous rather than eternal. Such examples indicate that words that express ideals need not involve "inquiry until the end of time" even if they refer to *perfect* inquiry.

Again, it is understood that our actual here-and-now beliefs, generally speaking, fall short of being knowledge. Fallibilism is essentially a direct corollary of a PJTB definition of 'knowledge'. Knowledge-that-p claims are thus meaningful not as claims to have attained the requisite perfection in one's justifications that p but rather as commitments that any further justificatory efforts will not finally disconfirm that p (in just the intended sense, etc.). This same commitment is conveyed by claims that "p" is true, given Peirce's characterization of truth. It is also conveyed by the simple assertion that p if such an assertion in itself is regarded as a judgment, that is, as what will not be disconfirmed by further inquiry (such that further inquiry may just as well cease as to whether p or not—as opposed, say, to positing "p" as an axiom or tentative assumption). Actual claims in this regard, while perfectly meaningful, are fallible. The difference between assertions of "I know that p," "It is true that p," and just "p" may simply come down to a difference of emphasis—namely, emphasis on one's degree of *commitment* that, while p may be questioned and while tentative disconfirming evidence may be seriously considered sooner or later, it will henceforth never be finally disconfirmed.

There are actually many knowledge claims that one can make with considerable confidence—claims, for instance, that $2 + 2 = 4$ in decimal arithmetic; or that the Moon orbits the Earth; or that smoking causes cancer, given the different kinds of observational and experimental efforts that have actually been made to test such a claim. If we take Gibson's ecological theory of perception (chapter 7 above) as an account of perception as a "fast" variety of *judgment*, then actually acting consistently in accordance with what we perceive is quite the same as an assertion of knowledge. Walking on what appears to be a solid and flat surface is an *assertion* of sorts involving a *wager* of sorts that such an affordance will in fact be afforded. We indeed assert such proto-knowledge claims continually throughout the waking hours of each day.

Democracy

Clear$_3$ definitions of various words will be affected by the preceding joint definition of 'truth', 'reality', and 'knowledge', but probably will not emerge without making some finer distinctions. Operations of inquiry with fixed beliefs as their tangible outcomes may be used to define other than those three words, but it might involve an appeal to more specific types of inquiry and/or, respectively, more specific types of tangible results. A case in point is the word 'democracy'.

Operational definitions of 'truth', 'reality', etc., hinge on the notion of perfect employment of scientific methods. Talisse (2007, 63–66) claims that there is a close connection between the notions of *science* and *democracy* by Peirce's lights. Namely, Peirce (1877) associated each of four types of inquiry (four ways of *settling opinion*) with a type of political order, namely, where a given type of inquiry will be able to be successful in maintaining fixed beliefs only in a respective political arrangement. So, for instance,

- the method of *tenacity* can succeed only in an apolitical *anarchy* (each to their own, a stateless society of hermits, etc.);
- the method of *authority* can succeed only in a totalitarian and/or theocratic *tyranny* (tenacity writ large, state coercion, intellectual slavery, etc.);
- the *a priori* method (the method of reason alone) can succeed only in an *aristocracy* (qua leisure class perhaps?—involving open discourse and consensus but only among those with the means to converse; an insular

glass bead game for those free to indulge in purely intellectual pursuits; what is "agreeable to reason [alone]" becomes conventionally intuitive and appealing; a provincial reasonableness prevails though being an accidental matter of parochial fashion and taste); whereas

- the method of *science* can succeed only in a *democracy* (ideally, involving participation of a whole community; not a community of consensus but a community of inquiry; not aimed at belief preservation for its own sake but continually driven to correct if not improve its theories and practices in the event that they prove to be inadequate in the face of *real* events; not answerable to any collection of independent or privileged special interests, but continually challenged by unfolding facts; otherwise employing a self-correcting method of inquiry concerned with the integrity and intrinsic worthiness of its progressive accomplishments; etc.).

Talisse concludes from this that scientific inquiry can be properly carried out only in a democratic political order (in a way echoing Putnam's assertion—in recommending a pragmatist conception of science over a logical-positivist conception—that science requires the *democratization of inquiry* (1995, 73)). But here is the present point: turning such claims inside out suggests a way to *operationally define* the word 'democracy'.

We may use Peirce's template.

To begin simply, a democracy is supposed to be a form of government "of the people, by the people, and for the people" where primary political power is vested in the governed, such power being exercised directly or through representatives under a free and fair electoral system, etc. One might want to add something about the rule of law, requiring legal institutions that guarantee formal equality of basic personal and political rights and privileges, with independent courts of law; or something about the separation of judicial, legislative, and executive powers more generally might be in order, not to mention the guarantee of religious freedom, separation of church and state, etc. But rather than *defining* features of democracy, the latter are only specific institutions established in a U.S.-style democracy. For instance, what is meant by the *rule of law* depends on the origins and development of the legal principles that it presupposes. Some would be quite accepting of such a maxim if what was meant is Sharia law, while others would not accept that. In any case, such rough-and-ready characterizations are not entirely clear.

To define the word 'democracy' operationally, note that we may characterize different political orders in terms of *how* their institutions are established and maintained (settled, fixed, stabilized). This gets us started:

1. The requisite *operations* would again be *inquiries*, but more specifically, inquiries as engaged in by a given community of inquirers dealing with matters that will include the community's own social, political, economic, and legal arrangements.

2. The *tangible results* of such activities would have to be not just beliefs as habits or rules of action but, more specifically, *institutions* as socially distributed habits—stable if not secure manners of *co*-operation that embody and otherwise substantiate broadly acknowledged agreements resulting from cooperative inquiry (reflecting of course the tight connection between belief, habit, and action spelled out by Peirce (1878a, sect. 2), though couched here in social externalist terms). Then,
3. what we should *mean* by 'democracy' is just the sustained and exclusive use of scientific methods in such institution-fixing inquiries (versus methods characteristic of anarchies, tyrannies, aristocracies, etc.).

This definition is remarkably simple, assuming we understand what scientific methods are. Even if it would not be easy to implement, it sets a clear and meaningful standard. It calls for impartial, rational, self-correcting methods for building and improving social, political, economic, and legal institutions; and it insists on perfect institutions even if having to settle in the short term for less than perfect. A democratic political order in this sense would, by Peirce's lights, be epistemically if not practically superior to other kinds of political orders precisely because of its built-in self-correcting methods and because of its explicit concern for distinguishing perfect from imperfect institutions.

Other kinds of political orders may be defined in much the same way: "anarchy" is just the perfectly sustained and exclusive use of methods of *tenacity* in such inquiries, etc. But the focus here is on methods of science.

Democracy—employing scientific methodology in political affairs—requires (ideally) that every citizen be able to participate fully as an intelligent member of a community of inquiry. With reference to forming and reforming a democratic society's institutions, *any citizen* would be free to formulate and analyze hypotheses and propose respective experiments to test them. Clearly this does not require nor does it call for government by a scientific elite. Rather, it presupposes (ideally) that every citizen (even if only as a voter) uses scientific sensibilities and methods in carrying out their civic responsibilities—scientific methods in some broad sense that of course needs to be better understood. (Dewey's attention to education as essential to the achievement of a true democracy is easily if not accurately understood in such terms.) Ideally, in a democracy, only citizens who understand scientific methodology actually deserve the right to vote. Ideally, only candidates who understand scientific methodology and put it into practice as the basis for their political views deserve to campaign. Without a doubt, democracy in the United States, in this ideal sense, is practiced in a crippled manner, at best, and at worst, not at all.

This is admittedly a demanding if not extreme conception of democracy by current lights. The emphasis on intelligent perfectionism cannot of course be regarded as pathological unless that is how we wish to characterize scientific inquiry.

The point rather is that democratic deliberation would be the best way of settling disputes and otherwise writing contracts, instituting social agreements, establishing social institutions (social habits), etc., precisely because (as scientific) it is the only kind of political order that continually strives to repair and improve such things. If we want to be able to say that democracy is the best way of establishing and maintaining social institutions, then, filling out Peirce's template, we would have to say that the latter should be done scientifically.

With all of that on the table, we can now more effectively turn to defining the word 'justice'.

Justice

So what exactly is *justice*? What is a *just* institution? We may of course start with a pedestrian conception of justice as fairness. But such a rough-and-ready characterization is not entirely clear. To define the word operationally, what types of operations and tangible results might we appeal to?

Again following Talisse (2011), we might take a cue from Rawls's social-contract theory of justice (1971; 2001). The question here is not whether Rawls is or is not a pragmatist or whether pragmatism is or is not Rawlsian. But Rawls's characterization of the "original position" with its "veil of ignorance" in large part provides the kind of operational perspective we are looking for to clarify the notion of justice. There may be other if not better options, of course, but this will allow us to illustrate the pragmatist method. Namely,

1. Yet again, appropriate types of *operations* will be scientific inquiries as engaged in by a given community of inquirers dealing directly with their own social, political, economic, and legal arrangements. But more specifically, we want to consider such inquiries that would attempt, for example, "to specify and assess the system of rules that constitute [...] basic institutions, and determine the fair distribution of rights, duties, opportunities, powers and positions of office to be realized within them" (Freeman 2008).
2. *Tangible results* of executing such operations would be *basic institutions* (viz. social, political, economic, and legal "habits of action") that embody and otherwise substantiate those specifications and assessments.
3. What should be meant by the phrase 'just institution', then, is the kind of institution that ultimately would be collectively achieved as the product of perfectly executed democratic deliberations of this particular type (concerning *basic* institutions, seeking *real* fairness, etc.).

Any of Peirce's four types of inquiry might be employed for such purposes, but the aim is to determine a *truly* fair distribution of rights, duties, etc. As we have already seen, democratic qua scientific methods constitute the only method of inquiry bent on properly distinguishing what would or would not *really* be fair.

As we try to make sense of this rubber-stamp application of Peirce's template, we find that Rawls's conception of the original position (etc.) depicts what perfectly impartial, universal, and equal participation in perfectly executed democratic inquiries would look like where *real fairness* is the aim—where otherwise one could not negotiate without preferential regard for one's own actual interests. The ideally disinterested negotiation that takes place in the original position depicts a high standard *in general* for what deliberations should look like in science and thus in a democracy. (Striving for such disinterestedness, as an ideal standard, is key to achieving the *objectivity* that is essential to legitimate science.)

Then, *justice* would on this account characterize social institutions "fated" to be established as the result of a perfect democratic process—with objectivity guaranteed by assuming Rawls's original position etc.—where the respective deliberation specifically addresses the nature of basic institutions that determined the distribution of goods. Social institutions (like habits/beliefs) that comport with what would be established in that perfect limit could be said to be *just*.

Like 'truth', 'reality', and 'knowledge', the words 'democracy' and 'justice' express ideals. Such perfect results often are not achievable in practice. We all know that it is unlikely that actual negotiations will always measure up to the high standards set by Rawls's depiction of the original position. Nevertheless, given such a definition, one may meaningfully claim, here and now, that some political arrangement or event is just (or unjust). Slavery is unjust. The Equal Pay Act of 1963 is just. Making such a claim simply commits one to the wager that further democratic inquiry will not eventually disprove it.

TEN
Twelve Misconceptions of Pragmatism

We now have a fairly definite proposal regarding what pragmatism is. Namely, ignoring common usage if need be and defining the terms 'pragmatic' and 'pragmatism' in line with how Peirce and James originally characterized pragmatism as a philosophical method or attitude, here, in summary form, is what we have so far been defending:

1. Pragmatism endorses a conception of *belief* where, as Peirce puts it, beliefs are formed as responses to respective doubts (they "appease the irritation of doubt") and as such "involve the establishment in our nature" of habits or rules of action (Peirce 1878a, EP1:129). It is not just that we act in accordance with our beliefs but that our beliefs are individuated in terms of rules of action. This accommodates various normative conceptions of rational, justified, warranted belief so long as these conceptions are explicable in terms of beliefs playing out (working) in ways that comport with the respective rules of action that constitute those beliefs.

2. Pragmatism endorses a corollary conception of *meaning* as formulated by the pragmatic maxim (Peirce 1878a, EP1:132). Namely, beliefs are couched in words and/or concepts such that a clear definition of a given word or concept will be in terms of the rules of action (stateable perhaps as "conditionals having their apodoses in the imperative mood") that would be constitutively involved in believing that the concept applies in a given case—rules of action that could be *brought to bear* as measures or standards to test such a belief. Since actions have "exclusive reference" to their effects or consequences, as Peirce puts it, we cannot mean anything by a given belief other than that various specific consequences should come about as results of acting in ways consistent with certain actions characteristic of that belief. This emphasis on actions and consequences can be understood in two ways:

    a. *Operationalism* emphasizes tangible effects of interactions with objects alleged to fall under a given concept.
    b. *Inferentialism* emphasizes implied consequences of holding a given belief when conjoined with other standing beliefs.

We would want to say then that to be a *pragmatist* is to acknowledge and consistently hold to these particular conceptions of belief and meaning.

On the other hand, being pragmatic is not the same as being a pragmatist. We might want to say that to be *pragmatic* is not just to be practical or prudent or down-to-earth but to think and work (saying what one means, formulating and implementing policies, etc.) in ways that comport with these respective conceptions of belief and meaning, whether one acknowledges them or not. More simply, in this latter *full* sense of the term, to *be* pragmatic is to *be like* a pragmatist. On this score, one may at times be pragmatic without being a pragmatist. One may also be disposed to being pragmatic as a matter of principle and thus in a sense be a pragmatist without necessarily acknowledging it or knowing anything about the origins and history of pragmatism as a philosophical attitude. One may simply adopt such an attitude or be disposed to such a temperament, as it were.

In any case, what it means exactly to be a pragmatist is what a careful analysis of the pragmatic maxim and a pragmatist conception of belief is designed to articulate.

References to *pragmatism* are not uncommon in political news and commentary, and they often have no apparent connection with pragmatism as a *philosophical* position. It is not likely in today's political climate, of course, that anyone caught up in the grind of governing would bother with a great deal of philosophical nitpicking. Nevertheless one would like to think that Obama's supporters and detractors have actually been cognizant of what it means when they label his attitudes or methods as pragmatist or pragmatic in nature (Keyes 2009; Obama 2008b; Sunstein 2008; Wickham 2008). If Peirce and James have anything to say about it, such a claim would not be untruthful if it is understood that pragmatism is based on a view such that our beliefs are individuated by the actions that they promote as a rule; that, in this light, it recommends a *method* for clarifying one's policies and is not itself a particular policy or political doctrine (it is at most a meta-doctrine—a methodological doctrine about doctrines, beliefs, etc.); and that this latter method is inferentialist but that, more fundamentally, it is operationalist. The issue of how or even whether any political official is a pragmatist then becomes a matter of sorting out the facts as evidenced by his or her actual methods and accomplishments—to see how and to what extent they meet these conditions.

But again, it would be disingenuous to suggest that Obama or anyone else should have in mind, e.g., the inferentialist-plus-operationalist view of the pragmatic maxim that has been presented here. We prefaced this book with some comments from numerous quarters concerning Obama's professed pragmatism. The term 'pragmatism' certainly means different things to different people. The meaning and appropriate use of the term 'pragmatism' has been contentious from the start, ever since Peirce started using it in the 1870s. As previously noted, Peirce appropriated the term from Kant and gave it a new twist. Yet the meanings Kant gave to it reflect long-standing usages of the term 'pragmatic' that are not easily dispensed with. In response to this diversity of meanings, we have come out in favor of a certain characterization of pragmatism primarily as a methodological attitude rather than a body of philosophical doctrine. With this view of pragmatism in mind, the goal of this chapter is to exhibit a substantial incongruity between, on one hand, various references to pragmatism in the political news and, on the other, American-style pragmatism as it was originally characterized by Peirce and James. We can fairly easily show how various uses of the word 'pragmatism' today do not always comport with pragmatism in the original sense of classical American pragmatism. One may draw one's own conclusions, but the intention here is to help change the way people use the term. It can't hurt to try.

The attention that Obama has brought to the whole business of pragmatism in politics is thus helpful just because it has inspired a number of responses in the political press that give hard evidence of the different ways that people think about pragmatism. In the preface (pages ix–xii above) we listed several statements of what pragmatism is so far as such views can be distilled from political news and commentary. We will take several of these statements one by one to assess how well they fit with the characterization summarized at the beginning of the present chapter. Utilizing the characterization developed here as a standard, it would appear that most people do not understand what pragmatism is and probably should not be using the term as they do.

So here are twelve misconceptions of pragmatism:

THESIS 1: *Being pragmatic means being practical. Pragmatism is the principle or attitude to the effect that practical considerations ground or otherwise trump all other factors in policy decisions, ethical decisions, etc., such that practicality is the basis of any kind of normativity.*

This misconception is probably not uncommon. According to this thesis, the meanings of the terms 'pragmatist' and 'pragmatism' are derived from the meaning of the term 'pragmatic', not the other way around as proposed earlier. But if the word 'practical' could stand in for the word 'pragmatic', as this thesis suggests, then why not say that pragmatism is just practicalism and that a pragmatist is a practicalist? In short, if the words 'pragmatic' and 'practical' are synonymous, why have two terms at all?

The answer is that they are not synonyms. Pragmatism is more specific about certain things than practicalism is. Namely, practicalism as just described requires no particular conceptions of belief or meaning and thus includes none of the essential features of pragmatism. So one may be a practicalist without being a pragmatist. This thesis thus misconstrues what it is to be pragmatic or to be a pragmatist. It does identify a position, namely, practicalism; but that is not pragmatism.

THESIS 2: *Being pragmatic means being prudent. Pragmatism is the principle or attitude to the effect that prudential considerations ground or otherwise trump all other factors in policy decisions, ethical decisions, etc., such that prudence is the basis of any kind of normativity.*

We can run the same kind of argument against this thesis that we ran against Thesis 1 to conclude that it identifies a position, namely, prudentism or prudentialism, which fails to include any of the essential features of pragmatism (i.e., pragmatist conceptions of belief or meaning). Thus pragmatism is not just prudentialism.

Note that Thesis 1 regarding pragmatism versus practicalism is not unrelated to the discussion in chapter 4 of why Peirce used the term 'pragmatism' and rejected 'practicalism' as a label for the views he was promoting in 1871. In that earlier discussion, we were addressing (in part) a Kantian use of the term 'praktischen', which is considerably different than the contemporary folk use of the English term 'practical' that was employed in the previous thesis. Hence our reasons for rejecting that thesis seem simpler and more straightforward. They seem simpler also because we have by now established a fairly definite proposal about what pragmatism is, so we have a clear standard for assessing such theses. The important point at this juncture is that the two discussions of pragmatism versus practicalism are related but different. In arguing against Thesis 1, we were not particularly concerned with how Kant used the terms 'pragmatisch' and 'praktisch'.

The present thesis, though, is more directly connected with how Kant used the term 'pragmatisch'—in the first *Critique* and elsewhere—and here I defer to Gregor's remarks in the introduction to her English translation of Kant's *Anthropology from a Pragmatic Point of View* (1798, xvi–xxi) where she indicates several ways that he used the term 'pragmatic', *none* of which exactly corresponds to how Peirce ultimately used it.

In his uses of the term, Kant was generally pressing connections with *prudence* in one form or another. This is evident in the passages from the first *Critique* that were quoted in chapter 4 above (pages 40f.). In those passages, *pragmatic* practical laws pertaining to the achievement of happiness (as the satisfaction of all of our desires) are termed "rules of prudence," in stark contrast with *moral* practical laws (laws of morality) that pertain to achieving *worthiness* of being happy.

On the other hand, Gregor's remarks about Kant's different uses of the terms 'pragmatic' and 'prudential' range more widely. She points out, for instance, that "anthropology," for Kant, could be pursued from several points of view, e.g., as *physiological* anthropology. Interestingly, Kant also might have written on anthropology from a *moral* point of view—an empirical study of humanity "directed to rules about the way they can use their natural powers and dispositions to make the practice of morality easier and more effective" (xvi). He chose rather to pursue a *pragmatic* anthropology—an empirical study of humanity attempting to formulate rules about how one can use others for one's own purposes (xvi, xix). To understand what that means, Gregor spends a few pages tracing different senses in which Kant used the term 'pragmatic' up through the writing of the *Anthropol-*

ogy. It is interesting to see how tightly the terms 'pragmatic' and 'prudential' are woven together in this discussion.

A relatively familiar sense of the term 'pragmatic' appears in the *Groundwork* (1785) where Kant distinguishes three kinds of imperatives or "objective practical principles: the technical, the pragmatic or prudential, and the practical or moral" (xviii). Moral imperatives are unconditionally necessary while hypothetical (technical and prudential) imperatives "prescribe certain actions as rationally necessary under the condition of our having certain ends to which those actions are the rational means" (xviii). The difference, meanwhile, between technical and prudential imperatives (between imperatives of skill and imperatives of prudence) is that the former prescribe means to arbitrary ends while the latter prescribe means to ends to which all people aspire, namely, happiness (xix). This is consistent with the discussion of "rules of prudence" in the first *Critique* (1781/1787, A800/B828, A806/B834), and it is echoed elsewhere in the *Groundwork* and in the *Anthropology* itself where prudential reasoning is characterized as "determining not only the means to happiness but the composition or content of the end itself: that is, determining which of the individual's desires can be satisfied in an integral whole" (xix). Something to note about this whole discussion is that the term 'prudential' could just as well be used wherever the term 'pragmatic' is used. Why not just say, then, that what Kant was doing was *prudential* anthropology, i.e., anthropology from a prudential point of view? It would surely be a more succinct and accurate description.

Gregor goes on to discuss how the term 'pragmatic' is given a meaning in the *Anthropology* that contrasts with the more familiar meaning outlined in the preceding paragraph. In the *Anthropology*, the term refers more narrowly "to skill in using other [people] for one's own purposes" (xix). That is, this seems to be anthropology from a *technical* rather than *prudential* point of view, aimed at providing "such knowledge of [people] as will enable us to formulate technical rules for using them"—as, for example, in being able to manipulate people for one's own purposes by playing on their "passions" and "manias" (xix–xx). In the *Anthropology* Kant somewhat off-handedly distinguishes wisdom and prudence (1798, Ak.VII:266), but Gregor points out that Kant elsewhere (in the *Groundwork*) actually characterizes prudence (*Klugheit*) in terms of wisdom, namely, as either "worldly wisdom" (*Weltklugheit*) or "personal wisdom" (*Privatklugheit*). Moreover, "worldly wisdom" refers here to a person's "skill in influencing others in order to use them for [one's] own ends" (xix). We thus see that the narrower sense of the term 'pragmatic' in the *Anthropology* is after all just the sense of the term 'prudential' in the *Groundwork*. Gregor might hesitate to connect these two senses so tightly, but she does go on to clarify the connection in more detail, particularly to examine the tighter relationship between skill and prudence in the *Anthropology* than one finds in the *Groundwork*. In any case, we have enough here to make our point. Kant might as well have been talking about prudence and never have used the term 'pragmatic'.

The alleged synonymy of the terms 'pragmatic' and 'prudential' in Kant's work is superfluous and otherwise unhelpful if we want to know what pragmatism is. He tells us what prudentialism is, but there is nothing to say that that is what pragmatism is. Simply claiming synonymy does not make it so.

The point of course is that, whatever Kant is talking about and whatever his terminology may be, it is not pragmatism in the sense outlined at the start of the present chapter precisely because (1) it assumes fairly specific notions of belief and meaning that run counter to what is essential to *pragmatism* so far as Peirce and James are concerned, and (2) the discussion itself deals with "skill in influencing others" etc., not with belief and meaning as such. Kant really was talking about something else—a specific kind of prudentialism, not pragmatism.

THESIS 3: *Being a pragmatist means being ideologically neutral in the interest of promoting post-partisan practicality.*

This is a misconception that appears to be fairly widespread in today's political discourse. It is a misconception because it assumes a false dichotomy between *being a pragmatist* and *having an ideology* and/or partisan commitments.

It is not clear that the following statements exemplify such a misconception—that is, they assume only a dichotomy between *being pragmatic* and *being a recalcitrant ideologue*—but Thesis 3 seems to be one of the take-away messages:

> STEVE PELLEY: You [just] said that Washington is dysfunctional.
>
> RAHM EMANUEL: Okay, is that breaking news? [...]
>
> STEVE PELLEY: That's the way it seems to you, running the third largest city in America. "*Dys*functional."
>
> RAHM EMANUEL: I think that, yeah—I mean, I have my own view of why, but—I think that [Washington has], on certain things, decided to—in my view—allow ideology to become an impasse to progress, where it is a mistake. You should not be more loyal—and more of a slave—to ideology. Be pragmatic. Make a decision. We're doing things in the city of Chicago that have nothing to do with philosophy, have nothing to do with ideology, [but] have to do with making sure that taxpayers get—and residents—get what they deserve. (CBS News 2012)

Politics aside, the point here is to focus on the use of the term 'pragmatic' and the distinction that is made between being pragmatic and being a slave to ideology. Is this what pragmatism versus ideological partisanship is about?

There are actually several interrelated misconceptions that need to be sorted out in this context. For instance, (a) if Peirce was right about its being only a method, pragmatism is not inconsistent with at least some ideologies though it does not by itself recommend any particular ideology. More importantly, (b) we need to understand the difference between being a *dogmatic* ideologue and being able to endorse a given ideology while remaining *open-minded*. Generally speaking, having an ideological bias by itself cannot legitimately be equated with holding to such a bias blindly or dogmatically. (Emanuel's remarks above seem to accommodate this point.) In another direction, (c) there is a difference between one's reasons being concrete at least some of the time versus being purely abstract all of the time. Pragmatism can emphasize the importance of grounding a given ungrounded ideology in concrete terms without rejecting that particular ideology (not to mention ideologies altogether). Or one may argue against proponents of a given ideology not on ideological grounds as such but because that ideology is not concretely grounded—a "logical" *reason* that is itself ideologically neutral. In yet another direction, harking back to the thesis about pragmatism and practicalism, (d) there is an apparent distinction between being practical versus acting from principle, but those are not incompatible. Etc.

A careful reading of Obama's statements indicates to his credit that he did not reject ideology as such but only "the *rigid* ideology and dysfunctional politics" that he and others attributed to the Bush presidency (and that Emanuel was to attribute to "Washington" four years later). He moreover recommended that "America [lead] with principle and pragmatism" (Obama 2008b), as if principles and pragmatism were not at odds after all—as if partisanship and pragmatism were not incompatible (Packer 2008; Worsnip 2012). That sounds right. But how is it possible? How might that make sense?

The answer is straightforward. Principles typically are systematized elements of some ideological framework. Ideologies and thus principles are couched in conceptual terms. As such, so far as pragmatism is concerned, for one's principles or ideology to be as clear as possible, their constituent conceptual terms must be operationally as well as inferentially articulated. That is, the pragmatic maxim applies to any concepts employed in any given ideology—political, scientific, or otherwise. To say that someone is a pragmatist means not that he or she has a particular ideology (e.g., liberal or progressive), nor that he or she has no ideology and thus holds to no principles, but that any ideological position that he or she does have will have been formulated in specific ways, namely, in ways that are inferentially coherent and operationally grounded.

Being fully enabled "methodologically" does not entail that a *pragmatist* (on grounds other than merely endorsing a pragmatist methodology) is ideologically neutral. Arguably, some kind of ideology is in fact unavoidable (Burke 2004). It is a part of human nature, whatever one's station in life may be. Pragmatism would be immediately refuted if it ruled out all forms of ideology (Hayes 2008). Indeed pragmatism does not force one to refrain from explicitly ideological or partisan discourse, but it does rule as unworthy certain kinds of ideology—particularly, any ideology that is unable to accommodate operational and/or inferential clarification of its basic concepts.

Pragmatism in a political arena, especially if characterized exclusively as inferential-role pragmatism (e.g., Rorty 1998), may seem to carry with it a default partisan commitment to progressivism as opposed to conservatism (Berkowitz 2009; Dionne 2009a; Hamburger and Wallsten 2009; Lowry 2009; Milligan 2009; Packer 2008; Schultz 2009; Sunstein 2008). But that misconstrues the nature of the possible flexibility inherent in the operationalizability of one's conceptual framework. Operationalism and empiricism are not particularly progressive or conservative attitudes. An emphasis on looking to facts as they emerge in the course of concrete actions on the ground neither recommends nor presupposes either a progressive or a conservative ideology. Experimentation as such is not the enemy of either a progressive or conservative ideology unless that ideology is hostile to exploring and accommodating new facts and new ideas. The pragmatist attitude easily accommodates an aversion to uncompromising if not mindless adherence to absolutes of either stripe; but that is a meta-ideological attitude—a *methodological* ideology, not a *substantive* ideological position as such.

So much for issues (a), (c), and (d). What about (b)? Open-mindedness in the face of the humble realization that one does not and cannot know everything there is to be known may be a fairly normal aspect of the pragmatist attitude. The problem with any particular ideology "is not its content but its form. Not the substance of ideology but the fact that [one is] too wedded to it, too rigid and dogmatic" (Hayes 2008). This is a good point that applies to *any* ideology, progressive or conservative. Pragmatism does not immediately avoid misconception (b), though neither is it particularly disposed to it. While promoting no particular ideology and offering no surefire cure for dogmatism, pragmatism only makes the methodological point that, at bottom, it is not what you think you believe—certainly not what you *say* you believe—but what you do, how you act in the world, that exhibits the content of your ideology insofar as such activities reveal the empirical contents of the concepts constituting that ideology. It is not just the propositional consequences of a belief that count but also the factual results of *acting* in accordance with the conceptual contents of your belief that determine what your ideology in fact *is*. Such an attitude is actually hard to maintain consistently insofar as it disallows institution of the leisure of mere thought as a fixed state separate from the labor of knowing what the thought is actually about.

Obviously, U.S. citizens would not want a president to be either inferentially incoherent or operationally disconnected. But even in the sense of being inferentially coherent and operationally grounded, one may be a pragmatist and still be rather close-minded. A pragmatist may well be an absolutist, or an ideologue, so long as one's ideology is to some extent inferentially coherent and in some way operationally grounded. Perhaps that is hard to imagine, and perhaps it is unlikely? But strictly speaking, it is not ruled out. Pragmatism in itself is not a cure for dogmatism, narrow-mindedness, or stupidity. There is nothing inherently virtuous or vicious about operationalizing one's concepts; and in any case, that can be done well or it can be done badly.

THESIS 4: *Being a pragmatist means that one emphasizes an opportunistic expediency, possibly at the expense of principles—ignoring, bending, breaking with, or holding to principles only for reasons of political expediency.*

This is a misconception that is not unconnected with the false dichotomy between "being pragmatic" and "being ideological." Previous discussion already touched on the related false dichotomy between being pragmatic versus holding to one's principles. If the latter is indeed a false dichotomy, then we should not use it to characterize pragmatism; and if pragmatism is as we have characterized it at the beginning of this chapter—as a particular conception of belief and a corollary conception of meaning—then it just does not entail what the present thesis says it entails.

One may be a pragmatist without emphasizing opportunistic expediency and without being willing to sacrifice one's principles in favor of political expediency. Again, being a pragmatist amounts to having a certain conception of belief and an operationalist-plus-inferentialist conception of meaning—conceptions one may hold to without being willing to compromise one's principles for short-term (opportunistic) benefits.

Conversely (for what it's worth), one may emphasize political expediency as such with no constraints otherwise, i.e., able to accommodate any concepts of meaning and belief. For instance, one may make a politically expedient move with temporary setbacks in order to get into a position to be able later to promote certain irrevocable dogmatically held beliefs couched in inflexible conceptual terms (in effect, to keep one's head down and live to fight another day). That is not pragmatism. It's not about meaning and belief at all. This is just politics from a prudential point of view.

Thus the entailment between pragmatism and opportunistic expediency goes neither way.

Indeed the notion of political expediency is closely related to Kant's notion of prudence as skillfulness in using others to promote one's own ends. This is a matter of effective political behavior, independent of moral concerns. By itself, to a large extent, it more directly echoes Machiavelli and Hobbes. Rather than anthropology from a prudential point of view (broadly conceived), Thesis 4 in a sense addresses politics from a Machiavellian and/or Hobbesian point of view. It would be naive to deny that actual political activity is often morally questionable, or to deny that the present thesis is getting at something crucially problematic about common political behavior. The misconception here is rather that this problem is a necessary feature of *pragmatism*. We have already dissociated pragmatism from prudentialism in the discussion of Thesis 2, and the same kind of argument shows Thesis 4 also to be misconceived.

Pragmatism thus does not entail a Machiavellian stance in politics, though it is not inconsistent with it either. And vice versa. In other words, the two are entirely independent. Indeed pragmatism does not foreclose the possibility of almost any manner of conflict between *kratos* and *ethos* in political spheres. Pragmatism alone will not analytically dispel problems like, for example, the paradox of the commons (Hardin 1968). It would be problematic to think it could do that. The latter problem is a moral, political, and/or economic problem, not one that can be cleared up by way of mere technicalities associated with this or that conception of belief or meaning, pragmatist or otherwise. A "maxim of logic," as it were, will probably not have moral entailments beyond normative constraints on what constitutes better and worse forms of inference.

That disposes of Thesis 4 so far as pragmatism and political expediency go. But we should perhaps say one more thing about pragmatism and the notion of expediency. Specifically, recall James's following statement:

> *"The true," to put it very briefly, is only the expedient in the way of our thinking, just as "the right" is only the expedient in the way of our behaving.* Expedient in almost any fashion; and expedient in the long run and on the whole of course; for what meets expediently all the experience in sight won't necessarily meet all farther experiences equally satisfactorily. Experience, as we know, has ways of *boiling over*, and making us correct our present formulas. (James 1907f, PMT:106)

By this account pragmatism surely has something to do with expediency; but this statement makes a point about what truth is, not about political expediency as such. It is about cognitive expediency (a factor in a pragmatist theory of belief)—cognitive expediency in which wholesale coherence is at issue and where different configurations of beliefs prove their worth by fostering such coherence. Several (many) such configurations ("coalitions") of beliefs may compete successfully in this regard—that is just James's *pluralism* in at least one of its guises—where such success is gauged not psychologically or politically but *logically* and thus "in the long run and on the whole of course." Rather than a matter of how people use other people to advance their own ends, this is a matter of how beliefs function with other beliefs to determine their own consequences. This is just inferentialism characterized in terms of cognitive expediency.

THESIS 5: *Being a pragmatist means focusing on what works, that is, on what gets things done, typically in response to a compulsion to implement what gets something done just when something needs to be done. To be a pragmatist is thus to do what one has to do so that* something *gets done even (oftentimes) if it is not quite what one would prefer.*

Typically the emphasis here is on the importance of making moves to get beyond mere deliberation in order to take concrete action. Being pragmatic in this sense often means acquiescing to the impulse to "settle for less" in order to break a stalemate or deadlock in deliberations about an issue at hand—as if one *occasionally* has to lower one's sights and be a pragmatist.

Despite the emphasis on "what works," this is a misconception in that it casts "pragmatism" as an attitude that one can pick up or put down as circumstances change. Certainly there are occasions when it is time to get off of one's duff and get something done—e.g., to stop merely talking about things and take concrete action. It is a mistake to say that it is only in this latter kind of move that one thereby becomes a pragmatist. At best, it may rather be an occasion in which one becomes pragmatic, temporarily becoming *like* a pragmatist—but even that is false, strictly speaking, if the only grounds for saying it is that one is compelled to take concrete action. We are back again, then, to Thesis 1.

The issue of "occasionally" being a pragmatist is something we have not yet discussed. One may occasionally but not always be pragmatic, rational, or empirical. But it would be strange if not deranged to be *occasionally* rationalist, or *occasionally* empiricist—for the same reasons that one cannot occasionally be a Christian or a Muslim or an American or a mathematician. One may "convert" from one such profession or nationality or philosophical stance to another, but not just move from one to another and back again as short-term circumstances change. Pragmatism is like that as well. One can be rational off and on, but one cannot be a rationalist off and on. One can be empirical off and on, but one cannot be an empiricist off and on. Similarly, one can be pragmatic off and on, but one cannot be a pragmatist off and on. As a consistent and comprehensive approach to things, pragmatism would rather characterize one's overall approach to problem-solving processes in general—the thinking aspects of the problem solving as well as the doing aspects, as it were—rather than be a pose that one temporarily adopts whenever it is time to "get real" and do something.

THESIS 6: *Being a pragmatist means focusing on what works in the sense of always stressing that, metaphorically speaking, "the proof of the pudding is in the eating."*

This thesis and the preceding one are alike in emphasizing concrete action, both being similar to the emphasis on practicality in Thesis 1. A similar response on that score may be given in each of these cases. The twist in the present case is the emphasis put on "what works" as some kind of test or proof of one's beliefs. This is not so much a misconception in itself as it just falls short of saying what pragmatism is. The misconception, in other words, would be in thinking that this is all it takes to say what pragmatism is.

The point is that focusing on what works is not a sufficient condition for being a pragmatist. Not all ways of focusing on what works would count as pragmatist. That is, what exactly is "the pudding" and what is its "eating"? Apparently the pudding will be some body of beliefs, and the eating is their application in actual circumstances. But such an attitude that beliefs need to be applied in order to validate them is not uniquely pragmatist. One may have any of several conceptions of belief and meaning and still stress that the proof of the pudding is in the eating.

Is this not obvious? What works or not might be gauged on purely rationalist grounds—*proving* rational consistency of a set of beliefs by way of meticulous step-by-step argumentation. And/or on purely empiricist grounds—weighing empirical implications of those beliefs against banks of actual empirical data. And/or as a matter of point-by-point comparison with some accepted body of doctrine—the Bible, the Constitution, or some other relevant authoritative text. Or maybe what works is what one can successfully endorse out of mere tenacity. This list of options of course echoes Peirce's list of methods of fixing belief in *The Fixation of Belief* (1877), the point being that there are many ways to conceive of and gauge "what works" that do not require pragmatist conceptions of belief and meaning.

By Peirce's lights, the best method for testing, proving, and thus fixing beliefs is the method of science—broadly conceived in such a way as to pertain to more than just the hypotheses of physics. This best method is something he promoted independently of his presentation of the pragmatic maxim, and he even makes the point that an appreciation of the superiority of scientific method will not follow necessarily from a pragmatist conception of belief (1877, EP1:121–123). Conversely, holding to the superiority of scientific method is clearly not sufficient for being a pragmatist, as evidenced by any number of scientists and philosophers who do the former but are not the latter: Newton, Lavoisier, Carnap, Quine—the list is varied and long. The point is that pragmatism cannot be identified simply with an emphasis on what works to prove one's beliefs, *even* when science is taken to be the measure of what works.

THESIS 7: *Pragmatism is merely a kind of data-driven evidence-based empiricism, given its emphasis on tangible results, particularly in political arenas where such empiricism entails an emphasis on techniques like cost-benefit analysis, risk assessment, multi-criteria decision analysis, game theory, and so forth.*

First, it should be pointed out that emphasizing the use of empirical methods is not specific to pragmatism as such. That is something one may do simply as an empiricist. Several chapters above have been devoted to spelling out the difference between empiricism and pragmatism. One may even recommend operationally grounded empirical methods and still not be a pragmatist (by ignoring or rejecting the inferentialist elements of pragmatism, for instance, or by endorsing a non-pragmatist conception of belief). Beyond promoting the importance of empirical methods, the pragmatist would at the same time have to point to the need both to *operationalize* and to *"inferentialize"* (as it were) the methods by which one obtains or otherwise characterizes empirical results.

This is particularly true in the case of cost-benefit analysis—say, as promoted and used by the Office of Information and Regulatory Affairs in the White House Office of Management and Budget.

> Many environmental advocates accuse [cost-benefit analysis] of being a rigged methodology that always seems to favor doing less for public health and the environment. For a long time, OIRA has been seen as the place where regulations go to die, and cost-benefit analysis—in combination with improper second-guessing of

scientific research produced by expert agencies—as the chief executioner. (Mooney 2009)

The fact is that a promotion (feigned or not) of *empiricism* by itself does not preclude a concern only for what works to successfully promote fixed, preconceived favored agendas or partisan causes (Butler 2010). We have already seen that pragmatism also does not preclude such proactive partisanship. One might expect, though, that by having to consistently operationalize and inferentialize its methods for assessing "costs and benefits," the OIRA would thus be compelled to make these allegiances more explicit—which in turn might serve (for better or worse) to make the regulatory processes more transparent. In any case, by pragmatist lights, this is the only way for the OIRA to be *clear* about what it does. All of this of course is more easily said than done.

The point here is that a conscientious and meticulous pragmatist may or may not utilize state-of-the-art empirical techniques; but when that is done, those techniques may have to be modified—more effectively operationalized and inferentialized—to be consistent with pragmatism as such, to be more than just "empirical." Using any particular empirical technique like cost-benefit analysis or risk assessment by itself, or together with other such techniques, is not what makes one a pragmatist.

THESIS 8: *Pragmatism is just anti-intellectual practicality.*

This is yet another common misconception. Pragmatism, for both Peirce and James, is anti-rationalist, and thus it is anti-intellectualist in James's sense. Several of Peirce's writings target Cartesian presuppositions and methods (1868b; 1878a; 1891). Rationalism was an even more frequent adversary in James's works (1905; 1907c; 1907f). James in one instance identified intellectualism as rationalism with idealist tendencies (1907b, PMT:12). In more incisive critiques, he points to the rationalist tendency to treat the intellect as having the capacity "of shooting over nature behind the scenes and knowing things immediately and directly" (1907g, PMT:249). In the course of not just ignoring but even denying any intermediaries between ideas and what they are about, rationalism commits what elsewhere he calls the fallacy of "vicious intellectualism" (1909b).

One can readily see that the culprit here is not use of the intellect but treating the intellect as a wholly independent and autonomous (self-contained, self-sufficient) faculty of knowledge about the world at large. Pragmatism does not therefore eschew rationality or intellectual deliberation. By pragmatist lights, one cannot be *too* intellectual. Problems arise rather when intellectual deliberations are not grounded in and balanced with the "practical bearings" of what one is deliberating about. Pragmatism is thus not anti-intellectual. It is anti-intellectual*ist*.

THESIS 9: *Pragmatism emphasizes consequences (ends) over means, even to the point of advocating that ends justify means.*

This thesis points to an alleged necessary condition of pragmatism, though (as an instance of affirming the consequent or not) an emphasis on consequences (etc.) is often regarded as well as a surefire sufficient sign of pragmatism.

It is of course a misconception to think that an emphasis on consequences is sufficient to characterize pragmatism. The pragmatic maxim (properly understood) states the nature and role of "effects" or "consequences" in a pragmatist conception of *meaning*, but it does not say that any and all ways of emphasizing consequences fit the bill. Utilitarian ethics emphasizes consequences, but that alone does not make it pragmatist in character. In particular, if there is no operationalization of the methods of determining "utility values," then that form of utilitarianism might simply reflect a purely empiricist or even a rationalist ethical stance.

As for "ends" necessarily being a focal component of pragmatism, recall James's summary of a discussion of Peirce's pragmatic maxim as follows:

> No particular results then, so far, but only an attitude or orientation, is what the pragmatic method means. *The attitude of looking away from first things, principles, "categories," supposed necessities; and of looking toward last things, fruits, consequences, facts.* (James 1907h, PMT:32)

Oddly enough, James lumps *facts* together with "last things" here. In any case, we have already quoted and discussed remarks by Peirce also concerning the focus on future consequences:

> All pragmatists will further agree that their method of ascertaining the meanings of words and concepts is no other than that experimental method by which all the successful sciences (in which number nobody in his senses would include metaphysics) have reached the degrees of certainty that are severally proper to them today;—this experimental method being itself nothing but a particular application of the older logical rule, "By their fruits ye shall know them." ... The most prominent of all our school and the most respected, William James, defines pragmatism as the doctrine that the whole "meaning" of a concept expresses itself either in the shape of conduct to be recommended or of experience to be expected. (Peirce 1907b, EP2:400–401)

These are just two of any number of statements indicating how centrally important the notion of consequences is for pragmatism. Nevertheless, it is surprising that such remarks about the role of "ends" in an account of meaning should be thought to support or even suggest the attitude that ends may justify means. The latter attitude is a wholly distinct way of emphasizing ends. Nothing in James's or Peirce's writings could legitimately serve as a basis for identifying these two ways of emphasizing ends.

A pragmatist conception of the relationship between ends and means, if there is any such definitive conception at all, would perhaps be that the distinction is anything from purely relative to virtually meaningless. Peirce seems to have had little to say about this distinction, but James and Dewey were quite the opposite. Actually James's conception of the means-ends distinction is mostly implicit in his view of experience as an ongoing burgeoning enterprise (1904a; 1904c), though the idea that ends *are themselves* means is evident in his statement that "theories thus become instruments [means], not answers to enigmas [ends], in which we can rest. We don't lie back upon them, we move forward ..." (1907c, PMT:32). In this sense, means are justified by how well they continue to function as means.

We have said rather little here about Dewey as a proponent of pragmatism, though his many critiques and mentions of the means-ends distinction essentially echo a Jamesian notion of experience as growth (for starters, see Dewey 1922, chap. 19; 1938a, chap. 7; 1938b, chap. 9), where finality in experience is always tentative and ends are always means to something else.

This way of talking is actually rather odd in the present context, but it was imposed here by proponents of Thesis 9, not by James or Peirce in their presentations of pragmatism. Sensible (tangible) effects do after all have a kind of secure finality in the sense that every successful measurement, functionally speaking, has a fixed and distinct outcome. Consequences of beliefs conjoined with other beliefs are as fixed and distinct as logical inference is able to distinguish and fix them. Those are the notions of "ends" that matter to pragmatism at least so far as a pragmatist conception of meaning goes.

The relevant point here, though, is that while certain conceptions of the (odd) means-ends distinction were promoted by two prominent pragmatists, they may not be, strictly speaking, a component of pragmatism in the minimalist sense that is being presented here. They may be components rather of pragmatism conjoined with a particular conception of experience that may not be shared by all pragmatists—unless it might be shown, for instance, that that conception of experience (as growth, etc.) is a necessary feature of the conception of belief that in part constitutes pragmatism.

However that may turn out, it is clear that Thesis 9 fails by a long shot to capture a pragmatist conception of the relationship between means and ends. Indeed, any conception of the relationship between means and ends will most likely not be enough by itself to say what pragmatism is.

THESIS 10: *Pragmatism entails fallibilism, epistemological modesty, and doxastic flexibility.*

Certainly such virtues are not *sufficient* conditions for pragmatism. They are consistent with any number of conceptions of belief and meaning, pragmatist or otherwise. Unfortunately or not, these virtues may also not be *necessary* aspects of the conceptions of belief and meaning that constitute pragmatism (though both James and Peirce were fallibilists).

For instance, doxastic flexibility, as a virtue, may be thought of as a mean somewhere between doxastic rigidity and a disposition to freely waffle. Pragmatism does not guarantee the attainment of such virtues though it easily accommodates the spectrum of possibilities between which such moderate positions lie. To someone who insists exclusively on rigidity in one's beliefs, such accommodation makes pragmatism too flexible—as if *any* flexibility is too much flexibility. If one thinks only in these black-and-white terms, then to acknowledge the possibility of doxastic flexibility is ultimately to promote unconstrained free waffling in one's beliefs (to suit circumstances, etc.). The problem here, one may argue, is with thinking only in black-and-white terms, not with the possibility of legitimate doxastic flexibility as such. The important point is that pragmatism allows such flexibility, in varying degrees, though it may not *entail* it.

The same kind of point can be made regarding fallibilism as a point of balance between attitudes of blind certitude and blanket skepticism. Epistemological modesty likewise is a kind of mean between wishy-washy ambivalence (timidity) and smug sanctimony (vanity, hubris) with regard to one's own epistemic judgments. Pragmatism easily accommodates such spectra of possibilities but does not obviously provide a formula for identifying or attaining balance between the extremes of excess and deficiency. To entail such epistemological virtues, something else is needed to supplement pragmatism as a merely logical attitude—something like additional principles of a pragmatist virtue theory. In that case, it would be the virtue theory that recommends such virtues, not pragmatism by itself.

THESIS 11: *Pragmatism, with its emphasis on consequences, is just utilitarianism or some such form of consequentialism.*

That cannot be right. Pragmatism is a stance regarding the nature of belief and a corollary conception of meaning. It is not a particular normative ethical theory, whereas utilitarianism and other forms of consequentialism are simply and only that.

THESIS 12: *Pragmatism, particularly because of its flexibility, entails ethical emptiness and thus an absence of moral guidance.*

Consider the characterization of pragmatism as a particular conception of belief along with a conception of meaning that is both inferentialist and operationalist. This easily accommodates "the better angels of our nature." But there are plenty of shortsighted self-serving forms of pragmatism out there that are no less pragmatist for all that. Pragmatism as such is neither praiseworthy nor blameworthy. It is neither a virtue nor a vice (Reich 2009). Pragmatism as such is not an ethical doctrine; it is a methodological stance.

So are we to be concerned that elected officials who espouse pragmatism may be moral relativists, steering the ship of state with no moral compass (Aboulafia 2008)? By itself, espousing pragmatism, if one is true to classical American pragmatism, says pretty much nothing one way or the other about moral sensibilities. But if a "compass" metaphor is in order, then we should consider it carefully.

We—whether as citizens or simply as human beings—can be said to build ideologies to make our way through life the way some of us build ships to navigate the world's oceans. A ship's captain and crew utilize compasses and related navigation tools to know where they are and where they are going—using locally manageable tools to get a sense of realities well beyond the confines of the ship itself. External realities like the local direction of the planet's gravitational and magnetic fields simply are what they are, independently of how the ship is built. The ship's compass, if it is to be of any use, has to be built to move freely on a pivot, not rigidly attached so as to be aligned always and only with the ship's deck.

If the analogy holds, one's "moral compass" should be connected and oriented, but not *rigidly*, with one's ideological conceptual framework, having a flexible sensitivity to a larger reality that (very likely) one's ideology does not fully encompass. Having a "moral compass" that is able to "pivot" in response to the "rocking" of one's ideology is surely the way to go—that is, if a compass analogy is at all appropriate.

What this means, literally, is that moral judgment requires an objective sense of history (garnered through experience) and interpretive skills oriented to a humble but alert appreciation of the fact that past and current circumstances as well as long-term future consequences of our actions propagate well beyond what we are able to discern by present lights. An engrained humility in this respect could be that on which a fully charged and reliable moral compass would pivot—not to allow flimsy waffling but to permit measured responsiveness to "more things in heaven and earth ... than are dreamt of" in our ideology.

So what does this have to do with pragmatism? If anything, the point would be that pragmatism easily accommodates this kind of moral sensitivity because of the conception of belief that it promotes. In line with the discussion of Thesis 10, pragmatism does not entail doxastic flexibility but very readily accommodates it. This is all we need in order to be able to conclude that pragmatism (coupled consistently with, say, a plausible form of virtue ethics) easily accommodates a robust ethics with the only kind of moral compass that has objective validity. If a particular government provides no moral guidance or is marked by ethical emptiness, it will not be simply because it is pragmatist in its methods.

Again, pragmatism is ethically neutral. So is rationalism. So is empiricism. If a public official were to claim to be a rationalist, it would be odd to hear his or her critics complaining that this provides no moral guidance, or that because of this rationalism, the government's methods are marked by ethical emptiness. It would be just as odd, conversely, to think that rationalism by itself is sufficient to provide a distinctively unique ethical perspective. The same goes for a public official claiming to be an empiricist, or a pragmatist.

If pragmatism is to be recommended, it should be preferred simply on methodological if not logical grounds. While pragmatism does not guarantee intelligent decision making, it is to be preferred over other known philosophical attitudes for the simple reason that, arguably, for better or worse, it more broadly reflects human nature. In particular, pragmatism encapsulates the best (workable) features of both empiricism and rationalism, and rejects their respective one-sidedness. For what it's worth, operationalist-plus-inferentialist pragmatism is applicable in the arts as much as the sciences, ethics and law, politics, and even religion if James (1896) and Peirce (1908) have anything to say about it. The working sentiment here is that pragmatism provides the conditions by which one may be wholly enabled, epistemically speaking, using a full complement of human faculties rather than being methodologically disabled in one way or another.

CONCLUSION
Belief and Meaning

So what have we accomplished, and what's next? Numerous issues remain open. Based almost entirely on some key writings of its two originators, the discussion in chapters 1–4 above yielded a characterization of pragmatism not as a doctrine but as a philosophical attitude or stance. This philosophical stance is marked, namely, by a certain conception of belief that is bound up with a notion of habits as rules of action. This is in turn coupled with a corollary conception of meaning as formulated by the pragmatic maxim—a maxim concerning how best to clarify one's concepts and define one's terms. More specifically, chapter 4 yielded an operationalist-plus-inferentialist conception of meaning based on two readings of the pragmatic maxim, that is, as calling for both inferential coherence and operational concreteness.

An inferentialist reading of the pragmatic maxim is not news, whereas an operationalist reading has not been given that much attention over the passing years. This is largely the result of a lack of appreciation of the difference between pragmatism and empiricism, beginning with James himself. Later chapters above have thus focused on the contrast between pragmatism and empiricism, looking from several angles at the implications of an operationalist characterization of the "sensible effects" and their "practical bearings" that were emphasized in Peirce's earliest presentation of the maxim. Chapter 5 showed that neither Carnap's atomistic empiricism nor Quine's holistic empiricism captures the active nature of observation that is proposed by operationalist pragmatism. Chapters 6 and 7 looked in turn at the (inter)active nature of measurement and perception, respectively, which should not be unexpected given an operationalist reading of the pragmatic maxim. In more detail, chapter 8 looked at an example from the social sciences where the difference between empiricism and pragmatism matters significantly when it comes to trying to understand the nature of science at work. Chapter 9, in turn, showed how to apply a schematic version of Peirce's method for defining 'reality' and 'truth' (and 'knowledge', for that matter) to the words 'democracy' and 'justice'—the point being not to engage in political philosophy so much as to simply illustrate Peirce's method. Chapter 10 put a cap on this discussion by showing how a dozen different more or less common misconceptions of pragmatism can be set aside as such if one adopts the view of pragmatism developed here.

What all of this accomplishes is to say what pragmatism is, or at least *was*, so far as Peirce and James were concerned. What might be *gained* by adopting this view of pragmatism? The two-part summary of what pragmatism is that was provided at the beginning of chapter 10 is by some standards too loose to accomplish much, yet it will seem arcane, obscure, obtuse, and otherwise nitpicky relative to other standards, e.g., those set by the political press and political discourse at large. Pulled in these different directions, can we be any simpler about what pragmatism is and isn't? Can we say something philosophically substantial that mass media can digest and assimilate without destroying its content?

Realistically, that is doubtful. Partisan spin is an unavoidable aspect of political journalism. At the same time, philosophers, like politicians, are on the whole a contentious lot, always looking for weak spots in an opponent's arguments. This compels one to be careful about how one formulates a philosophical position. Such care—just as in the sciences and other professions—engenders manners of discourse that are, well, arcane, obscure, obtuse, and otherwise nitpicky relative to common everyday discourse. Such concerns have influenced the present discussion to the point that some kind of spin will perhaps be needed just to make it suitable for public consumption. Nevertheless, the view of pragmatism that has been promoted here is for the most part relatively simple and not entirely unfamiliar, at least initially. It entails, for instance, that our discernment of observable *facts* is essentially theory-laden (that is one thing that inferentialism says) *and* that getting at the facts in any case involves active engagement in the world (that is what operationalism says).

The present view of pragmatism goes a bit further, though, to say that, when it comes to operationally grounding our conceptions of the facts, what we have is activity all the way down. *And* when it comes to fathoming the significance and thus the facticity of any given fact, what we have is inferential commitments all the way out. How quickly simplicity fades into vagueness and complexity. On this score, it would appear that where attention needs to be directed is not toward simplification and folk slogans. Rather, the resulting complexity needs to be surveyed and squared away to whatever degree that is possible. This will require a detailed exploration and technical development of the preceding sketch of pragmatism.

How should we proceed to do that? Where does one begin? Proponents of pragmatism may embrace pragmatism because it naturally accommodates an emphasis on practical actions and consequences that affect human forms of life in substantial if not important ways. One might hold that, while science may give us knowledge and understanding of a sort, it is religion or politics or the arts that make our lives meaningful—and it is just such meaningfulness that pragmatism is designed to explain. Or one might hold that pragmatist philosophy at the very least should address social and political endeavors of vital importance, as if pragmatism were designed especially for social and political philosophy.

Conclusion: Belief and Meaning / 163

This was not Peirce's focus, nor was it James's or Dewey's for that matter (at least not exclusively), though of course classical pragmatists recognized the applicability of pragmatism to all such matters insofar as all such matters require clarification of one's ideas. The original classical American pragmatists, in their different ways, were as much or more likely to emphasize the logical and methodological character of pragmatism as such. Of course, what pragmatism *is* remains open to further development, particularly in the direction of making it more concrete—for instance, rendering it so as to make it more obviously applicable to a wider range of subject matters and professions. Various generic technical details will need to be explored further as one pursues such applications. In particular, Peirce's conception of belief as employed in his derivation of the pragmatic maxim is neither as clear nor as detailed as it could be. It requires further clarification especially if it is to be reconciled with a Jamesian conception of truth as warranted believability. In another direction, it is not exactly clear what to make of the dual formulation of the pragmatic maxim in operationalist and inferentialist terms that has been proposed here. If nothing else, the formulation is a step in the direction of better reconciling the apparently disparate views of Peirce and James.

APPENDIX A
Optical Surface Area

The trigonometric formula used to produce Figures 3 and 4 in chapter 7 is not exactly complicated though it is not particularly trivial either.

The optical surface area of a given bit of terrain surface is the area of the solid angle determined by the projection of that terrain surface onto a sphere centered at a given observation point—the fraction of total ambient light converging onto the observation point from the given terrain surface. Measured in steradians, a *solid angle* is a three-dimensional analogue of a two-dimensional *angle* measured in radians. A full circle subtends an angle of 2π radians, while a sphere altogether subtends a *solid* angle of 4π steradians. One steradian is subtended by any surface on a sphere whose area is equal to the square of the sphere's radius (whereas one radian is subtended by any arc on a circle whose length is equal to the circle's radius).

The solid angle subtended by an arbitrary surface D from a given observation point P is defined as the surface area Ω_D covered by the projection of D onto a *unit sphere* centered at P. This can be written as

$$\Omega_D = \iint_D \frac{\vec{n} \cdot \mathrm{d}a}{r^2}$$

where $\mathrm{d}a$ is the differential area of a patch of surface D, $\vec{n}$ is a unit vector from the origin of the sphere toward that patch, and r is the distance from the origin of the sphere to that patch. In spherical coordinates, this becomes

$$\Omega_D = \iint_D \sin\varphi \, \mathrm{d}\varphi \, \mathrm{d}\theta$$

with coaltitude (polar angle) φ and longitude (azimuth) θ. In Cartesian coordinates, we have

$$\Omega_D = \iint_D \frac{\cos\varphi \, \mathrm{d}x \, \mathrm{d}y}{(x^2 + y^2 + z^2)} = \iint_D \frac{z \, \mathrm{d}x \, \mathrm{d}y}{(x^2 + y^2 + z^2)^{3/2}}$$

where $\cos\varphi = z/r$ and $r^2 = x^2 + y^2 + z^2$. These surface integrals can be difficult to use, but there are simpler ways to calculate solid angles in the present case.

APPENDIX A: OPTICAL SURFACE AREA / 165

First, with respect to spheres other than the unit sphere, the solid angle Ω_D subtended by an arbitrary surface D from a given observation point P is defined as the *ratio* of the surface area covered by the projection of D onto the sphere (with radius h centered at P) to the surface area of the sphere altogether (the latter being equal to $4\pi h^2$)—just as the angle determined by an arc on a circle with radius h is the ratio of the arc length to the total length (circumference) of the circle ($2\pi h$).

Second, the surface area of a spherical triangle can be calculated using Girard's Theorem—named after Albert Girard (1595–1632), a Flemish mathematician who first published it in 1626 though a statement and proof of it was discovered and recorded in 1603 in the unpublished notebooks of the English mathematician Thomas Harriot (c1560–1621). This theorem states how the area of a spherical triangle depends on its interior angles. Namely, the surface area of a spherical triangle $\triangle ABC$ with respective interior angles α, β, γ on the surface of a sphere with radius h is given as follows:

$$\text{Area}(\triangle ABC) = h^2(\alpha + \beta + \gamma - \pi)$$

This simple formula states that the surface area of the triangle is equal to the square of the sphere's radius times the amount that the sum of the interior angles α, β, γ exceeds π. The formula in Girard's Theorem is thus sometimes referred to as Girard's Spherical Excess Formula.

It follows that the associated solid angle subtended by $\triangle ABC$ on the concentric unit sphere is:

$$\Omega_{\triangle ABC} = \frac{\text{Area}(\triangle ABC)}{4\pi h^2} = \frac{1}{4\pi}(\alpha + \beta + \gamma - \pi)$$

In particular, the solid angle $\Omega_{0,n,0,m}$ subtended by a rectangle with one corner at the origin, with side lengths n and m, and lying in a terrain-surface plane at a depth h from the center P of a sphere of radius h is composed of two spherical triangles sharing the diagonal from $\langle 0,0 \rangle$ to $\langle n,m \rangle$ as a common side (Figure 5). We can thus calculate $\Omega_{0,n,0,m}$ by calculating and adding the respective solid angles subtended by these two triangles. We will show how this is done for one of the triangles, namely, for the one with vertices $\langle 0,0 \rangle$, $\langle n,0 \rangle$, and $\langle n,m \rangle$. The other solid angle is calculated similarly.

To facilitate this calculation, we can employ the law of sines for spherical triangles, namely,

$$\frac{\sin a}{\sin \alpha} = \frac{\sin b}{\sin \beta} = \frac{\sin c}{\sin \gamma}$$

where angles α, β, γ and opposite arcs a, b, c are as depicted in Figure 6. In this case, point A is the projection of $\langle n, 0 \rangle$ onto the sphere with radius h and centered at P. Point B is the projection of $\langle n, m \rangle$ onto the same sphere. Point C is likewise

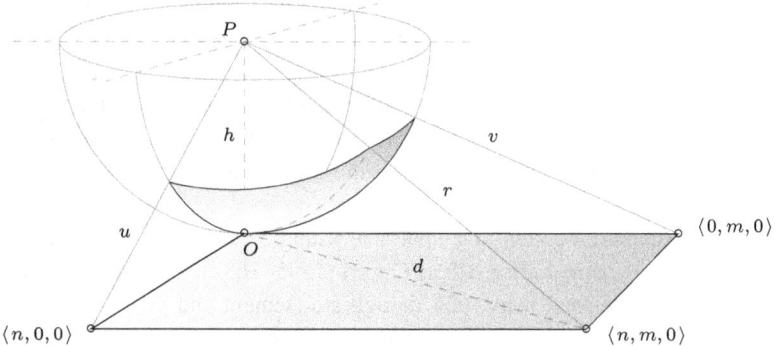

FIGURE 5: A solid angle subtended by a rectangular surface area with one corner at the toe-point O and another corner at the far point $\langle n, m, 0 \rangle$.

$d = \sqrt{n^2 + m^2}$ = step distance to the far corner $\langle n, m, 0 \rangle$.
$r = \sqrt{d^2 + h^2} = \sqrt{n^2 + m^2 + h^2}$ = distance from eye to far corner $\langle n, m, 0 \rangle$.
$u = \sqrt{n^2 + h^2}$ = distance from eye to corner point $\langle n, 0, 0 \rangle$.
$v = \sqrt{m^2 + h^2}$ = distance from eye to corner point $\langle 0, m, 0 \rangle$.

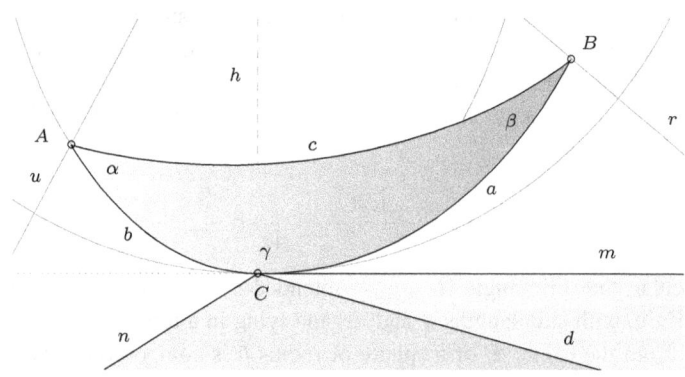

FIGURE 6: Girard's spherical excess formula and the law of sines for a spherical triangle $\triangle ABC$ with interior angles α, β, γ and respective opposite sides a, b, c:

$$\text{Area}(\triangle ABC) = h^2(\alpha + \beta + \gamma - \pi) \quad \text{and} \quad \frac{\sin a}{\sin \alpha} = \frac{\sin b}{\sin \beta} = \frac{\sin c}{\sin \gamma}$$

where arcs a, b, c lie on great circles of radius h centered at P.

the projection of $\langle 0, 0 \rangle$, which in the present case is just itself. The arcs a, b, c on the surface of the sphere lie on three respective great circles of radius h centered at P. Each arc thus determines a central angle in its respective great circle centered at P. An inspection of Figures 5 and 6 yields the following results:

APPENDIX A: OPTICAL SURFACE AREA / 167

$$\sin a = \frac{d}{r} \qquad \sin b = \frac{n}{u} \qquad \sin c = \frac{m}{r}$$

$$\sin \alpha = ? \qquad \sin \beta = ? \qquad \sin \gamma = \frac{m}{d}$$

where lengths h, n, m, d, r, u, and v are as depicted in Figure 5. The last four of these seven variables are easily calculated using the Pythagorean Theorem once the first three are given. We know the value of $\sin \gamma$ because arc b is tangent at point C to the respective side of the horizontal rectangle of which it is the projection, and arc a is tangent at point C to the horizontal rectangle's diagonal of length d running from $\langle 0, 0 \rangle$ to $\langle n, m \rangle$. The law of sines allows us to calculate $\sin \alpha$ and $\sin \beta$, namely:

$$\frac{\frac{d}{r}}{\sin \alpha} = \frac{\frac{n}{u}}{\sin \beta} = \frac{\frac{m}{r}}{\frac{m}{d}} = \frac{d}{r}$$

Thus $\sin \alpha = 1$ (so that $\alpha = \pi/2$, which may have already been obvious). And $\sin \beta = \frac{r}{d} \cdot \frac{n}{u}$. Then, the solid angle determined by this first spherical triangle is

$$\begin{aligned} \Omega_1 &= \frac{1}{4\pi}(\alpha + \beta + \gamma - \pi) \\ &= \frac{1}{4\pi}\left[\frac{\pi}{2} + \arcsin\left(\frac{r}{d} \cdot \frac{n}{u}\right) + \arcsin\left(\frac{m}{d}\right) - \pi\right] \\ &= \frac{1}{4\pi}\left[\arcsin\left(\frac{r}{d} \cdot \frac{n}{u}\right) + \arcsin\left(\frac{m}{d}\right) - \frac{\pi}{2}\right] \end{aligned}$$

Similarly, the solid angle determined by the other spherical triangle is

$$\Omega_2 = \frac{1}{4\pi}\left[\arcsin\left(\frac{r}{d} \cdot \frac{m}{v}\right) + \arcsin\left(\frac{n}{d}\right) - \frac{\pi}{2}\right]$$

Notice, next, that the sum of angles γ_1 and γ_2 in the two respective spherical triangles is $\pi/2$. That is,

$$\gamma_1 + \gamma_2 = \arcsin\left(\frac{m}{d}\right) + \arcsin\left(\frac{n}{d}\right) = \frac{\pi}{2}$$

With that fact in hand, we get the result that

$$\begin{aligned} \Omega_{0,n,0,m} &= \Omega_1 + \Omega_2 \\ &= \frac{1}{4\pi}\left[\arcsin\left(\frac{r}{d} \cdot \frac{m}{v}\right) + \arcsin\left(\frac{r}{d} \cdot \frac{n}{u}\right) - \frac{\pi}{2}\right] \end{aligned}$$

Finally, the solid angle of any rectangle that is in the first quadrant and is aligned with the axes can be calculated as follows:

$$\Omega_{n_1,n_2,m_1,m_2} = \Omega_{0,n_2,0,m_2} - \Omega_{0,n_2,0,m_1} - \Omega_{0,n_1,0,m_2} + \Omega_{0,n_1,0,m_1}$$

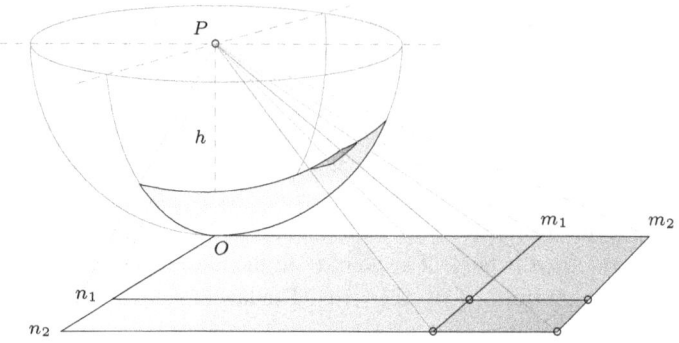

FIGURE 7: Solid angle subtended by an arbitrary rectangle.

assuming $0 \leq n_1 \leq n_2$ and $0 \leq m_1 \leq m_2$ (see Figure 7). This of course applies directly to each tile and each rectangular collection of tiles in Figures 2 and 3. The latter equation was used to produce the graphs in Figure 4 where

$$A_{n,m} = \Omega_{n-1,n,m-1,m}$$

for $1 \leq n, m$.

This kind of analysis has been used to calculate radiative heat transfer from the point position P_f of a fire to surfaces at various angles and distances from P_f (Forney 1991; Forney and Moss 1998). The analyses in these cases are entirely geometrical. The relevant "physics of heat" at most involves assumptions about heat radiating isotropically (uniformly in all directions) from the source point P_f.

In the present case we are using the same geometrical methods and results to analyze isotropic convergence of ambient light onto an observation point P. Ambient light and radiant light are to be distinguished when we consider the "physics of light" and the ecological nature of visual perception more broadly (Gibson 1979, chap. 4). Nevertheless the simple geometrical analysis outlined above is equally appropriate when applied to radiative heat from a point and to ambient light at a point so long as we do not equate the latter with an analysis of what is observed (seen, perceived, etc.) by an eye positioned at P. This analysis rather provides a model of what kind of information is available at point P—momentarily, on purely geometrical grounds, in a very simple (artificial) visual environment consisting exclusively of a regular array of step-sized square tiles stretching horizontally into the distance in a forward direction on a perfectly flat surface.

This analysis at bottom determines momentary optical surface area as a function of the lengths (distances) h, n, and m, the latter two in particular being measurable in terms of step lengths and otherwise being directly related to and thus informative as to affordances such as surface-walkability. Any number of other models may be involved in a visual creature's attunements to relations between optical surface area and surface orientation, depending on the nature of surfaces in actual environments typically negotiated by that creature. In the present case, the idea is that slight and not-so-slight movements of the point P relative to the given tiled surface will provide access to information comporting with the relation

$$A_{n,m} = \Omega_{n-1,n,m-1,m}$$

but across slight and not-so-slight changes of coordinates, respectively. If the "tiles" (as elements of texture) are reduced in size to minuscule fractions of a step length in length and width, then the effects of such changes of coordinates are respectively insensitive to alignments of perspective with sides of tiles. The large tile size in the preceding example is useful rather for accommodating a geometrical analysis. The more important point here is that as position P moves within such an environment, the relationship determining $A_{n,m}$ as a function of h, n, and m will nevertheless remain *the same*, i.e., *invariant*. However you might describe the surface—flat, horizontal, evenly textured, etc.—that invariance relation will be what is "sensed" in the flow of such information, and, e.g., a related degree of walkability may thus be what is "perceived," given other respective attunements involving relations among distance variables n and m and other variables (temporal, ergonomic, etc.) which have not yet been introduced into the discussion.

APPENDIX B
Material Inference

The discussion in chapter 5 suggested that operationalist pragmatism offers an alternative conception of (first-order) semantic structures based not on *things* but on *actions* and their *effects*. This idea was explored in chapter 7 as a way of characterizing Gibsonian notions of *invariants* and *affordances*, thus providing a non-trivial treatment of (types of) perceivable objects. The claim floated there was that the same strategy could be used—as a variation on a theme—to describe techniques for operationalizing the meanings of "hard words" and "intellectual concepts" in the sciences. To develop that kind of formal semantic theory would go a long way toward explaining what the pragmatic method is, or so the present claim goes.

Actually spelling this out is a challenge that operationalist pragmatism must contend with. Nothing conclusive will be accomplished here; but it will work against an operationalist reading of the pragmatic maxim if such an alternative formal semantics could not after all be made to work.

The pragmatic maxim (the operationalist version) says that conceptions are to be analyzed in terms of the effects of interactions with objects that purportedly fall under that concept, roughly speaking. Apparently this would be done in such a way as to specify what types of tangible effects will result from which types of actions: Do an action of type A_1 and you will get an outcome of type $Q_{11}^\top$ or $Q_{12}^\top$ or ... and *not* of type $Q_{11}^\bot$ or $Q_{12}^\bot$ or ...; *and/or* do an action of type A_2 and you will get an outcome of type $Q_{21}^\top$ or $Q_{22}^\top$ or ... and *not* of type $Q_{21}^\bot$ or $Q_{22}^\bot$ or ...; *and/or* do an action of type A_3 etc. Allegedly any given concept could be "made clear" by some such list of conceivable action/outcome specifications. This is well illustrated by Peirce's lithium example (pages 30f. above). Namely, much of what is involved in doing an action of type A_i consists of preparing certain initial circumstances and allowing matters to proceed independently from there. Presumably one would try to make this list as extensive as necessary to be as discriminating as one needs to be. This is the basic idea anyway of an operationalist reading of the pragmatic maxim.

But we may still question whether it is possible to capture these intuitions in a more systematic way. The idea of lists of operational recipes needs further clarification. How does this picture comport with the well-developed mathematical formalisms of Carnap and Quine? What can pragmatist operationalism do that mere extensionalism cannot? Whatever the differences may be, extensionalism by itself is inadequate in that, for one thing, it fails to explain material inference (or material deduction, more specifically).

Material inference is an old problem (Sellars 1953; Brandom 1994; Brigandt 2010). Brandom has explored an inferentialist account of conceptual content. Brigandt, on the other hand, has proposed an empiricist account. What might an operationalist account look like if the idea of lists of operational recipes is not adequate? Some examples will help to illustrate what is at issue.

For instance, how is it that we can justify the *deduction* that if a given thing θ is a diamond, then it is hard? Or first, more generally, how can we justifiably deduce that if a given thing θ is of kind P, then it is of kind Q? No first-order proof rule will sanction a deduction of a claim that θ is Q solely from a claim that θ is P for arbitrary predicate symbols P, Q. The standard inferentialist view is that we would have to stipulate some axioms beforehand that in some way establish an appropriate relationship between P and Q such that the claim that θ is Q could be deduced from those axioms in conjunction with the claim that θ is P. This was James's strategy in his discussion of substance and transubstantiation (pages 45ff. above) when, for the sake of discussion, he gives independent axiomatic status to belief in the *real presence* of Christ in the sacrament.

It is well known that this strategy will not work in general for first-order languages, due (for instance) to the Löwenheim-Skolem and compactness theorems for first-order languages. For example, it is not possible to characterize a standard conception of natural numbers inferentially using only a first-order axiomatic "vocabulary" since there are nonstandard models for any such axiomatization. The inferentialist strategy thus cannot focus solely on first-order languages.

Alternatively, if we are somehow given that the extension of 'P' is a subset of the extension of 'Q', then the claim that θ is Q is a semantic entailment or consequence of the claim that θ is P. This option of course begs the question regarding how such extensions are determined in the first place. Can they simply be stipulated once and for all as one would do in providing an interpretation of a given first-order language? That might work mathematically, but it will not fly in real-world scenarios where often we are working out what language to use as we work out how to interpret it.

For words denoting *kinds*, Peirce's strategy would be to *operationalize* 'P' and 'Q'. We know that much; and we have considered many examples. Look again at Peirce's later discussion of the hardness of diamonds (Peirce 1905b, EP2:356–357 and page 132 above). Peirce's focus there was on dispelling a nominalist reading of his 1878 presentation and illustration of the pragmatic maxim. In the midst of that argument we find the following remarks (quoted earlier but worth quoting again):

Being a diamond, it was a mass of pure carbon, in the form of a more or less transparent crystal (brittle, and of facile octahedral cleavage, unless it was of an unheard-of variety), which, if not trimmed after one of the fashions in which diamonds may be trimmed, took the shape of an octahedron, apparently regular (I need not go into minutiæ), with grooved edges, and probably with some curved faces. Without being subjected to any considerable pressure, it could be found to be insoluble, very highly refractive, showing under radium rays (and perhaps under "dark light" and X-rays) a peculiar bluish phosphorescence, having as high a specific gravity as realgar or orpiment, and giving off during its combustion less heat than any other form of carbon would have done. From some of these properties hardness is believed to be inseparable. For like it they bespeak the high polymerization of the molecule. (Peirce 1905b, EP2:356)

As already stated, this provides a preliminary outline for a precise and thorough operational definition of the word 'diamond'. Notice that in the last two sentences it also highlights a connection with a similarly precise and thorough operational definition of the word 'hard'. For the sake of discussion, we will say that such a definition of a given word specifies an *operational intension* of that word. In those last two sentences, Peirce is saying that some aspects of the given operational intension of 'diamond' are also aspects of an operational intension of 'hard' by way of an operational intension of the phrase 'highly polymerized'. For instance:

- The molecules in a *hard* material will be tightly bound either in a regular geometric lattice (e.g., crystals, metals, ice) or irregularly (e.g., glass). How to acquire evidence of such tight bonding would be part of the operational intension of the word 'hard', which can be specified in terms of resistance to penetration, indentation, or scratching as measured in various standard ways: Brinell tests, Mohs tests, Rockwell tests, etc.
- The molecules in a *highly polymerized* material will be tightly bound in a regular geometric pattern of respectively long chains of monomers—for which evidence may be obtained as results of protocols included in the operational intension of the word 'polymer'. More highly polymerized substances will have respectively higher melting and boiling temperatures, respectively higher viscosity and impact resistance, respectively reduced chain mobility and thus greater resistance to deformations and matrix breakup at respectively higher stresses and temperatures. A wide variety of laboratory techniques are typically used to determine these various properties of polymers.

So, the operational intension of 'diamond' shows such material to be a *very* highly polymerized material with long chains of carbon atoms arranged actually in a specific type of cubic lattice with strong macromolecular covalent bonding.

The operational intension of 'polymer' shows that very highly polymerized crystalline materials will have respectively greater resistances to elastic deformation, greater tensile strengths, etc.

It so happens that a positive correlation between tensile strength and hardness has been shown for a great many materials (born out by a number of different ways to measure tensile strength and hardness, respectively). This may be an essential piece of the inference from something being a diamond to something being hard if high polymerization is not itself directly correlated with hardness.

So here is the point. While we can use plain vanilla *set theory* as a primary technical tool in an extensional semantics, we have to be more cautious when characterizing operational intensions and formal relationships among operational intensions. What we want to emphasize here is that, as Peirce notes, some aspects of the operational intension of the term 'diamond' (particularly those that are aspects of the operational intension of the term 'high polymerization') are aspects of the operational intension of the term 'hard'.

Let $|P|$ be the extension of predicate symbol 'P', and let $\|P\|$ be its operational intension. Let '$\subseteq$' denote the standard subset relation, and let '$\sqsubseteq$' denote a yet-to-be-determined "part of" relation possibly holding among operational intensions. A schematic characterization of what we have now is that

$$|\text{diamond}| \subseteq |\text{highly polymerized}| \subseteq |\text{hard}|$$

while

$$\|\text{hard}\| \sqsubseteq \|\text{highly polymerized}\| \sqsubseteq \|\text{diamond}\|.$$

We would want to say then that the latter relations are what underwrite the *material inference* that diamonds are hard, which can be made explicit only if we have clearly$_3$ defined those terms in the sense of specifying operational intensions for those respective words. One might of course draw such valid material inferences more instinctively if one is *habituated* (routinized, attuned) to at least some variation of what is designated by these operational definitions. This supports the notion that, say, the "logic of perception" is literally just logic, period, though with reference to a particular characteristic range of natural inferential behaviors.

This schematic account of operational intensions and material inference ought to hold, then, for the discussion of 'truth' and 'knowledge' if not also 'democracy' and 'justice' in chapter 9. We may have to tweak some terminology here, but the operational intensions of the words 'truth' and 'knowledge' were couched in terms of the execution of *inquiries* with respective *fixed beliefs* as tangible results. A belief is a truth, or a true belief, just in case it could be "perfectly" fixed using scientific methods of justification (broadly conceived). A belief can be said to be known on exactly the same grounds except that the alleged knower actually would be cognizant if not the agent of some justificatory basis for such a claim. That was one of the main take-away points of the discussion in chapter 9, namely:

$$\|\text{truth}\| \sqsubseteq \|\text{knowledge}\|.$$

That is, claiming that p is *known* materially implies a claim that p is *true*, but (generally) not vice versa.

Likewise, considerable overlap was built into the operational definitions of 'democracy' and 'justice' in chapter 9. The definition of 'democracy' involved scientific inquiries of a community that *might* address the community's basic social, political, economic, and legal arrangements. The definition of 'justice' involved scientific inquiries of a community that *do* address such arrangements specifically (where the rules that constitute such arrangements are perfectly determined using scientific methods—the import of that being captured well enough by Rawls's depiction of the original position, etc.). Thus:

$$\| \text{democratic} \| \sqsubseteq \| \text{just} \|.$$

That is, if a functioning institution is said to be just, it may be materially inferred that it is democratic (simply because it has been established and is being maintained by perfectly scientific means). Again, this is a somewhat radical characterization of democracy in the way that it sets a rather high bar for what counts as such; but the main point here is to illustrate how material inference is tied to proposed operational intensions.

First-order Semantics

Inferentialist strategies cannot account for material inference in first-order languages given that first-order axiom systems tend to underdetermine their intended interpretations. At the same time, it has been argued that an operationalist strategy would be more successful. Explaining how that would work should suggest how we are to understand the operational-intensional part-of relation, '$\sqsubseteq$'.[1]

Consider the following simple example of material inference—simple in that it is easily couched in the familiar terms of "first-order" thing-thinking. Suppose you are told that a particular cup is sitting on a particular table and that the cup therefore is *above* the table. In one easy step, based on what is *meant* by the words 'above' and 'below'—based on their operational content—you may infer from what was said that the table is *below* the cup.

Let a denote the cup and let b denote the table. Then, in first-order extensional terms, the sentence Below(b, a) is a material deductive consequence of Above(a, b). Here is the interesting point. Both of these sentences are atomic, so a syntactic first-order proof theory alone cannot reflect this entailment relation without introducing non-trivial spatial axioms ad hoc, e.g., that $\forall x \forall y (\text{Above}(x, y) \leftrightarrow \text{Below}(y, x))$. Without such additional axioms, the usual slew of first-order rules of proof just do not handle this kind of "analytic" or "material" consequence.

Almost any first-order extensional language with interpreted predicate symbols can be used to illustrate a similar incompleteness of the respective first-order

---

[1] The following remarks are based on some technical work currently in progress (Burke ms). Though it soon took on a life of its own, the present book in fact began as an introduction to that work in an attempt to motivate and otherwise contextualize these technicalities.

proof system. How then do we account for the *meanings* of words like 'above' and 'below' so as to account in some principled way for such simple everyday inferences? This, as much as anything else, is a question of how to clearly specify the meanings of our words. This is exactly what Peirce's pragmatic maxim was designed to address.

So can we get a handle on this operationalist strategy in a formally rigorous way? Here is a proposal. As a first approximation, we need to work at two levels, distinguishing a lower-order "pre-language" and a higher-order "language" that includes the terms (like 'above' and 'below') that are to be defined or "clarified." As a simple though artificial example, (a) the higher-order language L could just as well be an extensional first-order language but where the task is to clearly$_3$ state what the various predicate symbols *mean*, i.e., to specify their operational intensions. (b) Those specifications will be couched in a language L_o that is a pre-language for L (such that L_o may itself not be verbal but might nevertheless be a "grammar" (so to speak) of the *logic* of perception—not spoken but embodied nonetheless in one's habits). At this point, much of the work that is required to explain material inference is to be done at this lower level (insofar as we are already familiar with the character of extensional first-order languages, for the most part).

First, then, at the lower level, we want to present a kind of lower-order grammar (and respective semantics) that takes operation-types (or action-types) and their respective outcome-types as primitive. This was exemplified by basic invariance detection activities in chapter 7, but we might also work with comparatively complex measurement activities (Brinell hardness tests, etc.) in this role. In this way, we will be able to accommodate operationalist pragmatism directly by grounding semantics in specifications of such lower-order grammars.

Second, at the higher level, we can then characterize the meaning of a given (first-order extensional) predicate symbol as a class of models for such lower-order grammars. The notion of lists or recipes of actions and results suggested by Peirce's lithium example would be recast then in terms of classes of models for lower-order operation-based grammars. These classes of models may be determined in any number of ways, though one simple way to do so, as was suggested in chapter 7, is to specify one or more lower-order "sentences" that must be true in all models in the class. These lower-order sentences would formulate law-like invariance relations among relevant sorted variables in the given lower-order operation-based "grammar."

It should be briefly noted that the distinction between lower-order and higher-order grammars here is vaguely analogous to the distinction in extensional semantics between various n^{th}-order grammars. In the present *pragmatist* view, though, there need be no "first" or "last" order of anything linguistic or grammatical. In particular, the grounds for any such delineation of orders is not geared to the standard distinction between things and their properties, or so-called particulars and universals. Rather, what might count as a so-called lower-order grammar is not arbitrary but is contingent upon the situation at hand in which operational clarification of terms is called for.

Three things that essentially characterize lower orders of grammars here are the requirements that (a) lower-order actions or operations must be executable as if they were black boxes (e.g., see page 105 above); (b) any detected tangible result of executing such an action is clearly distinguishable as such; *and* (c) each execution of such an action is a token thing-in-itself, suitable for being regarded as an "independent trial" (as in Foulis and Randall 1974a; 1974b; Randall and Foulis 1978a; 1978b). Of course, these are only functional stipulations. Black boxes might be opened up and analyzed so that a single lower-order operation may come into focus as a way of using a higher-order grammar. Likewise, a given higher-order grammar may in turn serve as the guts of lower-order operations assuming that an ability to *use* that higher-order grammar may become so engrained and routine as to work like a black box. Possible tangible outcomes might consist of various "sentences" in the higher-order grammar. Models for the higher-order grammar could also function as possible outcomes.

In any case, as already noted, parallels with the semantic view of scientific theories are not coincidental. In the two-level framework proposed here, the contents of first-order predicates will be characterized as "classes of models" of a certain type—namely, models for lower-order operation-based vocabularies and grammars of some appropriate type—whereas the semantic view of scientific theories is concerned with just that—scientific theories (Suppes 1960; 1962; 1967; Suppe 1977; 1989; Hughes 1996; van Fraassen 1980; 2000). The strategy here is simply to borrow the "class of models" idea, in place of Peirce's list suggestion, as the basis for developing a formal alternative to standard extensional semantics for a first-order language.

How and why such seemingly extravagant techniques should be employed may not be obvious when considering the diamonds-are-hard example, or the just-institutions-are-democratic-institutions example—or any other example that we have considered so far, for that matter. But we should note two things. First, Peirce's operational definition for 'diamond', for example, fails in many ways to capture the full operational content of that word though in some cases it may be more than enough by itself to ground useful inferences. The point is that, just as there are many ways to specify the extensions of a given predicate symbol depending on how the overall language is specified and what the universe of discourse may be, a word may have any number of operational intensions depending on the circumstances of its use. A plurality of operational intensions yields a plurality of models for the lower-order operation-based vocabularies and grammars in which they are couched—at least one such model per distinct operational intension, one would expect—and no one of them will trump the others except perhaps under specific concrete circumstances for which it happens to be tailored. More to the point, usually even a single operational intension will yield multiple models none of which is *the* single canonical or prototypical model. There need not be a single model in this sense for what an apple is, say. Nevertheless the word 'apple' should in principle be clearly definable by way of a plurality of alternative models—a class of models specifying a highly disjunctive operational intension.

Second, the technical framework outlined above should allow a fairly precise if not rich characterization of the operational-intensional part-of relation '⊑' (if not several such relations). Classes of models may be sub-classes of other classes, lower-order grammars may be fragments of other lower-order grammars, and so forth. Such relationships are of course generally analyzable in familiar set-theoretic terms.

A Semantic View of Legal Concepts

If it is not yet clear, the following example might better illustrate the "class-of-models" notion and how it possibly opens up a fruitful account of material inference. There is not enough space to develop the example at great length, but we can say enough here to get the main idea across.

Specifically, consider the nature of common-law legal concepts. By "common law" is meant a system of laws (precedents) based on judicial decisions and custom (as opposed to statutory and regulatory law, established by legislative and executive branches of government, respectively). This means that prior legal decisions serve as authoritative guides or justifications in subsequent cases with similar or analogous issues, facts, etc. A "precedent" is a legal principle or rule initially established in and by way of such a prior case and is to some degree authoritative in deciding cases of the same or similar type (their degree of authority presumably being somehow correlated with the degree of similarity of the respective cases).

> Common law courts generally explain in detail the legal rationale behind their decisions, with citations of both legislation and previous relevant judgments, and often an exegesis of the wider legal principles. The necessary analysis (called *ratio decidendi*), then constitutes a precedent binding on other courts; further analyses not strictly necessary to the determination of the current case are called *obiter dicta*, which constitute persuasive authority but are not technically binding. (Wikipedia 2012b)

Aspects of a given case will fall near or under various *legal concepts* that, in a glossary or dictionary for the language of common law, would be defined in terms precipitated from relevant prior cases. The legal concept of *fraud*, for instance, will have arisen in various cases and will have been formed and refined by its use in statements of the authoritative principles established in legal decisions respective of those cases. Such a glossary of common-law legal concepts, like any glossary or dictionary, would be a tangled affair with virtually everything inferentially defined in terms of everything else—exemplifying in essence an inferential-role semantics. But it is not just a glass-bead structure given that the principles which are couched in terms of such concepts are themselves derived from actual cases. Ultimately it is the actual dispositions of cases that are authoritative whereas respective precedents qua principles are hermeneutically (re)formulated and (re)interpreted as generalizations designed to apply to other cases *of that type*. Precedents thus are designed to reflect a type of case though they are derived from and oriented to actual token cases.

Then, to see how operational intensions of common-law legal concepts can be thought of as "classes of models" defined on some kind of lower-order operation-based proto-legal pre-language, consider an operation-based language in which the basic operations are various distinct legal procedures typically employed in legal cases with respective aspects of legal judgments serving as tangible results.

Specifically, following Lamond 2008, we might assume for the sake of simplicity that there are five kinds of operations associated respectively with the five aspects of a legal judgment:

- a recitation of the facts of the case;
- an identification of the legal issue to be resolved by the court;
- a rationale for the resolution of that issue, citing legislation and previous relevant judgments, and possibly including an exegesis of wider legal principles;
- the ruling resolving the issue put before the court; and
- the outcome of the case (which follows from the ruling).

Every actual token case is unique and yet is in some degree similar to other such cases so far as these five aspects of legal judgments are concerned. Each of these five operations may be conveniently regarded as a distinctive kind of inquiry designed to yield its respective piece of the legal judgment.

Each of these aspects of a given legal judgment must be *written* and thus is able to count as a *tangible* (sensible) result of having actually resolved the given case. It is for good reason that cases that do not result in written judgments do not establish precedents for future court decisions—for the same reasons that hearsay usually is not acceptable evidence (in a court of law or otherwise). The writing must also be clearly presented in the proper five-part format so that legal judgments may be compared and contrasted point-for-point on various common grounds.

Further still, these tangible results must have been produced by an appropriate "court of record." That is, it is not just the tangible nature of the result that serves to establish its legitimacy as a precedent. *How* that tangible result was obtained (the activity by which it was produced) also matters. For instance, a published account of the result independently devised and written by a newspaper reporter would not serve this purpose, strictly speaking, insofar as the tangible writing did not come about in the way specified by legal protocols. Token cases are like executions of experiments according to specific preestablished procedural methods. Newspaper reporters may witness but are not the executors of such experiments. Even if a newspaper article were by happenstance to match the written legal judgment word for word, it would not legitimately serve to establish a precedent because it would not have been produced in the right way. Both the tangible result and the methods used to produce the tangible result must be in order.

Thus we might assume for instance that there is some kind of written *legal manual* specifying how to recite facts of a case, how to identify legal issues, and so forth, so that there are clear protocols and standards for how each of the five aspects of a legal judgment are to be produced and presented. This will not be a mechanical process, but it should be principled nonetheless.

So, to construct a lower-order proto-legal pre-language (with respect to which individual legal cases may be regarded as (sets of) *models*), we may associate one or more *variables* with each of the five types of operations mentioned above. Any fact-finding process fitting the manual's specifications may be employed to obtain information included in the recitation of facts of the case, etc. Each of these variables may be thought of as ranging over a huge set of possible values, namely, a set of possible tangible results that could be included in that respective part of the legal judgment. The range of possible outcomes in each instance is limited only by the grammar of the written script (e.g., English) and whatever counts, respectively, as a statement of fact, as a statement of legal principle, and so forth.

Assume, further, that one if not the only *predicate symbol* in this lower-order pre-language is the identity symbol. With that alone, a language may then be recursively constructed from simple atomic formulas stating, e.g., that the value of a given variable is such-and-so (which will be true in a given case if the corresponding operation was executed and the value qua tangible result was admissible in the legal judgment), or that the value of one given variable and that of a second given variable of the same sort are the same. A recursive construction of a lower-order language might involve only truth-functional connectives but, voilà, we have a simple lower-order five-sorted proto-legal pre-language.

Again for the sake of simplicity, assume that a model for this pre-language will be a valuation defined over the given variables (mapping a specific outcome-type to at least one variable for each of the five kinds of operations)—which is essentially a truth assignment (a row in a truth-table) for some or all possible atomic formulas. The written legal judgment for any given case will be represented in this way by a set of these truth assignments if we allow partial truth assignments—which is a prudent thing to do given that legal discourse is in fact continually changing.

A *semantic view of legal concepts* would hold then that each truth assignment in effect determines a *type* of case, and any set of these truth assignments potentially determines a *legal concept*. In practice, certain sets of these truth assignments would stand out insofar as their member truth assignments would exhibit common features or otherwise resemble one another in some way.

One way to pick out "interesting" types of cases would be to use some kind of search mechanism or query tool, perhaps where the corpus of legal judgments is accessible in some digital form that supports automated queries. Searches for phrases like, say, "corporate fraud" or "actionable negligence" in one or more of the five parts of any judgment (record) in the search space (database) would yield respective subsets of these judgments. If one wants to survey the current operational content of the legal phrase 'corporate fraud', say, one might begin by compiling a compendium of some or all of the cases in the respective search results. Such searches may of course be quite detailed. One might search for legal judgments in which specific atomic or non-atomic sentences in the language are designated as true, or when certain atomic sentences come out false in cases where the legal issue is such-and-so, and so forth.

Notice, if it is not already obvious, that legal concepts in this sense are the operational contents of legal terms and phrases appearing in the very script that is used to write out the outcomes of the five respective types of legal inquiries. There is an interesting kind of reflexivity at work here that may not be typical, but we need not at present address the issue of whether or not it is typical. A distinctive feature of this particular illustration, though, is that, in the lower-order *proto-legal pre-language*, the possible outcomes of legal operations may be regarded as *quotations* of statements occurring in a respective higher-order *legal language*—the very language whose terms are targeted for "clarification." Or to put it another way, the operational clarification (definition) of terms in a given *legal language* will in one way or another be composed of *quotations* of statements in that same legal language.

It is interesting to note, moreover, that the *operational* content of various higher-order legal terms (words, phrases, etc.) will largely coincide with the *inferential* content of respective terms appearing (quoted) within scripted outcomes in the lower-order proto-legal pre-language. Essentially, an analysis of a compendium of the cases occurring among given search results for a specific legal phrase might proceed by looking at how that phrase is used (the function role of that phrase) in the various judgments appearing in the search results for that phrase. That collection of judgments (and thus cases) loosely establishes, as it were, a respective lower-order *functional space of usage*—one that potentially extends outside of a respective collection of search results insofar as those judgments may refer if not defer to other judgments that are relevant but do not literally use the exact search phrase and therefore do not themselves appear in the current search results. The inferential content of lower-order phrases will thus be constrained by the nature and the extent of this functional space of usage—the latter making sense only by virtue of the fact that *usage* is grounded in tangible results of the executions of actual token cases (qua experiments).

In this kind of framework, the matter of *material inference* with regard to legal concepts becomes fairly interesting and not exactly simple. It would involve, for instance, relationships among search spaces for different legal phrases in the permanent record. Many of the actual cases that are referred to in the search results for the term 'trespass', say, would be among the search results for other terms, for instance, 'injury'. *The* legal concept of *trespass* will almost certainly not be fully captured by any one such set of search results but we may suppose that the set of cases represented in these results, as a set of models, does determine at least a preliminary working conception that we might label as *trespass*$_1$. Similarly, the set of search results for 'injury' will yield a preliminary notion of *injury*$_1$. Depending on one's aim, more refined searches targeted in suitably specific ways will yield corresponding modifications to such search results. In any case, the notions of *trespass*$_1$ and *injury*$_1$ are sufficiently specific to make a couple of points about material inference in the present context.

Namely, material inferential connections between *trespass*$_1$ and *injury*$_1$ might be found in various relationships between the respective sets of cases that characterize these two notions. There is, again, an interesting wrinkle here in that these sets directly determine (as a first approximation) both the extensions (in the domain of past cases) and the intensions of the respective legal terms. The extensions of the terms will be (or include) the actual token cases that are referred to in the search results, understanding that such extensions may change as cases are subsequently added to the search space. The intensions of the terms will consist of a related set of case *types* (models), instances of which are exemplified by the token cases. Each such case determines a type of case, and the set of these types (as models for the lower-order pre-language) constitutes the operational intension of the respective legal term. One would suspect that purely formal set-theoretic relations between the respective sets of cases in either sense will tend to indicate substantive connections between the two legal concepts.

This does not exhaust the kinds of analyses that are possible in an effort to characterize material inferential connections between such concepts. The various cases that are involved are presented as models defined on a lower-order operation-based proto-legal pre-language such that the written results that are available for analysis will exhibit other tangible features besides those involving trespass or injury. Beyond the sets of cases as such, relationships among these sets of tangible features may also be fruitfully explored to uncover material connections between *trespass*$_1$ cases and *injury*$_1$ cases. The analysis would still be set-theoretic, as it were, but the emphasis would rather be on sets of *features* exhibited by cases in the respective search results.

The peculiar features of legal languages are especially interesting, but they are also perhaps atypical. To say much more about the use of operationalist methods in the legal arena calls for starting over and developing the preceding discussion in greater detail—in which case we will stop here. The main point presently is only a proposal for how common-law legal concepts may be characterized by a collection of cases, or more accurately, case-types. This is, essentially, a *semantic view of legal concepts*.

For what it is worth, one could ask whether and how any of this might pertain to Holmes's original version of legal pragmatism. Consider his famous statement that "[t]he life of the law has not been logic: it has been experience" (Holmes 1881, 1). This reflects Peirce's 1878a point that Cartesian "clarity and distinctness" are by themselves insufficient means for explicating one's terms and should be supplemented with higher grades of "clearness" grounded in practical considerations. When read in context, Holmes's point in making such a statement also parallels the contrast that is typically made between the so-called *semantic* view of scientific theories and the *syntactic* view proposed by logical positivists and logical empiricists. Namely, scientific theory may be cast as a collection of theorems derived from an appropriate axiomatization couched in some characteristic language (the syntactic view) or else as a possibly motley collection of *models* defined over any number of workable languages (the semantic view). In the latter case, the emphasis is on models rather than on theorems. As with scientific theories, so it is with legal concepts: the life of the law has not been in proving theorems but in working out in detail the tangible results of actual cases.

Consider another famous remark that "[i]t is the merit of the common law that it decides cases first, and determines the principle afterwards" (Holmes 1870, 1). This is consistent with the present view in the following sense. Statements initially presented by litigants in a given case will help to establish a preliminary vocabulary and thus a range of relevant legal concepts that may bear on that case. But eventually it will very likely turn out in the course of a trial that the token case is sufficiently unique that any precedent that *it* establishes may include modifications of if not conflicts with those of prior cases. Even if the rationale for the resolution of the respective issue turns up nothing new or different from those of prior cases, that is something that is affirmed only after the case is decided by virtue of following out the various contingent twists and turns of the actual legal proceedings.

The preceding discussion of legal concepts of course only suggests a kind of analysis that would proceed more easily if it were to begin more easily. In light of various complexities associated with the legal arena, one might instead want to focus first on simpler examples, e.g., simple extensional first-order languages as discussed earlier.

Admittedly, first-order grammars may seem like an odd place to focus one's attention. An operationalist reading of the pragmatic maxim seems most at home in places like quantum physics, social and behavioral sciences, or wherever it is obvious that interactive observational activities affect observed outcomes.

The claim, though, is that the pragmatic maxim is broadly and generally applicable across the board. The point of previous discussions has been to argue for the primacy of an operationalist orientation to actions and results versus an extensionalist orientation to things. This does not mean that we have to begin with examples where the observer effect, say, is a persistent complication. We might be better off to start simply, not to preclude such applications but to pursue an understanding of pragmatist methodology a few small steps at a time until we get the hang of it.

The present claim, again, is that any style of analysis that can say what we mean by comparatively simple words like 'above' and 'below' should be applicable to virtually any word or concept in any type of discourse (with variations and refinements as needed). As outlined above, the pragmatic maxim emphasizes types of actions and their results (their tangible effects) as the elements in terms of which meanings of words (like 'above' and 'below', 'trespass' and 'injury') are best clarified. By pragmatist lights, types of actions and respective types of tangible effects resulting from implementing such actions would be the initial focal point of semantic analysis—as opposed to the now standard focus on "things" and sets thereof. The latter familiar extensionalist approach to semantic matters makes sense, of course, and is fully available to supplement an operationalist semantics. In that case, the extensionalist approach would no longer need to be regarded as methodologically fundamental or basic, nor would it have to do all of the work that it has been expected to do.

Bibliography

Aboulafia, Mitchell. 2008. Obama's Pragmatism (or Move over Culture Wars, Hello Political Philosophy). *Up@Night*, 2008 December 14. ⟨http://msa4.wordpress.com/⟩.

Aboulafia, Mitchell. 2009a. Bronx on the Court, Empathy, and Obama's Pragmatism. *Up@Night*, 2009 May 27. ⟨http://msa4.wordpress.com/⟩.

Aboulafia, Mitchell. 2009b. Obama and Pragmatism. *Up@Night*, 2009 June 3. ⟨http://msa4.wordpress.com/⟩.

Aboulafia, Mitchell. 2009c. Obama: Conservative, Liberal, or Ruthless Pragmatist? *Up@Night*, 2009 May 7. ⟨http://msa4.wordpress.com/⟩.

Aboulafia, Mitchell. 2009d. Obama's Pragmatism and the Stimulus Package. *Up@Night*, 2009 February 2. ⟨http://msa4.wordpress.com/⟩.

Abrams, Laura S. 2003. Social Settlements. In Paula S. Fass, ed., *Encyclopedia of Children and Childhood in History and Society*, 762–764. Detroit: Gale Cengage Learning.

Acronym Required. 2010. Obama, The Disappointment? Acronym Required blog, 2010 January 21. ⟨http://acronymrequired.com/⟩.

Adams, Frederick, and Kenneth Aizawa. 2001. The Bounds of Cognition. *Philosophical Psychology* 14:43–64.

Adams, Frederick, and Kenneth Aizawa. 2008. *The Bounds of Cognition*. Malden, MA: Blackwell Publishing Ltd.

Addams, Jane. 1893a. The Objective Value of a Social Settlement. In Henry C. Adams, ed., *Philanthropy and Social Progress*. New York: Thomas Y. Crowell. Reprinted in Elshtain 2002, 29–45.

Addams, Jane. 1893b. The Subjective Necessity for Social Settlements. In Henry C. Adams, ed., *Philanthropy and Social Progress*. New York: Thomas Y. Crowell. Reprinted in Elshtain 2002, 14–28.

Addams, Jane. 1899. The Subtle Problems of Charity. *Atlantic Monthly* 83:163–178. Reprinted in Elshtain 2002, 62–75.

Addams, Jane. 1908. Chicago Settlements and Social Unrest. *Charities and the Commons* 20:155–166. Reprinted in Elshtain 2002, 205–223.

Addams, Jane. 1910. *Twenty Years at Hull-House*. New York: Macmillan. Reissued by University of Illinois Press (Urbana, 1990).

Answers.com. 2006. Settlement House Movement. In *Encyclopedia of American History*. New York: Answers Corporation. ⟨http://www.answers.com/topic/settlement-house-movement⟩, accessed May 18, 2009.

Austin, John L. 1950. Truth. *Proceedings of the Aristotelean Society, Supplementary Volume* 24:111–128. Reprinted in *Philosophical Papers*, ed. J. O. Urmson and Geoffrey L. Warnock (Oxford: Oxford University Press, 1961).

Austin, John L. 1962. *How to Do Things with Words*. Cambridge, MA: Harvard University Press.

Ayer, Alfred J. (ed.). 1959. *Logical Positivism*. Glencoe IL: Free Press.

Ayer, Alfred J. 1968. *The Origins of Pragmatism: Studies in the Philosophy of Charles Sanders Peirce and William James*. San Francisco: Freeman, Cooper.

Bain, Alexander. 1855. *The Senses and the Intellect*. London: J. W. Parker.

Bain, Alexander. 1859. *The Emotions and the Will*. London: J. W. Parker.

Barwise, Jon. 1985. Model-Theoretic Logics: Background and Aims. In Barwise and Feferman 1985, 1–23.

Barwise, Jon, and Sol Feferman (eds.). 1985. *Model-Theoretic Logics*. New York: Springer-Verlag.

Berkowitz, Peter. 2009. Pragmatism Obama Style: Surprise, It's Left-Wing. *The Weekly Standard,* 14(31): May 4, 2009.

Bernstein, Richard J. 1989. Pragmatism, Pluralism, and the Healing of Wounds. *Proceedings and Addresses of the American Philosophical Association* 63(3):5–18. Presidential address delivered to the Eastern Division Meeting of the American Philosophical Association, December 29, 1988. Reprinted in *The New Constellation: The Ethical-Political Horizons of Modernity/Postmodernity*, 323–339 (Cambridge, MA: MIT Press, 1992).

Bernstein, Richard J. 2010. *The Pragmatic Turn*. Cambridge: Polity Press.

Boas, Franz. 1897. *The Social Organization and the Secret Societies of the Kwakiutl Indians*. From the Report of the United States National Museum for 1895. Washington, DC: Smithsonian Institution.

Boas, Franz. 1911. *The Mind of Primitive Man*. New York: Macmillan. Revised edition, 1938.

Boersema, David. 2009. *Pragmatism and Reference*. Cambridge, MA: MIT Press.

Brandom, Robert B. 1994. *Making It Explicit: Reasoning, Representing, and Discursive Commitment*. Cambridge, MA: Harvard University Press.

Brandom, Robert B. 2000. *Articulating Reasons: An Introduction to Inferentialism*. Cambridge, MA: Harvard University Press.

Brandom, Robert B. 2008. *Between Saying and Doing: Towards an Analytic Pragmatism*. Oxford: Oxford University Press.

Bridgman, Percy Williams. 1927. *The Logic of Modern Physics*. New York: Macmillan.

Bridgman, Percy Williams. 1936. *The Nature of Physical Theory*. Princeton, NJ: Princeton University Press.

Bridgman, Percy Williams. 1938. *The Intelligent Individual and Society*. New York: Macmillan.

Bridgman, Percy Williams. 1950. *Reflections of a Physicist*. New York: Philosophical Library.

Bridgman, Percy Williams. 1959. *The Way Things Are*. Cambridge, MA: Harvard University Press.

Brigandt, Ingo. 2010. Scientific Inference Is Material Inference: Combining Confirmation, Discovery, and Explanation. *International Studies in the Philosophy of Science* 24:31–43.

Bronsther, Jacob. 2009. The Emptiness of Obama's Pragmatism. *Christian Science Monitor*, May 26, 2009: Opinion, page 9.

Bruner, Jerome S. 1960. *The Process of Education*. Cambridge, MA: Harvard University Press.

Bruner, Jerome S. 1966a. On Cognitive Growth. In Jerome S. Bruner, Rose R. Oliver, and Patricia M. Greenfield, eds., *Studies in Cognitive Growth: A Collaboration at the Center for Cognitive Studies*, 1–67. New York: John Wiley.

Bruner, Jerome S. 1966b. *Toward a Theory of Instruction*. Cambridge, MA: Harvard University Press.

Burke, F. Thomas. 2004. The Logical Necessity of Ideologies. In Elias L. Kahlil, ed., *Dewey, Pragmatism, and Economic Methodology*. London: Routledge; and Great Barrington, MA: American Institute for Economic Research.

Burke, F. Thomas. 2010. Empiricism, Pragmatism, and the Settlement Movement. *The Pluralist* 5(3):75–90.

Burke, F. Thomas. ms. *Pragmatism and Dynamic Logic: A Sorted Affair*. A work in progress.

Burke, F. Thomas, and Stephen W. Everett. 2013. Social-Psychological Externalism and the Coupling/Constitution Fallacy. In F. Thomas Burke and Krzysztof Piotr

Skowroński, eds., *George Herbert Mead in the Twenty-First Century*. Lanham, MD: Lexington Books.

Butler, Brian. 2010. Obama, Sunstein, Dewey and the Pragmatic Cost-Benefit State. Presented at the Fifth Atlantic Coast Pragmatist Workshop, UNC Charlotte, April 2010.

Carnap, Rudolf. 1928. *Der logische Aufbau der Welt*. Berlin-Schlachtensee: Weltkreis Verlag. English translation by Rolf A. George, *The Logical Structure of the World* (Berkeley: University of California Press, 1967).

Carnap, Rudolf. 1936. Testability and Meaning. *Philosophy of Science* 3(4):419–471 and 4(1):1–40 (1937). Corrected version, with extended bibliography, published by the Yale University Graduate Philosophy Club (New Haven, CT, 1950).

Carnap, Rudolf. 1950. *The Logical Foundations of Probability*. Chicago: University of Chicago Press.

Carnap, Rudolf. 1952. *The Continuum of Inductive Methods*. Chicago: University of Chicago Press.

CBS News. 2012. Rahm Emanuel: Washington is Dysfunctional. Partial transcription of an interview aired 2012 July 9 on *CBS Evening News with Scott Pelley*. New York: CBS Interactive Incorporated ⟨http://www.cbsnews.com/⟩.

Chang, Hasok. 2009. Operationalism. In *Stanford Encyclopedia of Philosophy*. ⟨http://plato.stanford.edu/entries/operationalism/⟩.

Clark, Andy. 1993. *Associative Engines: Connectionism, Concepts, and Representational Change*. Cambridge, MA: MIT Press.

Clark, Andy. 2001. Reasons, Robots, and the Extended Mind. *Mind and Language* 16(2):121–145.

Cohen, Patricia. 2010. In Writings of Obama, a Philosophy is Unearthed. *The New York Times,* October 28, 2010 ⟨http://www.nytimes.com/2010/10/28/books/28klopp.html⟩.

CPR. 2008. Cost-Benefit Analysis: Over-reliance on a Flawed Approach. Washington, DC: Center for Progressive Reform ⟨http://www.progressivereform.org/costBenefit.cfm⟩.

Crasnow, Sharon L. 2000. How Natural Can Ontology Be? *Philosophy of Science* 67:114–132.

Critchley, Simon. 2008. The American Void. *Harper's* 317.1902(Nov. 2008):17–20.

Deegan, Mary Jo. 1990. *Jane Addams and the Men of the Chicago School, 1892–1918*. Piscataway, NJ: Transaction Publishers.

Devitt, Michael. 1981. *Designation*. New York: Columbia University Press.

Dewey, John. 1916. The Pragmatism of Peirce. *Journal of Philosophy, Psychology, and Scientific Methods* 13:709–715. Reprinted in MW10:71–78.

Dewey, John. 1922. *Human Nature and Conduct: An Introduction to Social Psychology.* New York: Henry Holt. Reprinted in MW14.

Dewey, John. 1925. *Experience and Nature.* Chicago: Open Court. Reprinted in LW1.

Dewey, John. 1929. *The Quest for Certainty: A Study of the Relation of Knowledge and Action.* New York: Minton, Balch. Reprinted in LW4.

Dewey, John. 1934. *Art as Experience.* New York: Henry Holt. Reprinted in LW10.

Dewey, John. 1938a. *Experience and Education.* New York: Macmillan. Reprinted in LW13:1–62.

Dewey, John. 1938b. *Logic: The Theory of Inquiry.* New York: Henry Holt. Reprinted in LW12.

Dewey, John. 1976–1980. *The Middle Works*, vol. 1–15 (1899–1924). Ed. Jo Ann Boydston. Carbondale: Southern Illinois University Press. Citations of items in this edition are indicated by MW followed by volume and page numbers.

Dewey, John. 1981–1990. *The Later Works*, vol. 1–17 (1925–1953). Ed. Jo Ann Boydston. Carbondale: Southern Illinois University Press. Citations of items in this edition are indicated by LW followed by volume and page numbers.

Dionne, E. J., Jr. 2009a. Audacity Without Ideology. *The Washington Post,* January 15, 2009. Editorial, page A19.

Dionne, E. J., Jr. 2009b. Left of Center-Right. *The Washington Post,* March 12, 2009. ⟨http://www.washingtonpost.com/⟩.

Dunbar, Robin I. M. 1997. *Grooming, Gossip, and the Evolution of Language.* Cambridge, MA: Harvard University Press.

Eddington, Arthur Stanley. 1928. *The Nature of the Physical World.* New York: Macmillan.

Einstein, Albert. 1916. *Relativity: The Special and General Theory.* Authorized English translation by Robert W. Lawson. New York: Crown Publishers.

Elshtain, Jean Bethke (ed.). 2002. *The Jane Addams Reader.* New York: Basic Books.

Engel, Lawrence J. 2002. Saul D. Alinsky and the Chicago School. *Journal of Speculative Philosophy* 16(1):50–66.

Everett, Stephen. 2013. *Vehicle Externalism, the Coupling-Constitution Fallacy, and Dewey.* PhD thesis. University of South Carolina.

Fine, Arthur. 1984. The Natural Ontological Attitude. In Jarrett Leplin, ed., *Scientific Realism,* 83–107. Berkeley: University of California Press.

Fisch, Max H. 1964. Was There a Metaphysical Club in Cambridge? In Edward C. Moore and Richard S. Robin, eds., *Studies in the Philosophy of Charles Sanders Peirce, Second Series,* 3–22. Amherst: University of Massachusetts Press.

Fisch, Max H. 1981. Was There a Metaphysical Club in Cambridge?—A Postscript. *Transactions of the Charles S. Peirce Society* 17(2):128–130.

Fischer, Marilyn. 2009. Interpretation as Settlement Discourse: A Context for Addams's Analysis of Averbuch. A work-in-progress presented at the Fourth Atlantic Coast Pragmatist Workshop, University of South Carolina, 2009.

Fish, Stanley. 2010. Pragmatism's Gift. *The New York Times,* March 15, 2010: Opinionator Blog. ⟨http://opinionator.blogs.nytimes.com⟩.

Flower, Elizabeth, and Murray Murphey. 1977. *A History of Philosophy in America.* New York: G. P. Putnam.

Fodor, Jerry A. 1975. *The Language of Thought.* New York: Thomas Y. Crowell. Paperback edition: Cambridge MA: Harvard University Press (1979).

Fodor, Jerry A. 1983. *The Modularity of Mind: An Essay on Faculty Psychology.* Cambridge, MA: MIT Press.

Fodor, Jerry A., and Zenon W. Pylyshyn. 1981. How Direct is Visual Perception? Some Reflections on Gibson's 'Ecological Approach'. *Cognition* 9:139–196.

Forney, Glenn P. 1991. Computing Radiative Heat Transfer Occurring in a Zone Fire Model. Technical Report NISTIR 4709. US Department of Commerce, National Institute of Standards and Technology.

Forney, Glenn P., and William F. Moss. 1998. A Method for Computing Heat Transfer Between Connected Compartments in a Zone Fire Model. Technical Report NISTIR 6190. US Department of Commerce, National Institute of Standards and Technology.

Foulis, David J., and Charles H. Randall. 1974a. Empirical Logic and Quantum Mechanics. *Synthese* 29:81–111.

Foulis, David J., and Charles H. Randall. 1974b. The Empirical Logic Approach to the Physical Sciences. In A. Hartkämper and H. Neumann, eds., *Foundations of Quantum Mechanics and Ordered Linear Spaces,* 230–249. Marburg: Springer-Verlag.

van Fraassen, Bas C. 1980. *The Scientific Image.* Oxford: Oxford University Press.

van Fraassen, Bas C. 2000. The Semantic Approach to Scientific Theories. In Lawrence Sklar, ed., *The Nature of Scientific Theory,* vol. 2, 175–194. New York: Garland.

van Fraassen, Bas C. 2002. *The Empirical Stance.* New Haven, CT: Yale University Press.

Freeman, Samuel. 2008. Original Position. In *Stanford Encyclopedia of Philosophy.* ⟨http://plato.stanford.edu/entries/original-position/⟩.

Gerson, Michael. 2009. Obama in the Shallows: Is There Any Vision Behind the Pragmatism? *The Washington Post,* February 11, 2009: Editorial, page A19.

Gibson, Eleanor J., and Richard Bergman. 1954. The Effect of Training on Absolute Estimation of Distance Over the Ground. *Journal of Experimental Psychology* 48:473–482.

Gibson, Eleanor J., and Anne D. Pick. 2000. *An Ecological Approach to Perceptual Learning and Development*. Oxford: Oxford University Press.

Gibson, Eleanor J., and Richard D. Walk. 1960. The 'Visual Cliff'. *Scientific American* 202:64–71.

Gibson, James J. 1950. *The Perception of the Visual World*. Boston: Houghton Mifflin.

Gibson, James J. 1966a. The Problem of Temporal Order in Stimulation and Perception. *Journal of Psychology* 62:141–149. Reprinted in Reed and Jones 1982, 171–179.

Gibson, James J. 1966b. *The Senses Considered as Perceptual Systems*. Boston: Houghton Mifflin.

Gibson, James J. 1967. Autobiography. In Edwin G. Boring and Gardner Lindzey, eds., *A History of Psychology in Autobiography*, vol. 5. New York: Appleton-Century-Crofts. Reprinted in Reed and Jones 1982, 7–22.

Gibson, James J. 1977. The Theory of Affordances. In Robert E. Shaw and John Bransford, eds., *Perceiving, Acting, and Knowing*. Hillsdale, NJ: Lawrence Erlbaum Associates.

Gibson, James J. 1979. *The Ecological Approach to Visual Perception*. Boston: Houghton Mifflin.

Gibson, James J. 1982. Notes on Affordances. In Edward Reed and Rebecca Jones, eds., *Reasons for Realism: Selected Essays of James J. Gibson*, 401–418. Hillsdale, NJ: Lawrence Erlbaum Associates.

Gigerenzer, Gerd. 2004. Fast and Frugal Heuristics: The Tools of Bounded Rationality. In D. Koehler and N. Harvey, eds., *Blackwell Handbook of Judgment and Decision Making*, 62–88. Oxford: Basil Blackwell.

Gigerenzer, Gerd, and Reinhard Selten (eds.). 2001. *Bounded Rationality: The Adaptive Toolbox*. Cambridge, MA: MIT Press.

Girard, Albert. 1626. *Trigonométrie*. The Hague.

Goldberg, Jonah. 2010. Obama Appears Blinded by his Own Ideological Biases. *The Los Angeles Times*, Opinion. February 2, 2010. ⟨http://www.latimes.com/news/opinion/⟩.

Gordon, Bennett. 2009. The Limits of Obama's Pragmatism. *UTNE Reader*, 2008 May 19. Topeka, KS: Ogden Publications, Inc. ⟨http://www.utne.com/⟩.

Haack, Susan. 1993. *Evidence and Inquiry: Towards Reconstruction in Epistemology*. Oxford: Blackwell.

Hamburger, Tom, and Peter Wallsten. 2009. Squaring Pragmatism with Oval Office: Demands from All Sides Testing Obama's Style. *The Chicago Tribune*, January 18, 2009: News, page 4.

Hanson, Norwood Russell. 1958. *Patterns of Discovery*. Cambridge: Cambridge University Press.

Hardin, Garrett. 1968. The Tragedy of the Commons. *Science* 162:1243–1248.

Hayes, Christopher. 2008. The Pragmatist. *The Nation* 287(22):13–16.

Heft, Harry. 2001. *Ecological Psychology in Context: James Gibson, Roger Barker, and the Legacy of William James's Radical Empiricism*. Hillsdale, NJ: Lawrence Erlbaum Associates.

Hochberg, Julian. 1994. James Jerome Gibson, 1904–1979. In *Biographical Memoirs, National Academy of Sciences*, vol. 63, 150–171. Washington, DC: National Academies Press.

Holmes, Oliver Wendell, Jr. 1870. Codes, and the Arrangement of the Law. *American Law Review* 5:1–13. Reprinted in Holmes 1995, vol. 1, 212–221.

Holmes, Oliver Wendell, Jr. 1881. *The Common Law*. Boston: Little, Brown, and Company. Reprinted in Holmes 1995, vol. 3.

Holmes, Oliver Wendell, Jr. 1995. *The Collected Works of Justice Holmes: Complete Public Writings and Selected Judicial Opinions of Oliver Wendell Holmes*. In three volumes. Ed. Sheldon M. Novick. Chicago: University of Chicago Press.

Hughes, R. I. G. 1996. Semantic View of Theories. *Encyclopedia of Applied Physics* 17:175–180.

Hull-House, Residents of. 1895. *Hull-House Maps and Papers: A Presentation of Nationalities and Wages in a Congested District of Chicago, Together with Comments and Essays on Problems Growing Out of the Social Conditions*. New York: Thomas Y. Crowell. Reprinted with introduction by Rima Lunin Schultz (Urbana: University of Illinois Press, 2007).

Hurley, Susan. 1998. *Consciousness in Action*. Cambridge, MA: Harvard University Press.

Hurley, Susan. 2006. Active Perception and Perceiving Action: The Shared Circuits Model. In Tamar Szabó Gendler and John Hawthorne, eds., *Perceptual Experience*, 205–259. Oxford: Oxford University Press.

Ignatius, David. 2007. The Pragmatic Obama: He's Shaping the Debate on Foreign Policy. *The Washington Post,* August 23, 2007: Editorial, page A19.

James, William. 1881. Reflex Action and Theism. *Unitarian Review* 16:389–416. Reprinted in James 1897.

James, William. 1885. On the Function of Cognition. *Mind* 10(37):27–44. Revised as Chapter 1 of James 1909a.

James, William. 1896. The Will to Believe. *New World* June:327–347. Reprinted in James 1897.

James, William. 1897. *The Will to Believe and Other Essays in Popular Philosophy*. New York: Henry Holt. Reprinted in the *Works of William James* series (Cambridge, MA:

Harvard University Press, 1979). Page or chapter citations refer to the Harvard edition, indicated by HUP followed by page or chapter numbers.

James, William. 1898. Philosophical Conceptions and Practical Results. *University of California Chronicle* 1(4):287–310. Reprinted in McDermott 1977.

James, William. 1904a. Does "Consciousness" Exist? *Journal of Philosophy, Psychology, and Scientific Methods* 1(18):477–491. Reprinted in James 1912, HUP:3–20, and in McDermott 1977, 169–183.

James, William. 1904b. The Pragmatic Method. *Journal of Philosophy, Psychology, and Scientific Methods* 1(25):673–687. Reprinted in James 1912, HUP:3–20, and in McDermott 1977, 169–183. Much of it also appeared as Lecture III of James 1907h.

James, William. 1904c. A World of Pure Experience. *Journal of Philosophy, Psychology, and Scientific Methods* 1(20/21):533–543, 561–570. Revised and reprinted in James 1912, HUP:21–44, and in McDermott 1977, 194–214.

James, William. 1905. The Thing and Its Relations. *Journal of Philosophy, Psychology, and Scientific Methods* 2(2):29–41. Reprinted in James 1912, HUP:45–60, and in McDermott 1977, 214–226.

James, William. 1907a. A Defense of Pragmatism. *Popular Science Monthly* 70:193–206 and 351–364. Reprinted as Lectures I and II of James 1907h.

James, William. 1907b. The Present Dilemma in Philosophy. First part of James 1907a reprinted as Lecture I of James 1907h.

James, William. 1907c. What Pragmatism Means. Second part of James 1907a reprinted as Lecture II of James 1907h.

James, William. 1907d. Some Metaphysical Problems Pragmatically Considered. Lecture III of James 1907h. Partial reprint of James 1904b, which itself was a revision of much of James 1898.

James, William. 1907e. The One and the Many. Lecture IV of James 1907h.

James, William. 1907f. Pragmatism's Conception of Truth. *Journal of Philosophy, Psychology, and Scientific Methods* 4:141–155. Reprinted as Lecture VI of James 1907h.

James, William. 1907g. A Word More About Truth. *Journal of Philosophy, Psychology, and Scientific Methods* 4:396–406. Reprinted as Lecture VI of James 1909a.

James, William. 1907h. *Pragmatism: A New Name for Some Old Ways of Thinking*. New York: Longmans, Green. Reprinted in *Pragmatism and Other Essays* (New York: Washington Square Press, 1963) and in the *Works of William James* series (Cambridge, MA: Harvard University Press, 1975). Reprinted again together with James 1909a in James 1978. Page citations refer to the latest reprinted version in James 1978, indicated by PMT followed by page or chapter numbers.

James, William. 1909a. *The Meaning of Truth: A Sequel to Pragmatism*. New York: Longmans, Green. Reprinted in the *Works of William James* series (Cambridge, MA:

Harvard University Press, 1975). Reprinted again together with James 1907h in James 1978. Page citations refer to the latest reprinted version in James 1978, indicated by PMT followed by page or chapter numbers.

James, William. 1909b. *A Pluralistic Universe.* New York: Longmans, Green. Reprinted in the *Works of William James* series (Cambridge, MA: Harvard University Press, 1977). Page or chapter citations refer to the Harvard edition, indicated by HUP followed by page or chapter numbers.

James, William. 1912. *Essays in Radical Empiricism.* New York: Longmans, Green. Posthumous, ed. R. B. Perry. Reprinted in the *Works of William James* series (Cambridge, MA: Harvard University Press, 1976). Page or chapter citations refer to the Harvard edition, indicated by HUP followed by page or chapter numbers.

James, William. 1978. *Pragmatism* and *The Meaning of Truth.* Cambridge, MA: Harvard University Press. A combined reprint of James 1907h; 1909a with an introduction by A. J. Ayer. Items in this collection are indicated by PMT followed by page or chapter numbers.

Johnson, Mark. 1987. *The Body in the Mind: The Bodily Basis of Meaning, Imagination, and Reason.* Chicago: University of Chicago Press.

Kant, Immanuel. 1781/1787. *Critique of Pure Reason.* Trans. Norman Kemp Smith. New York: Macmillan (1929).

Kant, Immanuel. 1785. *Groundwork of the Metaphysic of Morals.* Trans. Herbert James Paton. New York: Harper and Row (1964).

Kant, Immanuel. 1788. *Critique of Practical Reason.* Trans. Lewis White Beck. New York: Macmillan (1993, Third Edition).

Kant, Immanuel. 1798. *Anthropology from a Pragmatic Point of View.* English trans. Mary J. Gregor. The Hague: Martinus Nijhoff (1974).

Kantor, Jodi. 2009. As Professor, Obama Held Pragmatic Views on Court. *The New York Times,* May 3, 2009: U.S. Politics, page A1.

Keyes, Charley. 2009. U.S. is 'Pragmatic' with China, Russia. *CNN U.S.*, 2009 December 14. Atlanta: Turner Broadcasting System, Inc. ⟨http://articles.cnn.com/2009-12-14/⟩.

Kloppenberg, James T. 2011. *Reading Obama: Dreams, Hope, and the American Political Tradition.* Princeton, NJ: Princeton University Press.

Koopman, Colin. 2009. Pragmatism in Obama's Inaugural. *Requiem for Certainty* blog, 2009 January 24. ⟨http://cwkoopman.wordpress.com/⟩.

Kripke, Saul A. 1980. *Naming and Necessity.* Cambridge, MA: Harvard University Press.

Kroft, Steve. 2008. Obama On Economic Crisis, Transition. *60 Minutes* interview, 2008 November 16. Produced by L. Franklin Devine, Michael Radutzky, and Andy Court. New York: CBS Interactive ⟨http://www.cbsnews.com/⟩.

Kyburg, Henry E. 1961. *Probability and the Logic of Rational Belief.* Middletown, CT: Wesleyan University Press.

Lakoff, George, and Mark Johnson. 1999. *Philosophy in the Flesh: The Embodied Mind and Its Challenge to Western Thought.* New York: Basic Books.

Lamond, Grant. 2008. Precedent and Analogy in Legal Reasoning. In Edward N. Zalta, ed., *The Stanford Encyclopedia of Philosophy* (Fall 2008 Edition). ⟨http://plato.stanford.edu/archives/fall2008/entries/legal-reas-prec/⟩.

Landler, Mark, and Helene Cooper. 2011. Obama Seeks a Course of Pragmatism in the Middle East. *The New York Times,* March 10, 2011. ⟨http://www.nytimes.com/2011/03/11/world/africa/11policy.html⟩.

Lashley, Karl Spencer. 1950. In Search of the Engram. In *Symposium of the Society of Experimental Biology, Vol. 4: Physiological Mechanisms in Animal Behavior.* New York: Academic Press.

Lee, David N. 1980. The Optic Flow Field: The Foundation of Vision. *Philosophical Transactions of the Royal Society of London* 290:169–179.

Lerner, Michael. 2009. Obama's Pragmatism Will Backfire. Politico.com blog, 2009 May 20. Arlington, VA: Capitol News ⟨http://www.politico.com/⟩.

Lim, Elvin. 2009. On Barack Obama's 'Pragmatism'. *OUPblog,* 2009 January 12. New York: Oxford University Press USA. ⟨http://blog.oup.com/⟩.

Lizza, Ryan. 2007. The Agitator: Barack Obama's Unlikely Political Education. *New Republic* 236(12):22–29.

Lowry, Rich. 2009. Barack Obama's Soaring Pragmatism. *National Review Online,* 2009 January 23. New York: National Review. ⟨http://www.nationalreview.com/⟩.

MacKay, Donald MacCrimmon. 1967. Ways of Looking at Perception. In Weiant Wathen-Dunn, ed., *Models for the Perception of Speech and Visual Form.* Cambridge, MA: MIT Press.

Makinson, D. C. 1965. Paradox of the Preface. *Analysis* 25:205–207.

Malinowski, Bronisław. 1922. *Argonauts of the Western Pacific: An Account of Native Enterprise and Adventure in the Archipelagoes of Melanesian New Guinea.* London: Routledge and Kegan Paul.

Malinowski, Bronisław. 1929. *The Sexual Life of Savages in North-Western Melanesia.* London: Routledge and Kegan Paul.

Malinowski, Bronisław. 1935. *Coral Gardens and their Magic: A Study of the Methods of Tilling the Soil and of Agricultural Rites in the Trobriand Islands.* New York: American.

Maturana, Humberto, and Francisco Varela. 1992. *The Tree of Knowledge: The Biological Roots of Human Understanding* (revised edition). Boston and London: Shamabala. Originally published in 1987 by New Science Library, Boston.

McDermott, John J. (ed.). 1977. *The Writings of William James: A Comprehensive Edition*. Chicago: University of Chicago Press.

McLeod, Peter, and Zoltan Dienes. 1996. Do Fielders Know Where to Go to Catch the Ball or Only How to Get There? *Journal of Experimental Psychology: Human Perception and Performance* 22(3):531–543.

Menand, Louis. 2001. *The Metaphysical Club: A Story of Ideas in America*. New York: Farrar Straus Giroux.

Milligan, Susan. 2009. Obama's First Year Marked by Pragmatism. *The Boston Globe*, December 27, 2009: News, national, page 1.

Mooney, Chris. 2009. A Close Look at Cass Sunstein's Take on Cost-Benefit Regulation. The Wonk Room blog, 2009 January 17. Washington, DC: Center for American Progress Action Fund. ⟨http://wonkroom.thinkprogress.org/⟩.

Moore, George Edward. 1907. Professor James' 'Pragmatism'. *Proceedings of the Aristotelean Society* 8:33–77. Also as "William James' 'Pragmatism'" in Moore 1922, 97–146.

Moore, George Edward. 1922. *Philosophical Studies*. London: Routledge and Kegan Paul.

Noë, Alva. 2004. *Action in Perception*. Cambridge, MA: MIT Press.

Noë, Alva. 2006. Experience without the Head. In Tamar Szabó Gendler and John Hawthorne, eds., *Perceptual Experience*, 411–433. Oxford: Oxford University Press.

Obama, Barack. 2008a. A More Perfect Union: Obama's 'Race Speech'. Delivered on 2008 March 18. Philadelphia, Constitution Center.

Obama, Barack. 2008b. The World Beyond Iraq. Delivered on 2008 March 19. Fayetteville Technical Community College.

Obama, Barack. 2009. President Obama's First Press Conference. 2009 February 9. Washington, DC: The White House.

Oxford American Dictionary. 2011. Ideal. In *The New Oxford American Dictionary*, 3rd edition. Oxford: Oxford University Press.

Packer, George. 2008. The New Liberalism. *New Yorker* 84.37(2008 November 17):84–99.

Packer, George. 2009. Keep Your Eye on the Ball. *The New Yorker* Online Only, 2009 March 13. ⟨http://www.newyorker.com/online/blogs/⟩.

Parker, Kelly. 1998. *The Continuity of Peirce's Thought*. Nashville, TN: Vanderbilt University Press.

Pavlov, Ivan Petrovich. 1927. *Conditioned Reflexes: An Investigation of the Physiological Activity of the Cerebral Cortex*. Translated and edited by G. V. Anrep. London: Oxford University Press.

Payne, Rodger A. 2008. Obama's Pragmatic Foreign Policy. *Rodger A. Payne's Blog*, 2008 September 6. ⟨http://rpayne.blogspot.com/⟩.

Peirce, Charles Sanders. 1868a. Questions Concerning Certain Faculties Claimed for Man. *Journal of Speculative Philosophy* 2:103–114. Reprinted in CP5:213–263, EP1, chap. 2, and WP2:193–211.

Peirce, Charles Sanders. 1868b. Some Consequences of Four Incapacities. *Journal of Speculative Philosophy* 2:140–157. Reprinted in CP5:264–317, EP1, chap. 3, and WP2:211–242.

Peirce, Charles Sanders. 1871. Fraser's *The Works of George Berkeley*. *North American Review* 113:449–472. Reprinted in CP8:7–38 and EP1, chap. 5.

Peirce, Charles Sanders. 1872. Toward a Logic Book, 1872–73. In WP3:12–108.

Peirce, Charles Sanders. 1877. The Fixation of Belief. *Popular Science Monthly* 12:1–15. Reprinted in CP5:223–247, EP1, chap. 7, and WP3:242–257.

Peirce, Charles Sanders. 1878a. How to Make Our Ideas Clear. *Popular Science Monthly* 12:286–302. Reprinted in CP5:248–271, EP1, chap. 8, and WP3:257–276.

Peirce, Charles Sanders. 1878b. Deduction, Induction, and Hypothesis. *Popular Science Monthly* 13:470–482. Reprinted in CP2:619–644, EP1, chap. 12, and WP3:323–338.

Peirce, Charles Sanders. 1884. Design and Chance. In EP1, chap. 15 and WP4:544–554.

Peirce, Charles Sanders. 1891. The Architecture of Theories. *Monist* 1:161–176. Reprinted in CP6:7–34 and EP1, chap. 21.

Peirce, Charles Sanders. 1893. The Essence of Reasoning. In CP4:21–79. Chapter 6 of *The Grand Logic* of 1893, a complete book for which Peirce could find no publisher. Paragraphs 53–79 are from an alternate draft.

Peirce, Charles Sanders. 1897. The Logic of Relatives. *Monist* 7:161–217. Reprinted in CP3:456–552.

Peirce, Charles Sanders. 1901. Laws of Nature. In EP2, chap. 7. From a longer paper "The Laws of Nature and Hume's Argument against Miracles," unpublished at the time.

Peirce, Charles Sanders. 1902a. Critical Analysis of Logical Theories. In CP2:1–78. Chapter 1 of *Minute Logic* (unfinished manuscript).

Peirce, Charles Sanders. 1902b. Pragmatic and Pragmatism. In James Mark Baldwin, ed., *Dictionary of Philosophy and Psychology*, vol. 2, 321–322. New York: Macmillan. Reprinted in CP5:1–4.

Peirce, Charles Sanders. 1903a. The Maxim of Pragmatism. Harvard Lectures on Pragmatism, no. 1. In CP5:14–40 and EP2, chap. 10.

Peirce, Charles Sanders. 1903b. On Phenomenology. Harvard Lectures on Pragmatism, no. 2. In CP5:41–56, 59–65, and EP2, chap. 11.

Peirce, Charles Sanders. 1903c. The Seven Systems of Metaphysics. Harvard Lectures on Pragmatism, no. 4. In EP2, chap. 13.

Peirce, Charles Sanders. 1903d. The Nature of Meaning. Harvard Lectures on Pragmatism, no. 6. In CP5:151–179 (in part) and EP2, chap. 15.

Peirce, Charles Sanders. 1903e. On Selecting Hypotheses. From the Eighth Lowell Lecture, titled "How to Theorize." In CP5:590–604.

Peirce, Charles Sanders. 1903f. Pragmatism as the Logic of Abduction. Harvard Lectures on Pragmatism, no. 7. In CP5:180–212 (in part) and EP2, chap. 16.

Peirce, Charles Sanders. 1903g. Sundry Logical Conceptions. Third section of *A Syllabus of Certain Topics of Logic*. In EP2, chap. 20.

Peirce, Charles Sanders. 1905a. What Pragmatism Is. *The Monist* 15:161–181. Reprinted in CP5:411–437 and EP2, chap. 24.

Peirce, Charles Sanders. 1905b. Issues of Pragmaticism. *The Monist* 15:481–499. Reprinted in CP5:438–463 and EP2, chap. 25.

Peirce, Charles Sanders. 1905c. The Architectonic Construction of Pragmatism. In CP5:5–10.

Peirce, Charles Sanders. 1905d. Unsigned letter to Mario Calderoni. In CP8:205–213.

Peirce, Charles Sanders. 1906a. The Basis of Pragmaticism in Phaneroscopy. In EP2, chap. 26.

Peirce, Charles Sanders. 1906b. Historical Affinities and Genesis [of Pragmatism]. In CP5:11–13 and EP2:399.

Peirce, Charles Sanders. 1907a. Pragmatism. In EP2, chap. 28.

Peirce, Charles Sanders. 1907b. Pragmatism. In EP2, chap. 28.

Peirce, Charles Sanders. 1908. A Neglected Argument for the Reality of God. *The Hibbert Journal* 7:90–112. Reprinted in CP6:452–491 and EP2, chap. 29.

Peirce, Charles Sanders. 1911. A Sketch of Logical Critics. In EP2, chap. 30.

Peirce, Charles Sanders. 1913. An Essay toward Improving our Reasoning in Security and in Uberty. In EP2, chap. 31.

Peirce, Charles Sanders. 1923. *Chance, Love, and Logic: Philosophical Essays*. Ed. Morris R. Cohen with an essay by John Dewey. New York: Harcourt, Brace, and World.

Peirce, Charles Sanders. 1931–1935/1958. *Collected Papers of Charles Sanders Peirce* (CP). Cambridge, MA: Harvard University Press. Vol. 1–6 ed. Charles Hartshorne and Paul Weiss; vol. 7–8 ed. Arthur W. Burks. Items in this collection are indicated by CP followed by volume and paragraph numbers.

Peirce, Charles Sanders. 1981ff. *Writings of Charles S. Peirce: A Chronological Edition* (WP). Ed. Peirce Edition Project. Bloomington: Indiana University Press. Items in this multivolume collection are indicated by WP followed by volume and page numbers.

Peirce, Charles Sanders. 1992/1998. *The Essential Peirce: Selected Philosophical Writings*, in two volumes. Ed. Peirce Edition Project. Bloomington: Indiana University Press.

Perry, Ralph Barton. 1935. *The Thought and Character of William James* (2 volumes). Boston: Little, Brown.

Perry, Ralph Barton. 1948. *The Thought and Character of William James*. Cambridge, MA: Harvard University Press. Abridged reissue of Perry 1935.

Pfeifer, David. 2011. Inquiry and the Fourth Grade of Clearness. Presented at the Fourth Nordic Pragmatism Conference, Copenhagen.

Piaget, Jean. 1936. *Origins of Intelligence in the Child*. London: Routledge and Kegan Paul.

Piaget, Jean. 1945. *Play, Dreams and Imitation in Childhood*. London: Heinemann.

Piaget, Jean. 1954. *The Construction of Reality in the Child*. New York: Basic Books.

Piaget, Jean. 1976. *The Grasp of Consciousness: Action and Concept in the Young Child*. Cambridge, MA: Harvard University Press.

Pick, Anne D. 1965. Improvement of Visual and Tactual Form Discrimination. *Journal of Experimental Psychology* 69:331–339.

Prinz, Jesse J. 2002. *Furnishing the Mind: Concepts and Their Perceptual Basis*. Cambridge, MA: MIT Press.

Prinz, Jesse J. 2006. Beyond Appearances: The Content of Sensation and Perception. In Tamar Szabó Gendler and John Hawthorne, eds., *Perceptual Experience*, 434–460. Oxford: Oxford University Press.

Putnam, Hilary. 1981a. A Problem about Reference. In Putnam 1981b, 22–48.

Putnam, Hilary. 1981b. *Reason, Truth, and History*. Cambridge: Cambridge University Press.

Putnam, Hilary. 1995. *Pragmatism: An Open Question*. Oxford: Basil Blackwell.

Quine, Willard van Orman. 1948. On What There Is. *Review of Metaphysics* 2:21–38. Reprinted in Quine 1953, 1–19.

Quine, Willard van Orman. 1951. Two Dogmas of Empiricism. *Philosophical Review* 60:20–43. Reprinted in Quine 1953, 20–46.

Quine, Willard van Orman. 1953. *From a Logical Point of View*. Cambridge, MA: Harvard University Press.

Quine, Willard van Orman. 1958. Speaking of Objects. *Proceedings and Addresses of the American Philosophical Association* 38:5–22. Reprinted in Quine 1969, 1–25.

Quine, Willard van Orman. 1960. *Word and Object*. Cambridge, MA: MIT Press.

Quine, Willard van Orman. 1968. Ontological Relativity: The Dewey Lectures 1968. *Journal of Philosophy* 65:185–212. Reprinted in Quine 1969, 26–68.

Quine, Willard van Orman. 1969. *Ontological Relativity and Other Essays*. New York: Columbia University Press.

Quine, Willard van Orman. 1973. *The Roots of Reference*. LaSalle, IL: Open Court Publishing.

Quine, Willard van Orman. 1981. *Theories and Things*. Cambridge, MA: Harvard University Press.

Randall, Charles H., and David J. Foulis. 1978a. A Mathematical Setting for Inductive Logic. In William L. Harper and Clifford A. Hooker, eds., *Foundations of Probability Theory, Statistical Inference, and Statistical Theories of Science, III*, 169–205. Dordrecht: D. Reidel.

Randall, Charles H., and David J. Foulis. 1978b. The Operational Approach to Quantum Mechanics. In Clifford A. Hooker, ed., *Physical Theory as Logico-Operational Structure*, 167–201. Dordrecht: D. Reidel.

Rawls, John. 1971. *A Theory of Justice*. Cambridge, MA: Harvard University Press.

Rawls, John. 2001. *Justice as Fairness: A Restatement*. Cambridge, MA: Harvard University Press.

Reed, Edward. 1982. An Outline of a Theory of Action Systems. *Journal of Motor Behavior* 14(2):98–134.

Reed, Edward, and Rebecca Jones (eds.). 1982. *Reasons for Realism: Selected Essays of James J. Gibson*. Hillsdale, NJ: Lawrence Erlbaum Associates.

Reich, Robert. 2009. Obama and Pragmatism: Thinking Through Values. *Robert Reich's Blog*, 2009 May 5. ⟨http://robertreich.blogspot.com/⟩.

Revesz, Richard L., and Michael A. Livermore. 2009. Cass Sunstein for Regulation Czar: Neither an Easy Ally, nor a Wilting Lily. Online commentary, 2009 May 12. New York: Forbes.com LLC. ⟨http://www.forbes.com⟩.

Rivas, Bruno. 2009. Obama contextualizá decisiones: Interview with Gregory Pappas. *El Comercio*, 2009 June 2. Lima, Peru: ⟨http://elcomercio.pe/impresa/⟩. Trans. A. Howard: ⟨http://www.obamaspragmatism.info/Pappas.htm⟩.

Rorty, Richard. 1998. *Achieving Our Country: Leftist Thought in Twentieth-Century America*. Cambridge, MA: Harvard University Press.

Rowlands, Mark. 2006. *Body Language: Representation in Action*. Cambridge, MA: MIT Press.

Russell, Bertrand. 1909. Pragmatism. *Edinburgh Review* 209(428):363–388. Reprinted in Russell 1910, chap. 4. Includes remarks on Dewey's *Studies in Logical Theory*.

Russell, Bertrand. 1910. *Philosophical Essays*. New York: Longmans, Green. A revised edition with a slightly different selection of essays appeared in 1966 (London: George Allen & Unwin).

Salam, Reihan. 2008. Obama's Pragmatism. *The American Scene: An Ongoing Review of Politics and Culture*, 2008 December 11. ⟨http://theamericanscene.com/⟩.

Schneider, Herbert Wallace. 1946. *A History of American Philosophy*. New York: Columbia University Press. Chapters 39–41.

Schultz, Bart. 2009. Obama's Political Philosophy: Pragmatism, Politics, and the University of Chicago. *Philosophy of the Social Sciences* 39(2):127–173.

Searle, John. 1969. *Speech Acts: An Essay in the Philosophy of Language*. Cambridge: Cambridge University Press.

Sellars, Wilfrid. 1953. Inference and Meaning. *Mind* 62(247):313–338. Reprinted in Sellars 2007.

Sellars, Wilfrid. 1974. Meaning as Functional Classification. *Synthese* 27(1974):417–437. Reprinted in Sellars 2007.

Sellars, Wilfrid. 2007. *In the Space of Reasons: Selected Essays of Wilfrid Sellars*. Edited by Kevin Scharp and Robert B. Brandom. Cambridge, MA: Harvard University Press.

Shapiro, Sidney A., and Christopher H. Schroeder. 2008. Beyond Cost-Benefit Analysis: A Pragmatic Reorientation. *Harvard Environmental Law Review* 32(2):433–502.

Shaw, Robert E., and Michael T. Turvey. 1981. Coalitions as Models for Ecosystems: A Realist Perspective on Perceptual Organization. In M. Kubovy and J. R. Pomerantz, eds., *Perceptual Organization*, 343–415. Hillsdale, NJ: Lawrence Erlbaum Associates.

Simkhovitch, Mary Kingsbury. 1906. Settlement Organization. *Charities and the Commons* 16:566–569.

Smith, Ben. 2008. Obama, Pragmatist. Politico.com blog, 2008 June 19. Arlington, VA: Capitol News ⟨http://www.politico.com/⟩.

Sosa, Ernest. 1980. The Raft and the Pyramid: Coherence versus Foundations in the Theory of Knowledge. *Midwest Studies in Philosophy* 5(1):3–25.

Stephens, James Fitzjames. 1863. *A General View of the Criminal Law of England*. London and Cambridge: Macmillan.

Strawson, P. F. 1966. *The Bounds of Sense: An Essay on Kant's Critique of Pure Reason*. London: Methuen.

Sunstein, Cass. 2002. *Risk and Reason: Safety, Law, and the Environment*. Cambridge: Cambridge University Press.

Sunstein, Cass. 2008. The Empiricist Strikes Back. *The New Republic* 239(4):9–10.

Suppe, Frederick. 1977. The Search for Philosophic Understanding of Scientific Theories. In Frederick Suppe, ed., *The Structure of Scientific Theories*, second edition, 3–241.

Urbana: University of Illinois Press.

Suppe, Frederick. 1989. *The Semantic Conception of Theories and Scientific Realism.* Urbana: University of Illinois Press.

Suppes, Patrick. 1960. A Comparison of the Meaning and Use of Models in the Mathematical and Empirical Sciences. *Synthese* 12(2/3):287–301. Reprinted in Suppes 1969, 10–23.

Suppes, Patrick. 1962. Models of Data. In E. Nagel, P. Suppes, and A. Tarski, eds., *Logic, Methodology, and the Philosophy of Science: Proceedings of the 1960 International Congress*, 252–261. Stanford, CA: Stanford University Press. Reprinted in Suppes 1969, 24–35.

Suppes, Patrick. 1967. What is a Scientific Theory? In Sidney Morgenbesser, ed., *Philosophy of Science Today*, 55–67. New York: Basic Books.

Suppes, Patrick. 1969. *Studies in the Methodology and Foundations of Science: Selected Papers from 1951 to 1969.* Dordrecht: D. Reidel.

Talisse, Robert B. 2007. *A Pragmatist Philosophy of Democracy.* London: Routledge.

Talisse, Robert B. 2011. Social Inquiry and the Challenges of Democracy: Why Pragmatists Must be Rawlsians. Fourth Nordic Pragmatism Conference, Copenhagen.

Talisse, Robert B., and Scott F. Aikin. 2008. *Pragmatism: A Guide for the Perplexed.* London and New York: Continuum International Publishing Group.

Tarski, Alfred. 1936a. The Concept of Truth in Formalized Languages. English translation in *Logic, Semantics, Metamathematics*, 152–278 (Oxford: Clarendon Press, 1956).

Tarski, Alfred. 1936b. On the Concept of Logical Consequence. English translation in *Logic, Semantics, Metamathematics*, 409–420 (Oxford: Clarendon Press, 1956). New translation as "On the Concept of Following Logically" by Magda Stroińska and David Hitchcock, in *History and Philosophy of Logic* 23(2002):155–196.

Tarski, Alfred. 1944. The Semantic Conception of Truth and the Foundations of Semantics. *Philosophy and Phenomenological Research* 4:341–375.

Taylor, Ken, and John Perry. 2006. American Pragmatism. *Philosophy Talk* (December 3, 2006). URL: ⟨http://www.philosophytalk.org/pastShows/Pragmatism.html⟩.

Thayer, Horace Standish. 1981. *Meaning and Action: A Critical History of Pragmatism*, 2nd edition. Indianapolis: Hackett.

Thompson, Manley. 1953. *The Pragmatic Philosophy of C. S. Peirce.* Chicago: University of Chicago Press.

Tindall, George Brown, and David Emory Shi. 2007. *America: A Narrative History*, seventh edition. New York: W. W. Norton.

Trattner, Walter I. 1998. *From Poor Law to Welfare State: A History of Social Welfare in America*, sixth edition. New York: Simon and Schuster.

Tuennerman-Kaplan, Laura. 2007. Settlement Houses. In Robert E. Weir, ed., *Class in America: Q–Z*, 753–755. Santa Barbara, CA: Greenwood Press.

Turvey, Michael T., Robert E. Shaw, Edward S. Reed,, and William M. Mace. 1981. Ecological Laws of Perceiving and Acting: In Reply to Fodor and Pylyshyn. *Cognition* 9:237–304. A reply to Fodor and Pylyshyn 1981.

Varela, Francisco, Evan Thompson,, and Eleanor Rosch. 1991. *The Embodied Mind: Cognitive Science and Human Experience*. Cambridge, MA: MIT Press.

Weisberg, Jacob. 2009. Getting to Know Obama: The Sides We're Just Starting to See. *Newsweek* 153.21(May 25, 2009):28.

Whitehead, Alfred North. 1920. *The Concept of Nature*. Cambridge: Cambridge University Press.

Wickham, DeWayne. 2008. Obama Insider Paints Portrait of 'Pragmatic' President-Elect. *USA Today,* November 11, 2008: Opinion, page 11A.

Wiener, Philip P. 1946. Peirce's Metaphysical Club and the Genesis of Pragmatism. *Journal of the History of Ideas* 7(2):218–233.

Wikipedia. 2009. Observer Effect. In *Wikipedia, The Free Encyclopedia*. ⟨http://en.wikipedia.org/wiki/Observer_effect⟩. Accessed May 15, 2009.

Wikipedia. 2012a. Chipset. In *Wikipedia, The Free Encyclopedia*. ⟨http://en.wikipedia.org/wiki/Chipset⟩. Accessed November 15, 2012.

Wikipedia. 2012b. Precedent. In *Wikipedia, The Free Encyclopedia*. ⟨http://en.wikipedia.org/wiki/Precedent⟩. Accessed April 16, 2012.

Worsnip, Alex. 2012. Against Pragmatism. *Prospect,* December 29, 2012. ⟨http://www.prospectmagazine.co.uk/blog/against-pragmatism-blair-cameron-clegg/⟩.

Zelizer, Julian. 2012. For President, Two Pragmatic Problem-Solvers. *CNN Opinion*, 2012 April 16. Atlanta: Turner Broadcasting System, Inc. ⟨http://www.cnn.com/2012/04/16/opinion/zelizer-two-pragmatists/⟩.

Index

a priori
    method of inquiry, 138
    rationalism, 61–62
    reasoning, 17, 32
abduction, 9, 25, 53, 112
    and pragmatism, 25
    logic of, 25
    perception as, 24, 112
    perfect, 24
abilities
    invariant-extraction, 102
        optical, 103
    lower-order, 90, 103, 116
    measurement, 105
    optical, 103
    routine, 116
Aboulafia, Mitchell, ix, x, 158
Abrams, Laura, 119, 122
absolutism, 6, 44, 65
    pragmatist, 150
abstract
    definition as distinctness, 51, 55
    entities, 67
Achilles and the tortoise, 25, 27, 33, 137
action, 126, 150, 170
    and enactivism, 115
    and evidence, 72
    and interpretation, 117
    and logic, 26
    and perception, 80–115
    and sensible effects, 7, 12, 15, 63, 66, 67, 115, 183
    as a black box, 105, 176
    as a thing, 67

conceivable, 22–24, 42, 53, 80
concrete, xi, 16, 19, 150–153
experience constituted by, 115
experimentation as, 26, 42
free, 40
habit as a manner of, 11
habit, and belief, 5, 10–12
higher-order, 116
intended, 61
lower-order, 100, 116, 175–176
practical, 162
principled, 149
prudent, 39
purpose of, 11
purposive, 26, 54
reform as, 125, 128–129
residence as, 129
rule of, 1, 10–11, 14, 161
    attunement as, 99
    habit as a, 1, 10–12, 14, 89, 140–144
    heuristic as, 114
sensorimotor, 81
systems, 84, 93
to be informed, 116, 117, 128
to perceive, 116, 117
to reform, 116, 117, 128
two conceptions of, 7, 63
types, 48, 67–68, 100, 175, 183
    invariant-extraction, 99
active
    intervention, 70
    observation, 70, 117
activity, 5, 37, 57, 110

204 / INDEX

bodily, 83
cognitive, 73
effects of, 16, 170
experimental, 15, 29, 57
investigatory, 34
laboratory, 21, 32
measurement, 21, 31, 57, 71
modes of, 69
observational, 15, 21, 58, 59
operational nature of, 60, 113
perceptual, 57
reflective deliberation as, 128
research as, 128
tactile, 73
vs. existence, 60
worldly, 80
actuality as temporal modality, 50
adaptation, 96, 100
attunement as, 99
Addams, Jane, xii, 116–125
affordances, 85–93, 97, 102, 103, 112–113, 138, 170
as constraints on behavior, 93
as ecological, 88, 92, 93
as higher-order invariants, 90–93
defined, 90–91
direct perception of, 87–94
for an animal, 87, 101
for an observer, 91
higher-order, 91
information about, 97
learned, 99
meanings as, 99
objective, 87
of an environment, 87, 91, 116, 168
of an object, 90, 101–102, 116
operational character of, 115
perceivable, 89, 103, 169
specified by
attunements, 99–102, 114, 169
habits, 100
higher-order invariants, 90–91, 101, 115, 169
systems of, 87
values as, 88, 99

vs. predictions, 100
vs. properties, 87
vs. stimuli, 92
aggregation principle, 136
agreement, 20, 25, 33
Aiken, Scott, 1–2, 20
Alinsky, Saul, x, xi
ambient optical array as information storehouse, 83–84, 108–111, 168
analytic
/synthetic distinction, 65
consequence, 174
empiricism, 26
philosophy, 2, 7, 26, 63, 71
anarchy, 138–140
anatomy, 93
Answers.com, 122
anthropology, 117
cultural, 118
moral, 146
physiological, 146
pragmatic, 146
prudential, 147, 151
social, 118
technical, 147
anti-foundationalism, 3
appearances, veil of, 33–35
apprehension
clearness of, 2, 9, 12, 51
approximation, 34
Aquinas, Thomas, 28
aristocracy, 138–140
Aristotle, 28
assertion, 138
assignment, inferential, 113–115
association
as ecological fact, 98
as higher-order stimulus, 98
as invariance of stimulus combinations, 91, 98
formation, 98
learned, 98
learning by, 93, 98
of variables of information, 98
atomism, 7, 44, 63, 68, 161

INDEX / 205

attention
  deictic, 31
  education of, 98
  perceptual, 84–85
  selective, 92
attributes, *see* tangible results
  as accidental, 46
  vs. substance, 45, 46
attunement, 93–103, 110
  as a rule of action, 99
  as achievement, 100
  as adaptation, 99
  as fit, 99–100
  as fixation, 99
  as habituation, 173
  as higher-order fixation, 97
  as invariance relation, 102, 113
  as law-like, 99
  mathematically formulated, 100, 101, 113
  organism/environment, 93, 99, 100
  successive, 96, 110
  systemic, 102
  to associations, 98
  to regularities, 108, 112, 113
Austin, John L., 57
authority, 17, 32, 89, 138, 154
Averbuch, Lazarus, 123
awareness, 84
  of objects, 86, 87, 113, 114
  vs. perception, 86, 87, 113
axiomatic method, 9, 44, 131, 171, 174, 182
Ayer, Alfred J., 2, 16, 44, 47

Bain, Alexander, 5, 36
Baldwin, James Mark, 6
Barwise, Jon, 56–57
beer, reality of, 35
behavior, 27, 84
  constrained by affordances, 92
  habitual, 29
belief, 1–6, 10, 11, 16–19, 36–42, 44, 45, 48, 143, 148, 151, 152, 159, 163
  ancient, 18
  and reference to the future, 50
  as an invariant, 88, 89
  as established habit, 1, 10, 12, 14, 89, 140, 143, 144, 161
  content of, 2, 150
  contingent, 38
  false, 32, 134
  fixation of, 10, 31, 88–90, 99, 154
  fixed, 99, 134, 138
    as a tangible result, 31, 32, 46, 134, 173
  flexible, 157–158
  formation, 41
  habit, and action, 5, 10–12
  instrumentality of, 116
  justifiable, 25
  justified, 18, 143
  moral, 38–41
  necessary, 39
  practical, as theoretically insufficient, 38
  pragmatic, 38, 40, 41
  preservation, 139
  primitive, 29
  psychology of, 44, 47
  rational, 136, 143
  rigid, 158
  settled, 32
    as a tangible result, 31, 32, 46, 134, 173
  tentative, 104
  true, 32, 33, 134
    perfectly justified, 134, 173
  vs. knowledge, 137
  warranted, 18, 143
  web of, 17, 26, 66
  workable, 10, 66, 116, 143
believability
  reasonably justified, 17
  warranted, 16, 18, 163
Bergman, Richard, 81
Berkeley, George, 6, 37
Berkowitz, Peter, ix, x, 150
Bernstein, Richard, 1, 3–5
betting, 38, 41
biological species, 88

as invariants, 89
black box, 176
   action as a, 105, 176
   language use as a, 176
   operation as a, 176
blood, 12, 43–45
   vs. wine, 43–45
Boas, Franz, 118
Boersema, David, 45
bounded rationality, 114
brain
   as a chipset, 111
   as a computer, 109, 110
   as a resonator, 94, 97
   as a storehouse, 94
   as an information processor, 94
Brandom, Robert, 1, 17, 44, 71, 171
Bridgman, Percy Williams, 44, 59, 60
Brigandt, Ingo, 44, 171
Bronsther, Jacob, ix, x
Bruner, Jerome, 44, 81–82
bundle theory of objecthood, 87, 102
Burke, F. Thomas, 84, 101, 149, 174
Butler, Brian, 155

Carnap, Rudolf, 7, 21, 26, 44, 56, 63–72, 78, 85, 126, 129, 154, 161, 170
cash-value, experiential, 20
catchable fly ball, 114
categorical imperative, 39
certainty, 39–41
   degrees of, 156
certitude, 39
   blind, 158
chance, 3
Chang, Hasok, 44
charity, 119–120
   pseudo-scientific, 121
   scientific, 120
   that imposes preconceptions, 121
   that promotes growth, 121, 123
   vs. settlement work, 124, 126
citizenship, xi, 120, 127
   and science, 140
   duties of, 123
   neighborhood, 120–126

clarification, 42, 48, 115, 144, 163
   and definition, 33, 80, 180
   as fixation, 96
   axiomatic, 9
   inferential, 149
   of basic terminology, 88
   of principles, xi, 149
   operational, 115, 149, 176
   scientific, 88
clarity, 41, 97–98, 122, 131
   and distinctness, 9, 36, 131, 182
   as familiarity, 9, 55
   conceptual, xi, 16, 161
   perceptual, 98
   resonant, 97
Clark, Andy, 81
$clear_N$, see clearness, N^{th} grade of
clearness, 12, 33, 46–55, 155, 182
   1st grade of, 9, 51, 55
   2nd grade of, 9, 51, 55
   3rd grade of, 9, 12, 36, 45, 46, 51, 54, 55, 88, 90, 131, 133, 175
   4th grade of, 36, 51, 54, 55, 88, 131
   as a logical matter, 9
   conceptual, xi, 16, 80
   ideological, xi, 149
   of apprehension, 2, 9, 12, 51
   of thought, 9, 10, 41, 54, 55
   perfect, 14
   resonant, 97
cognition, 44, 61, 73
   embodied, 81
   enactive, 82
cognitive
   activity, 73
   development, 44, 82, 121
      enactive, 81
      epistemic, 81
   effect, 46
   expediency, 152
   science, 44, 80, 101
      enactivist, 7, 63
Cohen, Morris R., 60
Cohen, Patricia, ix
coherence

conceptual, 17
deductive, 17
inferential, 149–150, 161
logical, 55
preservation of, 19
systemic, 17, 48, 152
theory of truth, 17
coherentism, 17–19, 44–45
fact-based, 58
inferentialist, 6, 58
quasi-, 56
commitments, 17, 135–138
ontological, 66–68
common law, 177–183
community of inquiry, 33, 140, 174
compactness theorem for first-order languages, 171
complementarity
ecological, 87, 92
of affordances, 88
of animal and environment, 87, 93, 99
computation, 56–57, 77, 85, 108–111, 114
as artificial enhancement, 111, 137
connectionist, 110
extended, 111
from an externalist viewpoint, 110
internal, 108
pencil-and-paper, 111, 137
science as, 69
solipsistic, 71
Comte, Auguste, 25
conceivable
actions, 22–24, 42, 53, 68, 80
circumstances, 11, 24, 29
conduct, 53
consequences, 52
effects, 2, 12, 22–24, 33, 42, 68, 80
experimental, 27
practical, 14
evidence, 34
ideal, 33
inferences, 51
operational recipe, 170
perfection, 32–34

practical bearings, 2, 11, 24, 27, 34, 42, 45, 50
vs. actual, 24, 34
vs. foreseeable, 24
concept, xi, 27–30, 48, 60, 156
abstract, 4, 29
clarification of, xi, 16, 80
constitution of, 117
intellectual, 28–29, 52–53, 133, 170
legal, 177–183
common-law, 178
non-trivial, 30
operationalized, xi
conception, 12, 22, 23
as rational purport of an expression, 27
meaning of a, 23, 24
of an object, 2, 9, 14
concrete
action, xi, 16, 19, 150–153
experience, 62
physiological effects, 78
reasonableness, 51–55, 89, 131
reasons, 149
reform, 117
situation, xi, 101
concreteness, xi, 19, 37, 163
and logical methods, 54
operational, 5, 20, 54–55, 131, 149–150, 161
conduct, 14, 24, 27, 44, 49–53, 121
and practice, 14
conceivable, 53
conditional, 28–29
consequences of, 41
controllable, 50–51
deliberate, 50–51
effects of, 14
ethical, 41
future, 50–51
habit of, 42
meaning refers to, 50
modes of, 15, 27, 66
of life, 27, 42
rational, 27, 49, 116
recommended, 29, 156

rule of, 14
self-controlled, 50
tangible results of, 53
connectionism, 110
conscientious thoroughness, 54
consciousness, 85
consensus, 138–139
consequence, 16, 42, 156–157
   analytic, 174
   as tangible result, 52, 143, 156
   deductive, 53, 174
   future, 50, 156
   logical, 2, 16, 17, 46, 143, 157, 171
      as tangible result, 52
   long-term, 159
   material, 174
   of conduct, 41
   of intended action, 61
   perceptual, 25
   practical, 14–16, 20, 53, 162
   propositional, 150
   testable, 44
consequentialism, 158
conservatism, 18–19, 66, 150
constancy, 90, 105
   across successive samples, 109
   as stability, 89, 105, 111
   detectable, 103
   of terrain texture, 103, 112
   relational, 109
content, 176
   conceptual, xi, 35, 150
      empiricist, 171
      inferentialist, 171
      operationalist, 171–179
   ideological, 150
   inferential, of lower-order terms, 180
   of belief, 2, 11
   of thinking, 60
   operational, 174–176
      legal concept as, 180
      of higher-order terms, 180
   pragmatic, xii
   semantic, xii
contingency, 3, 50, 53

continuity, 26
conventionalism, 17
conversational pragmatics, 31
correlation, 99
cost-benefit analysis, x–xi, 154–155
counterfactuals, 24
covariance, 99
   of tangible results, 99
Crasnow, Sharon, 4
creative intelligence, 127
Critchley, Simon, ix, x
Critical Common-Sensism, 49

Darwin, Charles, 37, 89, 96
decision
   analysis, multi-criteria, 154
   legal, 177
   practical, 145
   procedures, 135
   theory, x
deduction, 9, 53
   as experimentation, 52
   material, 171–174
deductive
   consequence, 53, 174
   logic, 56
Deegan, Mary Jo, 117, 122
definition, 16, 23, 30–33
   abstract, 9
      as distinctness, 55
   and clarification, 33, 80, 180
   complete, 27
   inferential, 177
   operational, 30–33, 49–50, 59–61, 90, 134, 180
      as 3rd grade of clearness, 55, 133
      method of, 133
      recipe version of an, 170
   pragmatist, 135
   precise, 9
deliberate
   conduct, 50
   control, 51
deliberation, 119, 142
   deadlocked, 152
   democratic, 141–142

intellectual, 155
political, 142
reflective, 128
scientific, 142
vs. action, 152–153
democracy, 8, 64, 71, 121, 138–142, 161, 173–174, 176
and science, 138–141
as a perfection, 131, 140–142
as an ideal, 140–142
social, 123
vs. justice, 174
dependencies
law-like, 102
regularity of, 99
sensory, 102
Descartes, René, 5, 6, 41, 101, 182
detached
measurement, 74
observation, 74, 78–80, 115
perception, 80, 115
reasoning, 26
spectator, 7, 63, 73, 74, 78–80, 115, 126
thought, 26
Devitt, Michael, 44
Dewey, John, xiv, 3, 4, 48, 57–62, 67, 81, 157
diagnosis, charitable, 124
diamond, 27, 43, 50, 132, 171–173, 176
dice, 137
Dienes, Zoltan, 114
Dionne, E. J., Jr., ix, x, 150
discourse
as an operation, 47
ethics, 71
forms of, 67
legal, 179
open, 138
distinctness, 10
as 2nd grade of clearness, 9, 131
as abstract definition, 51, 55
as precise definability, 9
formal, 12
dogmatism, 150

double-aspect
epistemology, 56
pragmatism, 7, 48–51, 55
doubt, 10, 18–19, 32, 37, 41–43, 48, 143
removal of, 104
tentative, 104
Dunbar, Robin, 120
duty
of citizenship, 123
professional, 123

ecological
externalism, 87, 110
physics, 83, 109–110, 168
psychology, 7, 56, 63, 81–115, 133, 138
vs. pragmatism, 88, 115
economics, 31
Eddington, Sir Arthur S., 59–60
education, 121
effects, 156
conceivable, 22–24, 33
of actions, 26, 48, 67, 170
of conduct, 14
practical, 14, 43
sensory, 69
Einstein, Albert, 31, 59–60, 77
Eldridge, Michael, xiv, 47
Elshstain, Jean Bethke, 119–121
Emanuel, Rahm, ix, 148–149
embeddedness, 116
interactive, 128
neighborhood, 124
empiricism, x, 35, 84, 154
analytic, 26
as a stance, 4
atomistic, 7, 63, 161
commonsense, 85–86
experimental, 60
holistic, 63, 68, 161
impressionist, 125
logical, 26, 182
modern, 65
occasional, 153
passive, 71, 125
pragmatist, 126

radical, 4, 24, 48, 65, 82, 92, 109
rationalistic, 69
sensationist, 7, 45–47, 56–63, 66, 71, 78, 115, 118, 125–126, 129
vs. operationalism, 56, 133, 150
vs. pragmatism, 7, 26, 47, 65–72, 115–117, 124, 129, 154–155, 159, 161
vs. rationalism, 16, 62
enactivism, 7, 44, 63, 73, 80–82, 85–86
and action, 115
and ecological psychology, 82–115
weak, 82
ends, 42
absolutely necessary, 39
and means, x, 155–157
as consequences, 155
as means, 157
as tangible results, 156
hypothetically necessary, 39
Engel, Lawrence, x, xi
enrichment theory of perception, 88, 93, 98–99
entailment, semantic, 171, 174
entitlements, 17
epistemology, 5, 18, 48, 101
coherentist, 45
double-aspect, 56
foundationalist, 45
foundherentist, 56
modern, 61
modest, 157–158
ethical
conduct, 41
emptiness, 158–159
neutrality, 42, 159
ethnographic fieldwork, 118
Euclid, 9
events, 67
affordances of, 87
Everett, Stephen, xiv, 84, 101
evidence, ix, x, 19, 43, 58, 72, 122, 126, 128
acquiring, 70–72, 172
and the observer effect, 76–78

conceivable, 34
disconfirming, 138
effects as, 22
empirical, 56, 69
facts as, 58
inferential role of, 117
inferentialist, 56
new, 58
observational, 69–70, 73
operational, 69, 117
perceptual, 56
sensory effects as, 69
supportive, 56
use of, 70
vs. hearsay, 178
evidentialism, 56
evolution, 88–89, 100, 110
and education, 121
successive, 96
evolutionism, 89, 96
excellence, 32–33
expediency, x, xi, 151–152
cognitive, 152
in the long run, 152
opportunistic, 151
political, x, 151–152
professional, 129
truth as, 152
vs. pragmatism, 151–152
vs. principle, x
experience, 17, 20, 35, 40, 48, 56, 61–62, 65–68
animal, 80
as growth, 157
as interactive, 68
as the life of the law, 182
burgeoning, 157
concrete, 62
constituted by action, 115
direct, 92
embodied patterns of, 81
expected, 29, 156
falsifying, 70
immediate, 65, 68
ivory tower conception of, 66

object of, 81
  relations as, 92
  perceptual, 81
  rational, 61
  recalcitrant, 66
  sensory, 66–68, 71
experimental
  conditions, 53
  empiricism, 60
  inquiry, 25
  method, 29, 37, 156, 178
  operations, 60
experimentalism, 35–37
experimentation, 15, 21, 27, 57, 69–72, 116, 137, 150
  and reasoning, 53
  as action, 26, 42
  as thought, 53
  disciplined, 91
  in chemistry, 53
  in mathematics, 52–53
  intelligently directed, 69
  legal case as, 178
  psychophysical, 91
  settlement house methods as, 119
  sociological, 119
explanation, 128
exploratory
  adjustments, 97
  perception as, 97
extension
  of a predicate symbol, 173, 176
  of legal terms, 181
  of predicate symbols, 171
  set-theoretic, 173
extensionalism, 43, 67
  first-order, 7, 63, 68, 171
  vs. operationalism, 170–174, 183
extensive abstraction, 60
externalism, xiv, 45, 84–87, 101
  and computation, 110
  boundary problem, 111
  cognitive, 101
  ecological, 87, 110
  empirical testability of, 101
  enactivist, 81
  explanatory power of, 101
  social, 140
  vehicle, 81
  vs. internalism, 101, 110

facts, ix, 15–19, 25, 29, 43, 50–54, 57–61, 65, 139, 156, 162, 177–179
  actual, 51, 126
  altered by observation, 78–79
  as evidence, 58
  as functional, 58
  as inferential, 59, 162
  as operational, 58–59, 162
  as results, 150
  controllable vs. inferable, 50
  emergent, 150
  existential, 29, 57
  experimental, 15
  facticity of, 162
  future, 50–51
  interpretation-laden, 123, 162
  legal, 179
  necessary, 51
  new, 19, 58, 150
  normal, 126–128
    reform of, 128
  objective, 29
  observed, 57
  of a case, 57, 178–179
  past, 51
  perceptual, 25
  practical, 54
  scientific accumulation of, 119–122
  selected for inferential purposes, 58
fairness
  justice as, 141
  real, 141–142
fallibilism, 3, 18, 70, 137, 150, 157–158
  operationalist, 6
fallibility, x, 136–138
falsification, 70–71
familiarity as clarity, 9, 51, 55
family resemblance, 102
fast and frugal heuristics, 114
Feferman, Sol, 56

fellowship, 123
Fine, Arthur, 4
first-order
    extensionalism, 7, 63, 68, 175
    incompleteness, 174
    language, 44, 66–68, 85, 171–176, 182
        as higher-order language, 175
        metatheorems, 171
        truth for a, 44
    logic, 56
    nominalism, 68
    ontological commitments, 66–67
    predicates, 176
    proof, 171, 174
    semantics, 67, 170, 174–177
    thing, 7, 63, 67, 85
    variables, 68
    vocabulary, 171
Fisch, Max, 37
Fischer, Marilyn, 123–125
fitness
    as an achievement, 100
    attunement as, 99–100
fixation, 37, 95–100, 114
    as clarification, 96
    higher-order, 89, 97
    learning as, 98
    lower-order, 89, 96
        visual, 97
    measurement as, 103–105
    of belief, 31, 88–90, 99, 154, 173
    of biological species, 89
    of institutions, 139–140
    of invariants, 88–89, 95
        higher-order, 96
        lower-order, 96
    perfect, 173
    tuning as, 96
flexibility
    doxastic, 157–159
    moral, 159
Flower, Elizabeth, 1
Fodor, Jerry, 110
force, 22, 132
Forney, Glenn, 168

Foulis, David J., 176
foundation
    abductive, 25
    logical, 26
foundationalism, 44–45
    anti-, 3
    quasi-, 6, 44, 56
foundherentism, 56
van Fraassen, Bas, 4, 102, 176
freedom, 40–41
Freeman, Samuel, 141
functionalism, 45, 58
    vs. operationalism, 80
future
    associated with possibility and necessity, 50
    conduct, 50–51
    consequence, 50
    facts, 50–51

game theory, x, 154
general
    class-names, 30
    description, 54
    ideas, 54
    notions, 25
    terms, 31
        as parts of verbs, 30
generality, 52–53
    and thirdness, 24
    in perceptual judgments, 25
geometry, 9, 22, 53, 88
Gerson, Michael, x
gestalt psychology, 82, 87
Gettier, Edmund, 135
Gibson, Eleanor, 81, 100
Gibson, James, 170
Gibson, James J., xii, 7, 56, 63, 82–115, 133, 138, 168
Gigerenzer, Gerd, 114
Girard, Albert, 165
glass bead game, 139
    inferential, 177
God, 43–44
going around, 131
Goldberg, Jonah, ix, x

good old-fashioned AI and robotics, 110
Gordon, Bennett, ix
gradient descent, 97
grammar, 175
    higher-order, 175–176
        models for, 176
    lower-order, 175–176
        legal, 178–182
        models for a, 175–182
        recursively constructed, 179
    of optical stimulation, 114
        models for, 103
    of sensory stimulation, 101, 114
        models for, 103
    operation-based, 175–176
Green, Nicholas St. John, 5, 37, 42
Gregor, Mary, 42, 146–147

Haack, Susan, 56
habit, 1, 14, 16, 48, 101–102, 116, 175
    action, and belief, 5, 10–12
    as a rule of action, 1, 10–12, 14, 89, 140–144, 161
    as attunement, 99–102
    distributed, 140
    of conduct, 42
    social, 140–142
habituation, 103
    as fixation, 99
    attunement as, 99–100, 173
Hamburger, Tom, ix, x, 150
happiness, 40–41, 146–147
    worthiness of, 40, 146
hard, 22, 27, 42–43, 50, 132, 171–173, 176
Hardin, Garrett, 152
Harriot, Thomas, 165
Hayes, Christopher, ix, x, 149, 150
Heft, Harry, 82, 92, 99
heuristic
    as higher-order rule of action, 114
    fast and frugal, 114
high polymerization, 132, 172–173
higher-order
    action, 116
    affordances, 91
    disturbance, 96

fixation, 89, 97
    of invariants, 96
grammar, 175–176
    models for, 176
information, 98
invariant, 90
    as law-like, 89
    optical, 91
needs, 96
purpose, 96
semantics, 175
    semantic view as, 175
sentence, 176
stimulus, 98
Hobbes, Thomas, 151
holism, 7, 44, 63–68, 161
Holmes, Oliver Wendell, Jr., 182
Holt, E. B., 82, 92
Hughes, R. I. G., 102, 176
Hull House, 118–123
    Residents of, 117, 122
Hurley, Susan, 44, 80
hypothesis
    admissible, 25
    nonsensical, 26
    testable, 19, 70–71
    unclear, 26
    verifiable, 25

ideal, x, xi, 33
    as a perfection, 8, 32–34, 135, 142
    as a standard of excellence, 32
    limit, 33–34, 137
        conceivable, 33
    neighborhood, 119
    reality as an, 33–34
    rigid moral, x
    science, 32–33, 134–142
idealism, 155
ideas, 53, 62
    as functional, 58–59
    as operational, 57–58
    as plans for action, 58
    as proposals, 57
    empirical origin of, 61
    inferential nature of, 60

new, 150
non-existential, 57
operational origin of, 61
validity of, 60, 70
ideology, 148
and principles, xi, 149
blind, 148
clarification of, xi, 149
conservative, 150
content of, 150
dogmatic, ix, 148, 150
inferentially coherent, 150
meta-, 150
methodological, 150
neutral, 148–150
open-minded, 148, 150
operationalized, xi, 150
political, 149
progressive, 150
recalcitrant, 148
rigid, 149
scientific, 149
unavoidable, 149, 158–159
ungrounded, 149
vs. practicality, 148
Ignatius, David, ix
imagination, 53
mathematical, 52
impartiality, 74, 121–122, 139–140
perfect, 142
imperatives
hypothetical, 147
moral, 147
of prudence, 147
of skill, 147
prudential, 147
technical, 147
unconditionally necessary, 147
impressionism, social, 125
impressions, 70, 125–126
empirical, 125
operationalist conception of, 126
spectator conception of, 71, 125–126
independent trial, 176
induction, 9, 25, 53, 69

industrialization, 118
inference, 50–57, 133, 152, 157, 175–176
abductive, 25, 112
and inquiry, 9
as an activity, 57
as an operation, 47, 51
conceivable, 51
deductive, 171–174
forms of, 9
inductive, 69
lower-order, 103
material, 170–183
example of, 171–175
in first-order languages, 174
instinctive, 173
perceptual, 113
principles of, 66
statistical, 55
inferential
-role semantics, 17, 44, 47, 177
assignment, 113–115
clarification, 149
coherence, 149–150, 161
content, of lower-order terms, 180
definition, 177
glass bead game, 177
holism, 65
pragmatics, 45, 47
reasonableness, 54
inferentialism, 2, 28, 55, 70–71, 116, 143, 152, 161–162
and reform, 129
as functionalism, 58
axiomatic, 171
Brandom's, 44
James's, 1–3, 16, 19, 28, 46, 62
Peirce's version, 49–55
pragmatist, 44–47, 122, 129–132, 144, 154
reducible to operationalism, 51
vs. coherentism, 6, 58
vs. holism, 7
vs. operationalism, 55–62, 130–132, 174–176
information, 94, 97, 116

about affordances, 97
ambient fields of, 83
  auditory, 83
  chemical, 84
  material, 83
  nutritive, 84
  optical, 83, 84, 108, 110, 168
  orientational, 83
  tactile, 83
  vibratory, 83
complex, 109
extraction, 57
flow of, 109, 169
higher-order, 98
invariant, 98
optical, 97, 108–109
redundant, 84
samples of, 109
sampling, 109
stimulus, 83–85, 93, 98–99
storage, 111
innovation, 123
inquiry, 9–10, 48, 58, 72, 89, 119, 135
actual, 137
and inference, 9
as an operation, 31–33, 51, 134, 139, 141, 173
  legal, 178–180
as fixation of belief, 90, 99, 134, 173
as interactive, 69
community of, 32–33, 139–141, 174
cooperative, 69, 139
democratic, 142
democratization of, 71, 139
doubt/belief depiction of, 18–19, 88–89
experimental, 25
four types of, 138–140
ideal limit of, 33–34, 137
idealized, 32–34, 134–142
intelligent, 78
legal, as an operation, 178–180
objective, 78
perfect, 32–33, 134–142
  scientific, 33, 135, 138, 173–174

scientific, 10, 32, 71, 134–135, 141
  and democracy, 139, 174
  and justice, 141–142, 174
  and knowledge, 173
  and truth, 173
  perfect, 33, 135, 138, 173–174
self-correcting, 139–140
spectator conception of, 71
theory of, 48
  pragmatist vs. empiricist, 68–72
thought as, 10
vs. consensus, 139
instinct, 116, 173
institutions
  as social habits, 140–141
  as tangible results of inquiry, 140
  basic, 141–142
    as tangible results, 141
  democratic, 140, 174
  fixed, 139–140
  just, 141, 174
  perfect, xi, 140, 174
instrumentalism, 17, 48, 60, 157
intellectual
  concept, 28–29, 52–53, 60, 133
  deliberation, 155
  instruments, 60
  predicate, 29
  purport, 27, 49–50
  significance, 61
  slavery, 138
intellectualism, 65
  vicious, 155
  vs. pragmatism, 155
intelligence, 48, 159
  creative, 127
  experimental, 69
  sensorimotor, 82
intension, operational, 172–181
  disjunctive nature of, 177
  of legal terms, 178–181
  of predicate symbols, 173–177
interaction, 42–43, 66, 80
  fact-changing, 78–79
  social, 123

interactive
  experience, 68
  immersion, 125–128
  inquiry, 69
  measurement, 7, 63, 71–79
  observation, 7, 63, 73–79, 117
  perception, 7, 63, 73, 79–80
internalism, 44, 101, 110
interpretation, 122–127, 159
  -laden facts, 123
  and action, 117
  and participant observation, 124
  authoritative, 123–125, 178
  competent, 123–124
  first-order, 171
  hermeneutic, 178
  reciprocal, 123
  underdetermined, 174
  valid, 124
invariance relation, 102–105, 109–114, 169, 175
invariant, 25, 82–85, 93–94, 170
  as a unit, 91
  as a value of a variable, 90, 100
  auditory, 83
  biological, 89
  chemical, 84
  complex, 91
  compound, 91
  detection, 83–90, 98–102, 112–115, 175
    as a tangible result, 90
    as sensory stimulation, 90, 169
    lower-order, 102
  evolutionary, 89
  extraction, 91–92, 97–99, 105, 115
    lower-order, 102–103
  fixation of, 88–89, 96
  higher-order, 89–92, 98
    as law-like, 89, 92, 99
    optical, 91
  information, 98
  is not a stimulus, 91–92
  lower-order, 90, 100
  material, 83
  mathematical description of, 91–92, 101, 108
  nutritive, 84
  of invariants, 90–91, 100, 112
    and affordances, 91
  optical, 83–86
  orientational, 83
  production, 113–115
  registration, 86, 105
  tactile, 83
  type, 100
  vibratory, 83
  vs. association of sensations, 91
inverse gnomonic projection, 106–108

James, William, xii, 1–9, 12–30, 36–37, 42–66, 69, 71, 82, 92, 109, 117, 126, 131–132, 143–145, 148, 152, 155–157, 160–163, 171
Jarrett, Valerie, ix, 144
Johnson, Mark, 81
judgment, 138, 158
  ampliative, 25
  fallible, 25
  legal, 177–179
    aspects of a, as tangible results, 178–179
    five aspects of a, 178–179
    searchable, 180–181
    written, 178–181
  moral, 159
  objectively valid, 35
  perceptual, 23–25
  theoretical, 23
just institution, 141, 174
justice, xi, 8, 64, 141–142, 161, 173–174, 176
  as a perfection, 131, 141–142
  as an ideal, 142
  as fairness, 141
  operational definition of, 141
  social-contract theory of, 141
  vs. democracy, 174
justification, 19, 25, 135
  empirical, 56
  epistemic, 56

imperfect, 136
perfect, 134–138, 173–174
scientific, 17

Kant, Immanuel, xii, 5, 6, 35, 37–42, 61, 80, 144, 146–148, 151
Kantor, Jodi, x, xi
knowledge, 8, 64, 134–138, 161
   as a perfection, 131, 134–135, 142, 173
   as an ideal, 131, 134–135, 142
   assertion of, 138
   by acquaintance, 21
   immediate, 155
   JTB conception of, 135
   PJTB conception of, 134–137
   vs. belief, 137
   vs. truth, 134–135, 173
Koffka, Kurt, 82
Koopman, Colin, ix
Kripke, Saul, 44
Kroft, Steve, ix
Kyburg, Henry, 135–136

labor, vs. leisure, 150
laboratory
   activities, 32
   operation, 32
Lakoff, George, 81
Lamond, Grant, 178
language, 65
   computer, 56–57
   first-order, 44, 66–68, 85, 171–176, 182
      as higher-order language, 175
      metatheorems, 171
   human, 57
   natural, 57
   of optical stimulation, 114
      models for, 103
   of sensory stimulation, 101, 114
      models for, 101, 103
   operation-based, 175–178
   use, 57
      as a black box, 176
Lashley, Karl, 93–94
Lavoisier, Antoine, 154

law, xi, 102
   a priori, 40
   absolute, 40–41
   common, 177–183
   ecological, 90
   empirically conditioned, 40
   hypothetical, 41
   life of the, 182
   necessary, 41
   of morality, 40
   of nature, 89, 99–100
      as an invariant, 89
      mathematically formulated, 100
   of physics, 65
   practical
      moral, 40–41, 146
      pragmatic, 40–41, 146
      pure, 40–41
   regulatory, 177
   rule of, 139
   statutory, 177–178
learning, 93–99
   as fixation, 98
   by association, 93, 98
   of affordances, 99
   of associations, 98
   of sensitivities, 97
   perceptual, 98
   to perceive, 99
Lee, David, 113–114
legal
   authority, 177
   case, 177–182
      as a model, 179–182
      as a thing-in-itself, 178
      as an experiment, 178, 180
      prior, 177, 182
      token, 178–182
      truth in a, 179
      type of, 178–181
   concept, 177–183
      as a class of cases, 179–182
      as operational content, 180
      common-law, 177
      semantic view of, 177–182

court of record, 178
decision, 177
dictionary, 177
discourse, 179
inquiry as an operation, 178–180
issue to be resolved, 178–179
judgments, 177–179
  aspects of, as tangible results, 178–179
  five aspects of, 178–179
  searchable, 180–181
  written, 178–181
manual, 179
methods, 178, 179
operation, 178
outcome, 178
pragmatism, 182
principles, 139, 177–179
  authoritative, 177
  precedents as, 177, 178
procedures, 178, 179
protocols, 178
rationale, 177, 182
  for resolution of the issue, 178
recitation of facts, 178–179
ruling, 178
term
  extension of a, 181
  higher-order, operational content of, 180
  lower-order, functional uses of a, 180
  operational intension of a, 181
Leibniz, Gottfried Wilhelm, 28
leisure, vs. labor, 150
length, 59
Lerner, Michael, ix
Lim, Elvin, ix, x
lithium, 30–32, 49, 132, 175
Livermore, Michael, x
Lizza, Ryan, ix–xi
logic, xii, 9, 22, 28, 48, 51, 53, 56–57
  and action, 26
  as the life of the law, 182
  deductive, 56
  mathematical, 56
  of abduction, 25
  of perception, 25, 113, 133, 173, 175
  of science, 133
logical
  atomism, 7, 63
  consequences, 2, 52, 171
  empiricism, 26, 182
  energy, 26
  foundation, 26
  methods, 53–54
  positivism, 7, 44, 63, 68, 139, 182
  thought, 26
long run, 18, 33, 137, 152
  expediency, 152
looming objects, 113–114
lottery paradox, 135–136
Löwenheim, Leopold, 171
Löwenheim-Skolem theorem for first-order languages, 171
lower-order
  ability, 90, 103, 116
  action, 100, 116, 175–176
  adjustments, 97
  features, 98
  fixation, 89, 96
    of invariants, 96
    visual, 97
  functional space of usage, 180
  grammar, 175–182
    legal, 178–182
    models for a, 175–182
    recursively constructed, 179
  inference, 103
  invariant, 90, 100
    extraction, 102–103
  operation, 176
  self-tuning, 97
  semantics, 175, 179
  sentence, 175
  variable, 90–92
    legal, 179
    stimulus, 91, 101–102, 114
  vocabulary, 176
Lowry, Rich, ix, 150

Mace, William, 100
Machiavelli, Niccolò, 39, 151
MacKay, Donald, 86
Makinson, D. C., 136
Malinowski, Bronisław, 118
material
   consequence, 174
   deduction, 171–174
   inference, 170–183
      example of, 171–175
      in first-order languages, 174
      in legal languages, 180–182
mathematics, 22, 51–53, 57, 170
   pure, 65
Maturana, Humberto, 44
maxim of pragmatism, 1–8, 12, 15–17, 20, 35–37, 46, 54, 66–68, 115, 130–132, 143–144, 161, 175, 183
   ambiguity of the, 1, 70, 113
   and animal experience, 80, 115
   as a maxim of logic, 2, 4, 48, 149, 152
   James's version of the, 15–16, 156, 161
   nominalist application of the, 22, 43, 132, 171
   recipe version of the, 170
   statement of, 2, 9, 23, 24, 27, 29, 49, 52, 54, 68, 170
McDermott, John, xiv
McLeod, Peter, 114
Mead, George H., 3–4, 48
meaning, 1, 4, 23, 24, 28, 34–37, 42–46, 148, 152
   and habits, 10–11, 16
   as a corollary concept, 3, 143, 158, 161
   as affordance, 88, 90, 93, 99
   beyond immediate content, 28
   clarification of, 19, 175, 183
   inferential, 36, 151, 158, 161
   instrumental, 48
   of 'meaning', 88
   of a belief, 17
   of a conception, 23–24, 29, 52, 156
   of a judgment, 23
   of a predicate, 42, 175
   of a thought, 10–14, 16, 28, 60
      of an object, 60
   of a word, 134, 156
   of the object of a thought, 11, 16, 28
   operational, 36, 48, 56, 151, 158, 161, 170
   perception of, 88
   practical, 16
   pragmatist conception of, 156–157
   refers to conduct, 50, 156
meaningfulness, 162
   degree of, 22
means, x
   and ends, 155–157
   functionally justified, 157
measurement, xi, 14, 21, 31, 57, 74
   as fixation, 103–105
   as interactive, 7, 63, 71–79, 161
   as invariant extraction, 104–105
   detached, 74
   direct, 22
   finality of, 157
   operations, 60, 67, 103, 175
   passive, 74
   psychophysical, 91
   quantitative, 91
   spectator conception of, 7, 63
memory, 50, 93–94
   trace, 93–94
Menand, Louis, 37
Metaphysical Club, 6, 37, 89
method, 89
   axiomatic, 9, 44, 131, 171, 174, 182
   experiential, 32
   experimental, 29, 37, 156
   legal, 178, 179
   logical, 53–54
   of a priori reasoning, 138
   of authority, 138, 154
   of intelligence, 48
   of operational definition, 133
   of science, 154, 174
   of tenacity, 138, 154
   pragmatist, 4, 29, 64, 133, 141, 144, 156, 182

scientific, 32–35, 48, 53, 139–140, 173
semantic, 65
statistical, 122
methodological solipsism, 69–70
methodology, 48, 118
    pragmatist, 130, 149–150
    settlement house, 117–129
modality
    objective, 50–51
    temporal, 50
model
    for a higher-order grammar, 176
    for a lower-order grammar, 175–182
    for language of
        optical stimulation, 103
        sensory stimulation, 101–102
    legal case as a, 179–182
    nonstandard, 171
    of an attunement, 108
    of regularities, 109
    theory, 56–57
    truth in a, 102, 175, 179
    valuation as a, 179
modesty, epistemological, 157–158
modularity, 110
Mooney, Chris, x
Moore, G. E., 17–18
moral
    belief, 38–40
    compass, 158–159
    judgment, 159
    law, 39–41
        practical, 40–41, 146
    principles, 39
    relativism, 158
    sensitivity, 159
morality, 146
    vs. politics, 151
Moss, William, 168
motherboard, 111
Murphey, Murray, 1
muscle systems, 84–86, 94

names, 45–46
natural
    frequencies, 93–96
    fixation of, 95
    selection, 88–89
necessity, 51
    absolute, 41
    as temporal modality, 50
    circumstantial, 50
    hypothetical, 38
needs, 92, 98
    and affordances, 93
    higher-order, 96
neighborhood
    citizenship, 120–126
    embeddedness, 124
    ideal, 119
    immersion, 125–126
    life, 125
    residence, 123, 127
    responsibility, 124, 127
    social services, 119
Newton, Sir Isaac, 22, 74, 108, 154
Noë, Alva, 44, 81–82
nominalism, 22, 43, 69, 171
    first-order, 67–68, 100
    formal, 67–69, 100
    vs. realism, 132
normative ethics, 41
normativity, xii, 145–146, 152

Obama, Barack, ix–xi, 144–145, 149
obiter dicta, 177
object, 14, 20, 57, 86–88, 170
    abstract, 67
    affordances of an, 87, 90, 116
    as a bundle of properties, 87, 102
    as a system of affordances, 87–90, 102
    awareness of an, 86–87
    character of an, 28
    ecological, 88
    falling under a concept, 16, 21, 43
    instantiating a concept, 116
    kinds of, 87, 102
    looming, 113–114
    of a conception, 2, 9
    of a word, 30–31
    of experience, 35, 81
    of perception, 85

of thought, 11, 16, 28
perception of, 88, 98, 170
value-free, 88
value-rich, 88
objective
  facts, 29
  modality, 50–51
  practical principles
    moral, 147
    prudential, 147
    technical, 147
  preference, 41
  validity, 159
objectivity, xi, 74, 78, 121–122, 139–140, 142, 159
  perfect, 142
  scientific, 142
  vs. conceit, 119
observation, 15, 21, 58, 69–72, 122
  active, 70, 117, 161
  as interactive, 7, 63, 73–79, 115–117, 126, 182
  bias, 74
  cooperative, 69
  detached, 74, 78–80, 115
  in science, 74–79
  operations of, 58
  ordinary, 79
  participant, 78, 115–127
  passive, 69–70, 74, 78
  sentence, 69–71
  spectator conception of, 7, 63, 69–80, 115, 125
  theory-laden, 26, 80
observer effect, 7, 63, 73–79, 183
  in astronomy, 76
  in computer science, 77
  in cultural anthropology, 78
  in electronics, 74
  in materials science, 75
  in medical research, 78
  in meteorology, 75
  in particle physics, 75
  in physics, 74
  in psychology, 77
  in quantum mechanics, 75, 182
  in social and behavioral sciences, 77, 182
  in special relativity theory, 77
  in thermodynamics, 75
Ockham, William of, 28
ontological
  commitments, 66–68
    first-order, 66–67
  promiscuity, 67
  relativism, 44, 66
operation, 15, 89
  as a black box, 176
  calculation, 60
  discourse, 47
  experimental, 60
  inferential, 47
  inquiry as an, 33, 134, 141, 173, 178
  invariant detection as an, 90
  laboratory, 20, 32
  legal, 178
  lower-order, 176
  measurement, 60, 67, 175
  observational, 57–58
  types, 67, 133, 175
operational
  analysis, 59
  clarification, 115, 149, 176
  concreteness, 5, 20, 54–55, 131, 149–150, 161
  content, 174–176
    legal concept as, 180
    of higher-order terms, 180
  definition, 30–33, 49–50, 59–61, 90, 115, 131–134, 170, 172, 180
    as 3rd grade of clearness, 55
    conceivable, 170
    method of, 133
    recipe version of an, 170
  evidence, 117
  facts, 57
  ideas, 57–58
  intension, 172–181
    disjunctive nature of, 177
    of legal terms, 178–181

222 / INDEX

    of predicate symbols, 173–177
    semantics, 47, 62, 170, 175
        as lower-order semantics, 175
operationalism, xi, 2–3, 7, 14–16, 19–20,
        35, 44, 55, 62, 68, 143, 161–162
    and residence, 129
    as functionalism, 58
    Bridgman's, 59–60
    Dewey's, 57–62
    Eddington's, 59–60
    Einstein's, 31, 60, 77
    first-order, 171
    pragmatist, 29, 43–47, 60, 67–70,
        115–118, 122, 129–132, 144,
        154, 161
    vs. empiricism, 56, 133, 150
    vs. extensionalism, 170–174, 183
    vs. functionalism, 80
    vs. inferentialism, 55–62, 130–132,
        174–176
operationalized
    concept, xi, 31, 116
    ideology, xi
    principle, xi
opportunism, x, 151–152
optic flow field, 113
optical
    abilities, 103
    illusions, 112
    information, 108–109, 168
    surface area, 105–111, 164–169
        of a coin, 106
    texture, 112–113
        density, 102–113
optimizing adjustments, 97
ordinary language philosophy, 45
original position, 141–142, 174
Ostwald, Wilhelm, 15
outcome, 71
    as a tangible result, 67, 134, 138, 161,
        170, 178
    legal, 178–180
    measurement, 104, 157
    numerical, 67
    observational, 73, 182

    perceptual, 93
    possible, 67, 176
    types, 170, 179
        invariant-extraction, 104, 175

Packer, George, ix, x, 149, 150
Papini, Giovanni, 6
paradox
    lottery, 135–136
    of the commons, 152
    preface, 136
Parker, Kelly, 51
part-of relation, $\sqsubseteq$, 173–174, 177
participant observation, 78, 115–127
    and residence, 122, 126–127
partisanship, ix, x, 148, 162
    and pragmatism, 149–150
    proactive, 155
passive
    empiricism, 71
    information channels, 73
    measurement, 74
    observation, 69–70, 74, 78, 115
    perception, 70, 115
    reception of impressions, 70
    receptivity, 73
    sensation, 66–68, 71
    spectator, 7, 63, 73
        detached, 74
past, associated with actuality, 50
Pavlov, Ivan Petrovich, 99
Payne, Rodger, ix, x
Peirce, Charles Sanders, xii, xiii, 1–70, 73,
        88, 89, 96, 99–100, 112, 115,
        117, 120, 129–148, 154–157,
        160–163, 170–176, 182
Pelley, Steve, ix, 148
pendulum, 95–97
    clock, 95–96
perception, 11, 24–26, 44, 52, 57, 73,
        80–89, 94, 111, 115, 129, 138
    ampliative, 25, 80
    and action, 80–115
    animal, 73
    as abductive, 26, 112
    as active, 81, 161

as enacted, 81
  as exploratory, 97
  as interactive, 7, 63, 73, 79–80
  as passive, 70, 115
  as perfect abductive faculty, 24
  as pickup of associated variables of information, 98
  as touch-like, 73, 81
  detached, 80, 115
  direct, 24, 85–87, 103, 111–112
  dynamic, 83
  ecological, 84
  efficient, 99
    law-like, 100
  enactive, 82
  enactivist conception of, 81
  enrichment theory of, 88, 93, 98–99
  fallible, 25–26
  logic of, 25, 113, 133, 173, 175
  object of, 85
  of affordances, 24, 85–88, 92–94, 114, 169
  of meaning, 88
  of objects, 88, 98, 170
  of space, 88
  of thirdness, 24
  ordinary, 80
  raw elements of, 86
  spectator conception of, 70, 80, 86, 115
  veridical, 85, 112
  visual, 83, 168
  vs. invariant detection, 86
  vs. representation, 111
  vs. sensation, 85, 115, 169
perceptual
  acquaintance, 30–31
  attention, 84–85
  consciousness, 81
  development, 81, 98
  judgments, 23–25
  kinds, 133
  prediction, 25
  systems, 83–86, 89, 93, 133
perfect
  clearness, 14

  fixation, 173
  impartiality, 142
  inquiry, 32–33, 134–142
    scientific, 33, 135, 138, 173–174
  institution, xi, 140, 174
  justification, 134–138, 173–174
  objectivity, 142
  political order, 140
  sampling, 137
  tangible results, 32–33, 142
perfection, 33, 134, 137
  as an ideal, 8, 32–34, 135, 142
  conceivable, 32–34
  democracy as a, 131, 140–142
  highest, 24
  justice as a, 131, 141–142
  knowledge as a, 131, 134–135, 142, 173
  reality as a, 8, 33–34, 134, 138, 142
  truth as a, 8, 32–34, 131, 134, 135, 138, 142, 173
perfectionism, xi, 14, 24, 32–34, 138
  intelligent, 140
  long-run, 131
  scientific, 133–135
Perry, John, xiv
Perry, Ralph Barton, 2
perspective, 70
  single-point, 106
  spherical, 106–108
Pfeifer, David, 51
philanthropy, 120
photons, 86
physics, 22–23, 30, 59, 74
  ecological, 83, 109–110
  laws of, 65
  mathematical, 67
  Newtonian, 22, 74, 108, 154
  of heat, 168
  of light, 168
  quantum, 76, 182
  terrestrial, 83, 115
π, 34
Piaget, Jean, 81–82
Pick, Anne, 81, 100

place
  affordances of, 87
  as a relation, 20
pluralism, ix, 3, 152
  intensional, 176–177
political order, 138–140
  anarchic, 138
  aristocratic, 138
  democratic, 139, 140
  Machiavellian, 151
  perfect, 140
  tyrannical, 138
polymer, 172
Popper, Karl, 70
positivism, logical, 44, 63, 139, 182
possibility
  as temporal modality, 50
  objective, 21
practical, 40
  applications, 129
  bearings, 2, 9, 24, 31, 34, 42–49, 155, 161
    actual, 24
    counterfactual, 24
  belief, 38
  consequences, 14–16, 20, 53, 162
  considerations, 11, 19, 52–54, 66, 145, 182
  difference, 14, 19–20
  effects, 43
  facts, 54
  laws
    moral, 40–41, 146
    pragmatic, 40–41, 146
    pure, 40–41
  point of view, 38
  principles, objective
    moral, 147
    prudential, 147
    technical, 147
  problems, 51, 55
  validity, 39
  vs. pragmatic, 66, 145–147, 153
  with reference to morality, 39
  with reference to skill, 39

practicalism, 37–40, 146
  vs. pragmatism, 145–146, 149
practicality, 8, 13–16, 144
  anti-intellectual, x, 155
  conceivable, 11
  post-partisan, ix, 148–150
  vs. ideology, 148
pragmatic, ix, x, 40–42, 143–146, 153
  belief, 38, 41
  inferentialism, 45
  maxim, see maxim of pragmatism
  method, 13–14, 29, 65
  practical laws, 40–41, 146
  vs. ideological, 148
  vs. moral, 40
  vs. practical, 66, 145–147, 153
  vs. prudent, 40, 66, 145–148
  vs. prudential, 146–148
pragmaticism, 6, 28, 49–50
  as operationalist pragmatism, 49
pragmatics, 44
  conversational, 31
  inferential, 45, 47
pragmatisch, 37–41, 146–148
pragmatism, ix, xiv, 1, 13, 27, 36, 42, 115, 129–131, 143–162
  absolutist, 150
  and abduction, 25
  and partisanship, 149–150
  and principle, x–xi, 149–151
  as a conversation, 3–5
  as a doctrine, 3–4, 16, 29, 37, 144–145, 156
  as a method, 4–5, 16, 37, 49, 120, 143–145, 148, 159, 163
    of clarification, 144, 170
  as a methodological ideology, 150
  as a stance, xi, 4–6, 36, 69, 120, 161
    methodological, 158
  as a style, 4
  as a temperament, 4, 144
  as an attitude, xi, 4–5, 16, 36, 143–145, 150, 156, 161
  as ideologically neutral, 148–149
  as meta-ideological, 150

close-minded, 150
coherentist, 66
Dewey's, 59, 157
double-aspect, 7, 48–51, 55, 69, 71, 113–115, 131, 143–144, 158, 161–163
enactivist, 7, 63
examples
  affordances, 90
  blood, 43, 45
  catchable fly ball, 114
  democracy, 7, 64, 138–141, 161, 173–174, 176
  diamonds, 27, 43, 50, 132, 171–173, 176
  ecological theory of perception, 115
  ∈, 44
  evolution, 45
  force, 22, 132
  freedom, 45
  God, 43–44
  going around, 13–14, 131
  hard, 22, 27, 42–43, 50, 132, 171–173, 176
  high polymerization, 132, 172–173
  justice, 7, 64, 141–142, 161, 173–174, 176
  knowledge, 7, 64, 131, 134–138, 161, 173
  legal concepts, 177–183
  length, 59
  lithium, 30–31, 49, 132, 175
  looming objects, 113–114
  matter, 45
  personal identity, 45
  polymer, 172
  rainy weather, 43
  reality, 7, 22, 30–31, 42–43, 51, 64, 131, 133–134, 161
  relation, 51
  step distance, 113
  substance, 45, 50–51, 171
  time, 50–51
  transubstantiation, 12, 45, 132, 171
  truth, 7, 20–22, 30–32, 43, 64, 131, 133–134, 161, 173
  walkable surface, 103, 112–113, 168–169
  weight, 22
  wine, 42–43, 45
history of, 1
inferentialist, 3, 7, 16, 26, 44–47, 55, 63, 71, 116, 122, 129–132, 144, 149, 154, 158, 161
legal, 182
misconceptions of, 145–161
occasional, 152–153
operationalist, 7, 29, 30, 43–45, 47, 55, 60, 63, 67–70, 73, 115–118, 122, 129–132, 144, 154, 158, 161, 170–175, 182
political, 8, 145, 149
Quine's, 66–68
shortsighted, 158
three cotary propositions of, 24, 32
vs. consequentialism, 158
vs. dogmatism, 150
vs. empiricism, 7, 47, 65–72, 115–117, 124, 129, 154–155, 159, 161
vs. expediency, 151–152
vs. ideological partisanship, 148–151
vs. intellectualism, 155
vs. logical positivism, 7, 44, 63, 68–72, 139
vs. practicalism, 145–146, 149
vs. prudentialism, 145–148, 151
vs. rationalism, 65, 155, 159
vs. utilitarianism, 158
pragmatist
  analysis, 117
  definition, 135
  emphasis on consequences, 155–157
  method, 32, 64, 130, 133, 141, 150, 182
praktisch, 37–41, 146
precedent, 177–179, 182
  legitimate, 178, 179
precept, 23, 30–31, 49
predicate

extension of, 171
intellectual, 29
meaning of, 42
symbol, 171
   extension of, 173, 176
   lower-order, 179
   operational intension of, 173–177
vs. subject, 46
prediction, 100
perceptual, 25
preface paradox, 136
principle, x, 16, 40
acting from, 149
and pragmatism, x–xi, 149–151
authoritative, 177
clarification of, xi, 149
empirical, 40
legal, 139, 177–179
   precedent as a, 177, 178
moral, 39
objective practical
   moral, 147
   prudential, 147
   technical, 147
of significance, 35
operationalized, xi
vs. expediency, x
Prinz, Jesse, 86
problem solving, 123, 127–128
production
of invariants, 113–115
operational, 115
Progressive Era, 118
progressivism, 150
projection, inverse gnomonic, 106–108
proof
as a thing, 57
as argumentation, 153
as experimentation, 52–53
first-order, 171, 174
of the pudding, 153
proper names, 30
property, 67, 88, 175
accidental, 46
bundles, 87, 102
ecological, 93
inherent, 85
physical, 67, 74
sensible, 85
vs. affordance, 87
proposition
basic, 67
categorical, 30
justified, 136
subject of, 31
protocol sentence, 21
prudence, x, 39–40, 66, 144–148
and skill, 147
as wisdom, 147
Machiavellian, 39, 147, 151
professional, 129
rules of, 40, 146–147
vs. wisdom, 147
prudentialism, 145–148, 151
psychology, 48
ecological, 56, 63, 81–115, 133
   vs. pragmatism, 88
enactivist, 85
gestalt, 82, 87
rationalist, 20–21
purpose, 39
achievement of a, 41
fixation of belief as a, 41
higher-order, 96
inferential, of selecting facts, 58
of action, 11
of thought, 10
rational, 37–38
removal of doubt as a, 41
Putnam, Hilary, 7, 44, 63, 68–71, 139

quasi-coherentism
foundherentist, 56
inferentialist, 56
quasi-foundationalism
foundherentist, 56
operationalist, 6, 44
Quine, Willard van Orman, 2, 7, 26, 44, 63, 65–71, 85, 100, 154, 161, 170
quotation, 180

radiative heat, 168
radical empiricism, 4, 24, 48, 65, 82, 92, 109
Randall, Charles H., 176
ratio decidendi, 177
rational, 153
   acceptance, 135
   assertion, 136
   believability, 6, 136
   conduct, 27, 49, 116
   consistency, 153
   experience, 61
   life, 53
   purport, 42
   thought, 26
rationalism, 9, 20–21, 61, 153
   a priori, 61–62
   and intellectualism, 155
   Cartesian, 9
   modern, 65
   occasional, 153
   vs. empiricism, 16, 62
   vs. pragmatism, 65, 155, 159
rationality, bounded, 114
Rawls, John, 141–142, 174
realism
   scholastic, 43, 49
   vs. nominalism, 132
reality, xi, 20, 22, 30–34, 37, 42–43, 51, 64, 133–134, 137, 161
   agreement with, 20
   as a perfection, 8, 33–34, 134, 138, 142
   as an ideal, 8, 33–34, 134, 142
   first-class, 67
   independent of thought, 31, 33, 42, 159
   mathematical, 137
   moral, 159
   of a diamond, 27
   of beer, 35
   Peirce's definition of, 31–34, 133–134
reasonableness, 52, 54–55
   concrete, 51–55, 89, 131
   global, 55
   inferential, 54
   provincial, 139

reasoning, 10, 25, 52, 54
   a priori, 17, 32, 41
   and experimentation, 53
   conclusion of, 50
   deductive, 52–53
   detached, 26
   fruitful, 51–52, 55
   guiding principles of, 9
   mathematical, 52–53
   precise, 52
   prudential, 147
reasons, 128
   abstract, 149
   concrete, 149
   ideologically neutral, 149
   subjective, 19
recognition, 94
reconstruction
   civic, 124
   reciprocal, 124
Reed, Edward, 83–84, 100
reference, 45
reflective deliberation as activity, 128
reform, 116–119, 122, 127–128, 133
   and inferentialism, 126, 129
   as action, 128–129
   as applied science, 122
   concrete, 117
   social, 117–119, 122
regularities, 20, 99–102, 108
   as invariants, 100
   attunement to, 108
   attunements as, 100
   dynamic, 93, 100
   ecological, 101
   law-like, 100
   models of, 109
   natural laws as, 100
Reich, Robert, x, 158
relation, 51, 67
   as parts of experience, 92
   as simple datum, 92
   commonsense, 20
   directly experienced, 92

invariance, 102–105, 109–114, 169, 175
  law-like, 22, 92, 100–101, 112, 175
  physical, 67
  static, 57
remembering, 94
representation, 43, 111
  as enactive, 81–82
  externalist conception of, 81
research, 116, 119, 122, 127, 133
  as activity, 128
  as search for solutions, 123, 128
  methodology, 118
residence, 118–129, 133
  and operationalism, 129
  and participant observation, 122, 126–127
  as action, 129
  as embedded interaction, 128
  neighborhood, 124, 127
    entails duties of citizenship, 123
    promotes fellowship, 123
    requires sympathy, 123
resolution process, 84
resonance, 93–95
  clear, 97
  precise, 97
  sympathetic, 94
  to information, 94
  vague, 97
resonant frequencies, 94–96
resonator, 94
  self-tuning, 94
Revesz, Richard, x
risk assessment, x, 154–155
Rivas, Bruno, ix
Rorty, Richard, 1, 3, 149
routine, xi, 34, 89
  automatic, 116
  evolved, 89
Rowlands, Mark, 44, 81, 86
Royce, Josiah, 28
rule of
  action, 1, 10–11, 14
    attunement as, 99
    habit as a, 1, 10–12, 14, 89, 140–144
    heuristic as, 114
  conduct, 14
  law, 139
  prudence, 40, 146–147
Russell, Bertrand, 17–18

saccadic movements, 109
Salam, Reihan, ix
sampling, 70, 109
  binocular, 109
  coffee beans, 137
  optical, 83
  perceptual, 97
  perfect, 137
  subsurface core, 11, 34
  successive, 109
  throws of a die, 137
  voter populations, 76
satisfaction, 19, 41
  of all desires, 40, 146
  semantic, 43, 57
Schiller, Ferdinand Canning Scott, 28
Schneider, Herbert, 1
Scholastic Realism, 43, 49
Schroeder, Christopher, x
Schultz, Bart, ix–xi, 150
science, 7, 17, 32, 48, 53, 65, 71, 73, 88–89, 116
  and democracy, 138–141
  and service, 122
  anthropological, 118
  as computation, 69
  cognitive, 7, 44, 63, 80, 101
  ethnographic, 118
  idealized, 32–33, 133–142
  in political affairs, 140
  logic of, 133
  method of, 139–140, 154, 173–174
  Newtonian, 22, 74, 108, 154
  self-correcting, 139–140
  social, 31, 77–78, 117, 122, 161
  social and behavioral, 78, 115, 118, 182
  sociological, 118, 122, 133

vs. metaphysics, 156
self, social character of, 3
Sellars, Wilfrid, 2, 44, 171
Selten, Reinhard, 114
semantic view
  as higher-order semantics, 175
  of legal concepts, 177–182
  of perceptual object-types, 103, 112, 114
  of scientific theories, 102, 176, 182
semantics, 48, 65
  conceptual-role, 44
  extensional, 67, 171, 175–176, 183
  first-order, 67, 170, 174–177
  higher-order, 175
    semantic view as, 175
  inferential-role, 17, 44, 177
    empiricist, 47
  lower-order, 175, 179
  many-sorted, 67, 175, 179
  of computer languages, 56–57
  operational, 43–47, 62, 183
    as lower-order semantics, 175, 179
  passive-empiricist, 71
  pragmatist, 71
  traditional, 56–57
  truth-conditional, 43
sensation, 12–14, 26, 60, 66, 84, 88–89, 109
  as first and last, 15
  passive, 66–68
  physiological mechanics of, 66
  spectator conception of, 66
  visual, 86, 91, 169
  vs. perception, 85, 169
sensationism, 7, 24, 45–47, 56–63, 66, 71, 78, 115–118, 126, 129
  impressionist, 125
  sociological, 125
sense data, 26, 60
sensible
  attributes, 46
  circumstances, 11, 16
  effects, 7, 12, 15, 24, 27, 31, 49–50,
    see also attributes

  as invariants, 101–103, 109
  as operational outcomes, 161
  as surface irritations, 66
  as values of variables, 67, 100–102, 113
  conceivable, 12, 22, 42, 52, 80
  covariation of, 99, 102
  finality of, 157
  in an inferentialist sense, 113
  in an operationalist sense, 113
  of actions, 11–12, 16, 19, 22, 26, 37, 46, 63, 113–115
  of experimentation, 21
  of measurement, 21, 157
  of observation, 21
  possible, 27
  practical, 46
  types of, 134
  properties, 87
sensitivity, 97, 109
  learned, 97
sensory
  dependencies, 102
  excitation, 86
    as perception, 85
    as stimulation, 85
    flow of, 86, 90, 100, 102
  stimulation, 102, 114
    as invariant detection, 86
    atomic, 92
    syntax of, 101
  stimulus, 86
    as an invariant, 86, 89
sentence, 57, 69
  as a symbol, 49
  atomic, 174, 179–180
  conditional, 23
  higher-order, 176
  lower-order, 102, 175
  observation, 69–71
  protocol, 21
settlement
  house, 117–128
    as an information and interpretation bureau, 123

as passive spectator, 126
experimentation, 119
methodology, 117–125
life, 125
movement, 7, 63, 116–130, 133
  methods, 124
  three Rs of, 122, 126
  work, 119–126
    three stages of, 124–126
    vs. charity, 124, 126
    vs. social work, 124
Shapiro, Sidney, x
Shaw, Robert, 100
Simkhovitch, Mary Kingsbury, 7, 63, 117–118, 124–127
simplicity, 66
situation, 101, 176
  concrete, xi, 101
  existential, 57
  problematic, 58, 123, 127
skepticism, 158
skill, 38, 41
  Machiavellian, 147–148, 151
Skolem, Thoralf Albert, 171
social
  contract theory, 141
  engineering, 122
  externalism, 140
  habits, 140–142
  impressionism, 125
  interaction, 123
  needs, 92
  reform, 117–119, 122
  relationships, 123
  science, 31, 77–78, 117, 122, 161
  self, 3
  service, 119
    neighborhood, 119
  work
    vs. settlement work, 124
    vs. sociology, 121
sociology, 117, 120–122, 133
  urban, 118
  vs. social work, 121
solid angle, 105, 112

Sosa, Ernest, 44–45
space, 88, 105
  perception of, 88
spectator conception of
  impressions, 71, 125–126
  inquiry, 71
  measurement, 7, 63
  observation, 7, 63, 69–80, 115, 125
  perception, 70, 80, 86, 115
  sensation, 66
  settlement house methods, 126
speech act theory, 45, 57
stability, 89, 105, 111
Starr, Ellen Gates, 118
statistical methods, 122
Stephens, James Fitzjames, 5, 36
stimulus, 91
  -response, 84, 92, 98
  combinations, 91, 98
  events, 82
  higher-order, 98
  information, 83–85, 93, 98–99
  sensory, 86, 102
    as an invariant, 86, 89, 100
    to action, 11
  variables, 91, 100–103, 113
    lower-order, 91, 101–102, 114
    relations among, 112–113
Strawson, P. F., 35
subject/predicate distinction, 29, 46
substance, 12, 22, 27, 45, 50–51, 171
  affordances of, 87, 98
  dualism, 94, 101
  vs. attribute, 46
substance, highly polymerized, 172
Sunstein, Cass, ix, x, 144, 150, 154
Suppe, Frederick, 102, 176
Suppes, Patrick, 102, 176
supportive evidence, 56
surface-walkability, 103, 113, 168, 169
symbol, 31, 49
  predicate, 171
  systems, 49
sympathy, 123–124
syntactic view

of legal concepts, 182
of scientific theories, 182
syntax
  of optical stimulation, 114
    models for, 103
  of sensory stimulation, 101–102, 114
    models for, 102–103
    sentences in, 102
  operation-based, 175–176

Talisse, Robert, 1–2, 20, 32, 138–141
tangible
  circumstances, 11
  initial conditions, 11
  results, xi, 143, 176, 183, *see also* sensible effects
    as detected invariants, 90, 115
    as invariants, 101
    as operational outcomes, 134, 138, 161, 178
    as values of variables, 67, 100–179
    basic institutions as, 140–141
    conceivably, 53
    covariation of, 99
    idealized, 33
    legal, 178–182
    of actions, 5, 11, 63, 89, 133, 143, 170, 183
    of conduct, 53
    of inquiry, 31–32, 46, 134, 138, 140, 173
    of measuring, 157
    of observation, 58
    operational outcomes as, 67
    perfect, 32–33, 142
    politically, 154
    practical, 11–12
    settled beliefs as, 31–32, 46, 134, 138, 173
    written, 178–181
Tarski, Alfred, 43–44, 67, 71
Taylor, Kenneth, xiv
tenacity, 17, 32, 89, 138, 140, 154
  writ large, 138
terrain
  surface area, 103–105
  texture, 112
testability, 44
texture
  optical, 112–113
  terrain, 112
Thayer, Horace Standish, 1
theorem, 182
theory, scientific, 176
thing, 45, 67–68, 175
  first-order, 7, 63, 67, 85, 170, 174
  in itself, 176
thinking
  as planning, 61
  clearness of, 9–10, 41, 54–55
  content of, 60
thirdness, directly perceived, 24
Thompson, Manley, 51
thought, 11, 84, 99
  as inquiry, 10
  clearness of, 9–10, 41, 54–55
  detached, 26
  experiments as operations of, 53
  function of, 10–12
  higher, 15
  interpretable, 28
  logical, 26
  meaning of a, 10–14, 28, 60
  motive of, 10
  object of, 11, 16
  of an object, 14, 28
  purpose of, 10
  rational, 26
  silent and dark, 53
three Rs, 122, 126
time, 50–51
  and memory, 94
  end of, 137
tradition, 89
tragedy of the commons, 152
transubstantiation, 12, 45–46, 51, 132, 171
Trattner, Walter, 122
treatment, charitable, 124
triangulation, 109
truth, 2, 5–6, 20–22, 30–34, 48, 57, 64, 133–137, 161

ancient, 19
as a perfection, 8, 32–34, 131–135, 138, 142, 173
as agreement, 20
as an ideal, 8, 32–34, 131–135, 142
as eventual verification, 20
as expediency, 152
as warranted believability, 163
as what works, 18–19
coherentist, 17
conditions, 43
in a legal case, 179
in a model, 102, 179
James's theory of, 5, 16–21, 30, 47
new, 18
objective, 19
older, 18–19
Peirce's definition of, 30–33, 48
plasticity of, 18
process, 20–21
subjective, 19
vs. knowledge, 134–135, 173
Tuennerman-Kaplan, Laura, 118, 122
tuning, 94, 96
 a clock, 96
 as fixation, 96
 self-, 94, 96
  higher-order, 97
  lower-order, 97
Turvey, Michael, 100
tyranny, 138, 140

universals, 175
 as things, 67
usage
 functional space of, 180
 word, 8, 135, 180
usefulness, 126
 inferential, 176
 professional, 127–129
utilitarianism, 156–158
utterance, 45

validation, 20
validity, 20, 58, 60
 inductive, 56
 objective, 159
 of ideas, 60
 practical, 39
value
 as affordance, 88, 99
 cognitive, 61
 of a variable, 66–68, 90, 100–103, 113, 115
  predicted, 100
  tangible result as, 179
 of ideas, 62
 quantitative, 67
 utility, 156
Varela, Francisco, 44
variable, 22, 90
 assignment, 103, 113–115
 first-order, 68
 invariant-detection, 90
 invariant-extraction, 102
 lower-order, 90–92
  legal, 179
 optical, 84, 97, 110, 113
 production, 105, 113–115
 sorted, 67, 100, 175, 179
 stimulus, 91, 100–103, 112–114
  lower-order, 91, 101–102, 114
 value of a, 66–68, 90, 100–103, 113, 115, 179
  predicted, 100
  tangible result as, 179
variation, 83
veil
 of appearances, 33–35
 of ignorance, 141
verification, 20–21, 43
 atomistic, 7, 63, 68
 by induction, 25
 empirical, 7, 63, 68
 holistic, 7, 63–68
 primary vs. indirect, 20
verificationism, 24, 44, 71
 reductionist, 69
virtue
 epistemological, 157–158
 ethics, 159

vocabulary, 44, 124
   first-order, 171
   lower-order, 176
   of physics, 59

Wald, Lillian, 118
Walk, Richard, 81
Wallsten, Peter, ix, x, 150
warranted believability, 16, 48, 163
weight, 22
what works, ix, x, 18–21, 43, 66, 70, 152–154
   as proof, 153
   momentarily, 18, 152
   truth as, 19
Whitehead, Alfred North, 60
Wickham, DeWayne, ix, 144
Wiener, Philip P., 37, 88–89
wine, 12, 42–45
   vs. blood, 43–45
wisdom
   personal, 147
   vs. prudence, 147

worldly, 147
word, xi, 33, 45, 48, 82, 143
   as a symbol, 49
   content of a, xii
   conversational uses of a, 47
   definition of a, 31
      operational, 33, 133, 135, 139, 141
   general, 30
   hard, 4, 29, 115, 134, 170
   meaning of a, 4, 29, 33, 43–44, 49–51, 131, 156
   object of a, 30–31
   rational purport of a, 27
   that signifies an ideal, 8, 32–33, 142
   usage, 8, 135, 180
workings, ix, 19, 21, 33, 48
   inferential, 48, 116
   long-term, 18
   operational, xi
Worsnip, Alex, ix, x, 149
Wright, Chauncey, 37

Zelizer, Julian, ix

F. Thomas Burke examines the philosophies of William James and Charles S. Peirce to determine how the original "maxim of pragmatism" was understood differently by these two earliest pragmatists. Burke reconciles these differences by casting pragmatism as a philosophical stance that endorses distinctive conceptions of *belief* and *meaning*. In particular, a pragmatist conception of *meaning* should be understood as both *inferentialist* and *operationalist* in character. Burke unravels a complex early history of this philosophical tradition, discusses contemporary conceptions of pragmatism found in current U.S. political discourse, and explores what this quintessentially American philosophy means today.

F. Thomas Burke is Professor of Philosophy at the University of South Carolina. He is author of *Dewey's New Logic: A Reply to Russell* (1994) and co-editor of *Dewey's Logical Theory: New Studies and Interpretations* (2002) and *George Herbert Mead in the Twenty-First Century* (2013).

www.ingramcontent.com/pod-product-compliance
Lightning Source LLC
Chambersburg PA
CBHW060117170426
43198CB00010B/923